Wordsworth
in His Major Lyrics

The Art and Psychology

Wordsworth
in His Major Lyrics

of Self-Representation

Leon Waldoff

University of Missouri Press
Columbia and London

Copyright © 2001 by
The Curators of the University of Missouri
University of Missouri Press, Columbia, Missouri 65201
Printed and bound in the United States of America
All rights reserved
5 4 3 2 1   05 04 03 02 01

PR
5892
.S38
W35
2001

Library of Congress Cataloging-in-Publication Data

Waldoff, Leon, 1935–
    Wordsworth in his major lyrics: the art and psychology of self-representation / Leon Waldoff.
      p. cm.
    Includes bibliographical references and index.
    ISBN 0-8262-1329-4 (alk. paper)
      1. Wordsworth, William, 1770–1850—Criticism and interpretation.
2. Self in literature. 3. Wordsworth, William, 1770–1850—Psychology.
4. Psychology in literature.   I. Title.

PR5892.S38 W35 2001
821'.7—dc21
00-066599

♾™ This paper meets the requirements of the
American National Standard for Permanence of Paper
for Printed Library Materials, Z39.48, 1984.

Text design: Elizabeth K. Young
Jacket design: Susan Ferber
Typesetter: BOOKCOMP, Inc.
Printer and binder: The Maple-Vail Book Manufacturing Group
Typefaces: Centaur, Coronet

Acknowledgment is made for the permission to quote from:
Waldoff, Leon. "Romantic Recognitions." *American Imago* 47 (1990), 337–65.
© The Johns Hopkins University Press. Reproduced with the permission of
The Johns Hopkins University Press.

This book is published with the generous assistance of the Department of
English, University of Illinois at Urbana–Champaign.

To Fay Botnick

Contents

Acknowledgments ix

Introduction 1

1. The Lyrical "I" as a Self-Dramatization: Wordsworth's Transitional Self 15

2. The Dramatics of Self-Representation in "Tintern Abbey" 47

3. In the Mind's Eye/"I": "Resolution and Independence" 77

4. The "I" of the Ode: Public Performance, Subjective Transformation 103

5. "Elegiac Stanzas": The Poet in His Letters and the "I" of the Poem 130

6. Conclusion: *The Prelude* as a Major Lyric . . 152

Works Cited 165

Index 175

Acknowledgments

I want to thank the following individuals for reading early versions of one or more chapters or of the completed manuscript and for helping me gain a better understanding of the issues I address in this book than I could possibly have done without their challenging questions and suggestions: Leon Chai, Dan Majdiak, Carol Neely, Cliff Spargo, Jack Stillinger, Jessica Waldoff, and Brian Wilkie. I am especially indebted to Richard Matlak and Douglas Wilson for criticisms and suggestions that forced me to rethink or develop further certain parts of the argument, as well as for their continuing interest in and enthusiasm for the project. During much of the writing I was fortunate to have the advice and friendship of the late Stuart Sperry. I have learned a great deal from discussions of Wordsworth with many students, both undergraduate and graduate, particularly in seminars and independent study courses. An early version of Chapter 5 was presented as a paper at the 1993 MLA Convention in Toronto and I benefited from the criticisms provided by my fellow panelists, Kevis Goodman, Alan Liu, and Cliff Spargo. I am grateful to the editors of *American Imago* and to The Johns Hopkins University Press for permission to reprint portions of my 1990 essay "Romantic Recognitions" in revised form. Jesse Delia, Dean of the College of Liberal Arts and Sciences at the University of Illinois, and Dennis Baron, Head of the English Department, provided financial support of the project. Bill Ogg at the University of Illinois Library was consistently helpful with many requests, and Julie Schroeder at the University of Missouri Press rescued me from numerous errors.

To my wife, Alice, and my daughter, Jessica, for many and varied forms of support, I owe far more than I can acknowledge. I dedicate this book to my sister, Fay Botnick, who gave me my first book, and much else.

Urbana, Illinois
February 2001

Wordsworth
in His Major Lyrics

Introduction

This book is concerned with a number of critical questions about the identity and role of the "I" or speaker in Wordsworth's major lyrics. If the poems are autobiographical, as Wordsworth repeatedly says or implies in his prefaces, letters, notes, and remarks to Isabella Fenwick, to what extent can the speaker be thought of as "the poet in his own person" (to use a phrase Wordsworth invokes several times in his prefaces)? If the speaker is indeed the poet in his own person, how is a reader to account for the frequently conflicting differences between the so-called empirical Wordsworth (familiar to us from his letters, his sister's journals, and other biographical sources) and his self-representations in the poetry? If, on the other hand, the speaker is not really the poet but rather a self-representation, partly autobiographical and partly fictional, to what extent is that self-representation an authentic expression of the poet's self and to what extent is it an attempt to construct a self? These and the related questions I shall raise have long persisted in Wordsworth studies, stemming from the poems themselves, but despite the voluminous critical literature that has grown up around the poetry we still have no critical book focused primarily on them and the larger question of the identity, conception, and function of the "I" in the poetry.

It should be acknowledged from the start that the larger question is not one to which there can be a definitive answer, given the fact that there are so many literary, biographical, psychological, historical, social, and other dimensions to it. For this reason more than any other, perhaps, readers, teachers, and critics have tended to prefer practical answers to the question while reading or teaching or writing about a particular poem. The most common and seemingly reasonable answer, of course, is that the speaker is Wordsworth, though it is haunted by our awareness that substituting the proper noun *Wordsworth* for the "I" of a poem begs the question of how the self or subjectivity of the "I" is constituted. An answer more alert to the problematic nature of the question avoids an unqualified substitution and allows for a fictional dimension in the character of the speaker. In their introduction to the Romantic period in *The Norton Anthology of English Literature*, the editors write that "in the Romantic lyric the 'I' often is not a conventionally typical lyric speaker, such as the Petrarchan lover or Cavalier gallant of Elizabethan and seventeenth-century love poems, but has recognizable traits of the poet's own person and circumstances." They go on to say that in the poems of Wordsworth, Coleridge, Shelley, Keats, Smith, Letitia Landon, and others, "the experiences and states of mind expressed by the lyric speaker often accord closely with the known facts of the poet's life and with the personal confessions in his letters and journals."[1] While they emphasize the autobiographical character of the lyric speaker, they do not equate him with the poet; his experiences and states of mind "accord closely" but not exactly with those of the poet. As careful as this answer is, however, it is not intended to address some of the more complex questions we have about specific differences between the poet and the speaker, the relation of autobiography to fiction in the poet's representation of himself as the "I" of the poem, or the problems of defining and conceptualizing the subjectivity of the "I."

In recent years variations on these two basic answers have multiplied and quite different versions of the self of the Wordsworthian speaker have been set forth in the critical literature in psychoanalytic, New Historicist, intertextual, psychobiographical, feminist, and other terms. What the existence of so many different versions indicates, more than the impossibility of answering the question in a definitive way or the clear possibility of answering it in multiple ways, is that the identity of the speaker and the problems of conceptualizing it remain important issues in Wordsworth criticism. Although most of the critical studies in which these versions have appeared have not been explicitly concerned with this question, and have instead generated only implicit answers to it while investigating other issues that impinge on it, they have problematized our conception of the speaker's self in valuable ways and in doing so made possible a richer understanding of it.

Yet, as a result of the strong concern in much recent criticism with issues relating to the literary, social, historical, and cultural constructedness of the speaker's self, the individual dynamics of the speaker's selfhood have tended to be neglected, along with a number of formalist and psychological issues relating to the complexities of self-representation in poetic form. In deconstructive approaches, for example, where the issue is language, the speaker in the poem or the self represented in it is explained

---

1. *The Norton Anthology of English Literature*, General Editor, M. H. Abrams, 2:7.

in terms of the problems of signification and meaning posed by language. Since the word *self* has no stable or definite referent, no transcendental signified to refer to, its meaning can be clarified only by working out the differences between it and other signifiers.[2] The aim of a deconstructive analysis, however, would not be to wholly discredit the notion of a "self" but to contextualize or situate it in language.[3] Because the idea that there is nothing outside the text means that there is nothing outside of a system of signification and representation, the word *self* or *presence* can be defined only by, or in relation to, other signifiers. As a result, the speaker of a poem or the idea of the speaker's "self," like the idea of authorial presence, tends to be displaced by or subordinated to the importance of a "text" as a construct of language. This is the reason J. Hillis Miller, in his reading of the Lucy poems, defines "Wordsworth" as "his writing." Miller's point is not to deny biographical, psychological, historical, or other determinants of the poet's empirical self but to emphasize what he calls the most important aspect of "the human predicament," which is "to remain, always, within language."[4]

Despite its genuine heuristic value, however, both in developing new and more exacting methods of close reading and making us aware of uncertainties inherent in language that radically problematize essentializing concepts, deconstruction has the effect of discouraging an investigation of the problems of defining the "I" of the lyric speaker and conceptualizing the subjectivity it represents. By privileging the importance of language, it relegates to issues of minor importance biographical and psychological questions relating to the "I" of the poem and the self of the speaker. Because the self is the text, and the speaker a representation

---

2. For the idea that "self," or "presence," or "self-presence" is a "chimera," and that "The sign, the image, the representation, which come to supplement the absent presence are the illusions that sidetrack us," see Jacques Derrida, *Of Grammatology*, 154.

3. See Jacques Derrida, "Structure, Sign, and Play in the Discourse of the Human Sciences," 271.

4. J. Hillis Miller, "On the Edge: The Crossways of Contemporary Criticism," 32. In his commentary on Walter Benjamin's essay on Goethe's *Elective Affinities*, Miller says: "The self of the author is not the explanatory origin of the work. That origin, or rather the apparent origin, metaleptically reversing cause and effect, is another, more genuine self. This self is made up by the work" (*Fiction and Repetition: Seven English Novels*, 11–12).

in language impossible to define with any sense of certainty, the idea of an actual, empirical self is placed in such suspension that the word *self* almost becomes a term of critical embarrassment. In effect, the lyric speaker is cut off from the self of the poet and critical thought becomes disengaged from the issues that arise out of that relationship. Not entirely unlike the old New Criticism, deconstruction figures the lyric speaker as a persona, a fiction, though of course its linguistic and philosophical premises enable it to explore cultural depths in the idea of the speaker as a textual representation that were undreamt of in New Criticism.

New Historicism, with its materialist emphasis, provides a radically different conception of the speaker's self in the Romantic lyric. Rather than a persona, the speaker is thought of as the empirical self of the poet. Yet because the poet is shown to have submitted to a body of illusions represented by the ideology of the age, the idea that he is speaking "in his own person" no longer carries the authority that it did when Wordsworth used the phrase. The speaker or the poet is now defined by what Jerome McGann calls a "false consciousness." In *The Romantic Ideology: A Critical Investigation*, McGann discusses "The Ruined Cottage" and "Tintern Abbey" as examples of poems that displace and elide specific social, economic, and political problems and discontents, as well as historical facts that serve as a background for the poems (bad harvests, poverty, war, the French Revolution, and transients and beggars). To the extent that the poems posit or recommend a transcendent or transhistorical (spiritual, religious, or psychological) solution to human problems, they are illusory. "The idea that poetry, or even consciousness," McGann writes, "can set one free of the ruins of history and culture is the grand illusion of every Romantic poet." McGann does not discuss the speaker or the "I" as such, but takes the speaker to be Wordsworth and concludes his discussion of the Intimations Ode with the statement that "Wordsworth's is . . . a false consciousness," though the statement, it should be noted, is not intended as an indictment of the poem's greatness.[5]

As important as New Historicism has been for Romantic studies in the last fifteen years, however, it has a tendency to reduce our conception of the poet's psyche or the speaker's self to a preoccupation with acts of exclusion and repression. In *Wordsworth's Great Period Poems: Four Essays*, for

---

5. Jerome McGann, *The Romantic Ideology: A Critical Investigation*, 91, 90.

example, Marjorie Levinson defines the mind or consciousness of the speaker of "Tintern Abbey" by its blindness to the social and economic conditions of the valley or society through which he walks. He cultivates and valorizes the inner life solely as a means of denying the transient nature of material and social existence and supporting the enabling fiction of his transcendence of it. He is overtaken by a "blindness which assumes autonomy of the psyche, its happy detachment from the social fact of being."[6] Although the speaker is situated in his social, economic, and historical context by Levinson in great and illuminating detail, his psyche is treated in discussion as constituted almost entirely by a single mechanism, repression. In his important study, *Wordsworth: The Sense of History*, Alan Liu takes a similar view of the speaker's subjectivity and, in his review of David Simpson's *Wordsworth's Historical Imagination: The Poetry of Displacement*, he identifies different versions of repression (displacement, distortion, and denial) used by New Historicists.[7]

In dialogic and intertextualist studies the issue has been Wordsworth's borrowings from and responses to Coleridge's poems and the extent to which the self in a Wordsworth poem is the intersubjective creation or product of that dialogue. Paul Magnuson's *Coleridge and Wordsworth: A Lyrical Dialogue* presents a strong argument that the poems of the two poets constitute the Coleridge-Wordsworth canon and that individual poems are fragments of a dialogue. "A radical implication of a dialogic reading insists," Magnuson points out, "that individual poems or individual lyric effusions have no meaning in themselves, any more than an individual stanza within an ode or other lyric has meaning in itself."[8] As a result, the dialogue tends to displace the poet as an individual, and a reader's conception of the poet or speaker as a man with a personal history—someone with moods, preoccupations, and an inner world of feeling, thought, and remembered experiences—tends to disappear. The creative process in the individual poet writing out of

---

6. Marjorie Levinson, *Wordsworth's Great Period Poems: Four Essays*, 48.
7. Alan Liu, *Wordsworth: The Sense of History*. The "I" of "Tintern Abbey" is seen as a "Spirit" denying historical reference: " 'I' am everywhere in history, Wordsworth's Spirit declares, and yet nowhere in particular in history. 'I' am the empire of the light of setting suns, of the round ocean and the living air, of the blue sky, and of the mind of man.... And though my very being is denial, 'I' will not be denied" (217).
8. Paul Magnuson, *Coleridge and Wordsworth: A Lyrical Dialogue*, 28.

desire and inner conflict is replaced by a generative process of the two poets in dialogue and the conception of the poet-speaker's self is based largely on his poetic interaction with the other poet. In Gene Ruoff's *Wordsworth and Coleridge: The Making of the Major Lyrics, 1802–1804,* the focus on what is called intertextual genetics is similar and an emphasis on the intersubjective makeup of the speaker's self is pronounced, though Ruoff remains concerned throughout with various psychological and developmental issues.

Feminist criticism has provided one of the most important revisions of critical thinking about the lyrical "I." In bringing attention to the numerous women readers and writers of the early nineteenth century, to attitudes toward gender embedded in the culture, and to the gendered constructions of subjectivity in the works of the six major Romantic poets, it has provided a new understanding of the lyrical "I" in Romantic poetry. Margaret Homans, Marlon Ross, Anne Mellor, and others have shown how these poets appropriate the voice of the female, display a masculine bias in the representation of the female, and rely upon a masculine image of conquest in the construction of the speaker's subjectivity.[9] In a recent study Elizabeth Fay has argued that Wordsworth was so dependent on Dorothy's agency, and his poetry so much the result of a collaborative effort, that one is justified in taking the proper noun "Wordsworth" to mean "both brother and sister together at once."[10]

Still other critical perspectives might be mentioned, but my purpose in this brief survey has not been to summarize all the critical literature relevant to the issue of subjectivity in Wordsworth.[11] Nor has it been to dismiss critical studies and theoretical perspectives that have changed

---

9. See Margaret Homans, *Women Writers and Poetic Identity: Dorothy Wordsworth, Emily Brontë, and Emily Dickinson,* and Homans, *Bearing the Word: Language and Female Experience in Nineteenth-Century Women's Writing;* Marlon Ross, "Naturalizing Gender: Woman's Place in Wordsworth's Ideological Landscape," and Ross, *The Contours of Masculine Desire: Romanticism and the Rise of Women's Poetry;* and Anne Mellor, *Romanticism and Gender.* See also Mellor, ed., *Romanticism and Feminism,* which includes important essays by Stuart Curran, Alan Richardson, Susan Wolfson, and others.

10. Elizabeth Fay, *Becoming Wordsworthian: A Performative Aesthetics,* 17.

11. Among the relevant critical approaches that might be mentioned, I would include the following: the lyrical "I" as "the poet in a poet" who responds to his precursors in Harold Bloom's *The Anxiety of Influence: A Theory of Poetry;* the dialogic "I" situated in a social context in Don Bialostosky's *Making Tales: The Poetics*

our understanding of Wordsworth and his poetry in valuable ways and that I shall refer to throughout this study. It has been rather to call attention to a tendency in recent criticism to explain the poet's "self" or the "I" of the poetry exclusively or largely in relation to concerns with language, political and social consciousness, intertextual relationships, and social and cultural history. As important as these concerns are, the focus on them has resulted in a neglect of certain formalist and psychological issues that are central, I believe, to an understanding of the "I" of Wordsworth's major lyrics and the subjectivity it represents.

Put in its simplest form, the assumption with which this study begins is that the individual self of the speaker, his preoccupation with it throughout the poem, and his efforts to represent it and act out a transformation of it are of central importance. The answers to many of the questions we have about the identity, conception, and function of the "I" in the poetry depend on an understanding of the art and psychology of self-representation at work in each poem. I deal with these questions by focusing on Wordsworth's major autobiographical lyrics, "Tintern Abbey," "Resolution and Independence," the Intimations Ode, and "Elegiac Stanzas," as well as, though more briefly, *The Prelude*. Although these poems have been and remain ideal works in which to trace aspects of Wordsworth's psychological, intellectual, and artistic development, his development is not my concern in this study. It is rather with the act of self-representation. That concern shifts the critical focus from the poem as a document that often reveals hidden aspects of Wordsworth's life and career (in his relationship with Dorothy Wordsworth, in his dialogic and intertextual relationship with Coleridge, in his political biases,

---

of Wordsworth's Narrative Experiments; the philosophically contextualized "I" given to experiences of visionary solipsism in Charles J. Rzepka's *The Self as Mind: Vision and Identity in Wordsworth, Coleridge, and Keats;* the historically shaped "I" implicit in an audience study such as Jon Klancher's *The Making of English Reading Audiences, 1790–1832;* the hermeneutically constructed "I" in relation to the supplementing role of the reader in Tilottama Rajan's *The Supplement of Reading: Figures of Understanding in Romantic Theory and Practice;* the psychobiographical self of the poet defined by personal relationships in Richard E. Matlak's *The Poetry of Relationship: The Wordsworths and Coleridge, 1797–1800;* and the "autographical" cultural self (rather than the autobiographical self) that creates itself and its identity in a text in Ashton Nichols's *The Revolutionary "I": Wordsworth and the Politics of Self-Representation.*

in his indebtedness to precursor poets) to the poem as a dramatized lyrical utterance that reflects the poet's art and psychology of self-representation. It requires that greater attention be given to the poetics and psychology of appearing, being, and becoming in a text than to the biographical or historical or other aspects of Wordsworth's life and experience revealed in the text.

In an important new biography of the young poet, *The Hidden Wordsworth: Poet, Lover, Rebel, Spy*, Kenneth R. Johnston persuasively uses the idea or theme of self-creation to tie together the myriad strands of thought and action in Wordsworth's life that led him to assume the role of "the Poet" during the period of revolution and national crisis when he wrote most of his great poetry. "Wordsworth's poetic self-creation was . . . intimately connected with an idea of his poetry *and* his life forming a model for national regeneration."[12] The implied definition of *self* in Johnston's use of the term *self-creation* emphasizes Wordsworth's construction of a public identity based on an image and idea of the Poet as possessed with a strong social and historical consciousness, though Johnston remains alert to (and often incorporates) other critical perspectives on many aspects of Wordsworth's life and writings.

By contrast, the definition of "self" implicit in this critical study of four poems, and particularly in my use of the term *self-representation*, is centered on issues of art and psychology, not on the larger issues of social and historical consciousness that Johnston's biography addresses. In other words, my concern is with the poems as lyrical utterances in which the speakers attempt to act out and achieve a self-transformation rather than with the poems as works in which Wordsworth attempts to construct a public identity for himself. Such a concern is different from but certainly not incompatible with the perspective developed in Johnston's biography or with other perspectives in various critical studies. I argue that the major lyrics are poems in which a speaker presents a self-dramatizing performance and attempts, through the dramatics of his utterance, to transform the sense of individual self represented in a moment of lyrical expression. While the immediate aim of the self-dramatization is self-transformation, the ultimate aim is the ideal of self-realization that has long been recognized as a central motivation for the expressivist impulses of the Romantic lyric.

12. Kenneth R. Johnston, *The Hidden Wordsworth: Poet, Lover, Rebel, Spy*, 603.

I use the term *self-dramatizing*, defining it in relation to Freud's theory of the transference and D. W. Winnicott's notion of the transitional self, to refer to a speaker's acting out the feelings and thoughts that he expresses in lyrical form.[13] Although the term calls attention to his preoccupation with himself, it does not, in my usage, include any pejorative connotation of affectation or histrionics, as it often does in ordinary usage. The Lucy poems provide examples in miniature form of the self-dramatizing nature of the major lyrics. Unlike the major lyrics, whose deep elegiac strains are ultimately for the speaker's self, the Lucy poems are short elegies for another person. Yet the central irony of them is that the self-dramatizing speaker makes himself both the mediator for and the object of the sympathy he invokes for the dead or soon-to-die Lucy. He uses several self-dramatizing strategies that recur in the major lyrics, including self-quotation or some representation of dialogue, a narrative structure ensuring that the lyrical utterance will lead to a climactic moment of recognition or new awareness, a splitting of the self between pre- and postconsciousness of Lucy's mortality, and the staging of the recognition or new awareness as a turning point in his life. But while the Lucy poems employ these and other self-dramatizing strategies to achieve their poignant effects ("oh, / The difference to me!"), they remain limited in scope and do not engage in the more complex act of self-representation and in-depth exploration of self that we find in the major lyrics.

The act of self-dramatization by the speakers of the major lyrics, more specifically their efforts both to perform and to achieve a self-transformation, is what primarily distinguishes them from the Wordsworth we find in the letters, notes, prefaces, and other self-representations of the poet. The self-dramatizing character of each speaker's utterance

---

13. In *Revolutionary "I,"* Nichols also uses the term *self-dramatizing*. His use is similar in its concern with Wordsworth's "dramatized projections" of versions of the self in a number of poems, but different in its conception of the self in historical and cultural rather than psychological terms and in attributing to it a philosophical rather than personal anxiety as the motivation for the self-dramatization: "Wordsworth felt a need to reconstitute the secular and postenlightenment view of the self out of the dissolving hierarchy that had represented the earlier ideal of 'soul.' . . . [and] to dramatize a version of himself that might solidify a new form of personal authority in the wake of the destabilizing effect of eighteenth-century anxieties about the 'soul' and the 'self'" (29–30).

calls for a critical approach that will not only focus on his use of dramatic strategies (apostrophe, the staged return or encounter, dialogue, the abrupt transition, the reenacted moment of new awareness, self-quotation) but also provide an explanation of his motives for the performance. The intensity of the speaker's concern with dramatizing his presence and utterance, the deliberateness with which he employs dramatic strategies, and the persistent concern he shows with self-transformation and self-realization require a way of defining and conceptualizing his subjectivity that will give greater recognition to the psychological dimension of his experience (his aspirations, traumatic memories, defensive strategies, internalized objects, countertraumatic and wish-fulfilling resolutions) than it has been customary in recent critical practice to do.

Since the term *major lyrics* has at times been used to refer to others of Wordsworth's poems than the four I have selected for this study, my use calls for some explanation.[14] First, these four poems represent his highest level of artistic achievement in the longer lyric, something that cannot be said, I believe, for other longer lyrics such as "Nutting" and "Ode to Duty." It is not an accident that these four are among his best-known poems, are the most frequently anthologized of his longer poems, and have figured prominently in numerous critical studies not only of Wordsworth but of Romantic poetry and thought. Although "Resolution and Independence" might be defined more strictly as a lyrical narrative similar to "Michael" rather than as a longer lyric, its two most important features—the prominence of the first-person speaker, with extended self-reflections that are characteristic of the speakers of the other longer lyrics I discuss, and the strongly autobiographical character of the speaker—distinguish it from narrative poems such as "Michael" and "The Ruined Cottage" and mark it, for my purposes, as

14. For example, Geoffrey Hartman, in a chapter entitled "1801–1807: The Major Lyrics," included "Michael," "Resolution and Independence," the Intimations Ode, "Ode to Duty," and "Elegiac Stanzas" (*Wordsworth's Poetry, 1787–1814*, 260–91). Gene Ruoff, on the other hand, included in his *Wordsworth and Coleridge: The Making of the Major Lyrics, 1802–1804* only the two most important poems by Wordsworth composed in the given years, "Resolution and Independence" and the Intimations Ode. It is clear in each case that chronology was a determinant of the poems to be included as "major." Had the chronological focus been different, more poems or fewer would perhaps have been included.

one of the major lyrics. Second, and more important, these four lyrics present longer, more searching, and more fully developed explorations by a lyric speaker of memories, experiences, states of feeling, reflections, and elevated moments of consciousness than are to be found in any of Wordsworth's poems other than *The Prelude*. If he had never written *The Prelude*, they might well be taken as his most autobiographical poems, though less for what they tell us about specific experiences, events, and activities than for what they reveal about the mind that interpreted them. The autobiographical nature of these poems brings me to the final consideration in selecting them for study. Because of the substantial body of extratextual material surrounding them (particularly Wordsworth's notes to Isabella Fenwick, his notes to editions of his poems, and his letters to various people), they offer a special critical opportunity not merely to observe differences between the self-representations in them and those in prose forms but to sharpen the focus on the distinctive characteristics of the lyrical "I" in these poems and develop an understanding of the subjectivity it represents.

The fact that "Tintern Abbey" and the other poems I discuss are dramatic lyrics, as well as the fact that many others of Wordsworth's lyrics are dramatic in fundamental ways, has not gone unnoticed. Forty years ago Robert Langbaum, in his important study *The Poetry of Experience: The Dramatic Monologue in Modern Literary Tradition*, observed that "It is the dramatic nature of the romantic lyric which distinguishes it not only from the lyrics of the older poets but from the traditional lyrics of the romantic poets themselves," and then went on to note several of the Romantic lyric's dramatic features, particularly "the arrangement of its events, the role of its observer and the dialogue-like style of its address."[15] Since then other critics have called attention to some of the dramatic features of Wordsworth's poetry. In an essay entitled "Rhetoric as Drama: An Approach to the Romantic Ode" (1964), Irene Chayes showed that the features of plot discussed in Aristotle's *Poetics* are not confined to genres such as epic and drama and may be found in lyric poems, "with the speaker playing the role of a protagonist whose 'actions' are contained in his words and who is brought to a Reversal or Discovery

---

15. Robert Langbaum, *The Poetry of Experience: The Dramatic Monologue in Modern Literary Tradition*, 53–54.

by what he himself says."[16] In *The Art of the "Lyrical Ballads"* (1975), Stephen M. Parrish demonstrated that many of Wordsworth's poems in *Lyrical Ballads* were "experiments in dramatic form," that a speaker such as the "loquacious narrator" in "The Thorn" (as Wordsworth referred to him in the Advertisement to *Lyrical Ballads*) is a dramatic character, and that this poem, like other lyrical ballads, "is, in effect, a dramatic monologue."[17] Other critics, among them Paul Sheats in *The Making of Wordsworth's Poetry, 1785–1798* (1973), Don Bialostosky in *Making Tales: The Poetics of Wordsworth's Narrative Experiments* (1984), and Stuart Curran in *Poetic Form and British Romanticism* (1986), have discussed some of the dramatic features of one or more of the major lyrics.

Yet it remains a fact that the dramatic nature of Wordsworth's major lyrics has still not received the kind of sustained critical analysis it deserves. A great deal of his poetic art has been devoted to dramatizing each speaker's utterance, but the dramatic strategies that are employed have yet to be identified, their psychological functions analyzed, and their aesthetic effects recognized. More important, the self-dramatizing character of the "I" of the major lyrics has been left unaccounted for. It has never been theorized and assimilated into an understanding of the subjectivity that it represents.

In the first chapter I address questions arising from the partly autobiographical and partly fictional nature of the "I" or speaker and deal with several problems inherent in attempts to define and conceptualize the self of the speaker. I identify his self-dramatizing character and relate it to a number of Wordsworth's ideas in his notes, prefaces, and essays about the way language and representation bear on issues of self-representation. I then develop a psychoanalytic explanation of it that employs Freud's concept of the transference and Winnicott's of the transitional object to establish a model for understanding the performative nature of the lyrical utterance and the transitional self of Wordsworth represented by the speaker. In the chapters that follow, I develop close readings of the four major lyrics and, in the final chapter, attempt to relate them to *The Prelude*. Since each of the major lyrics has received numerous and seemingly exhaustive critical readings, often

16. Irene Chayes, "Rhetoric as Drama: An Approach to the Romantic Ode," 67–68.
17. Stephen M. Parrish, *The Art of the "Lyrical Ballads,"* 99.

representing the best and most influential criticism on Wordsworth, a word of justification is called for. My readings are not intended as interpretations, though of course any critical analysis or commentary is necessarily interpretive to some extent, or as studies in Wordsworth's development. They are rather attempts to analyze the act of self-representation at the heart of each poem, to explore the critical problems involved when we try to conceptualize each speaker's subjectivity, and to present an understanding of each poem that takes into account the art and psychology that have gone into its representation of the speaker's subjectivity.

The readings address a number of formalist issues in their concern with the art of self-representation. In them I identify, analyze, and try to understand the ways various structural, rhetorical, stylistic, and other features of each poem (abrupt transitions, nominal addressees, apostrophes, moments of recognition or new awareness, experiences of the sublime) make it not only dramatic but, as the utterance of its speaker, self-dramatizing. The readings also address a number of psychological issues in their concern with the acts of self-representation. I use psychoanalytic theory in the first, methodological chapter to construct a model for understanding the act of self-representation in each poem, but also in succeeding chapters in employing the model and in exploring the dynamics of each speaker's act of self-representation, including fears and traumatic potentials mentioned or alluded to in his utterance, relationships to addressees, objects, and ideals, and strategies of self-representation such as splitting of the self, idealization, and internalization. Last but not least, I contrast the self-representations with the historical and biographical Wordsworth and distinguish the differences in self-representation among the four speakers.

Finally, I should mention that in frequently referring to *the* "I" of the major lyrics here and especially in the first chapter, I do not mean to suppress the differences that in fact I am concerned to emphasize. Nor do I want to suggest that there is a single, unchanging identity behind all the poems or that it would be possible or even desirable to construct a composite self or typology of self for the major lyrics, something that would involve the kind of reductionist critical practice I want to avoid. On the other hand, in emphasizing the differences among the four I do not want to give the impression that I think they are four wholly unrelated characters or personas in totally different lyrics. Despite the differences in occasion and experience at the centers of the four poems, in choice and degree of reliance on certain self-dramatizing strategies over others, and in the poetic forms giving shape to the speakers' utterances, there are marked similarities and continuities from one poem to another in the kinds of experience dealt with, in the aims of self-dramatization, and in the psychological defenses and dramatic and rhetorical strategies employed. The presence of these similarities and continuities suggests that we should not surrender the important common-sense awareness that, despite the differences among the speakers, as well as those among the various, repeatedly revised self-representations in *The Prelude*, there was after all a single, empirical self fashioning all these autobiographical self-representations. That self was not unchanging, of course, and was always in the process of reconstituting itself, but it was a self that also never lost, throughout the numerous revisions of *The Prelude* and the variations in self-representation in the major lyrics and other poems, the essential characteristics that continue to enable us to speak of their possessor as Wordsworth.

1 ⋅⋅ The Lyrical "I" as a Self-Dramatization

Wordsworth's Transitional Self

Of the various critical problems encountered by a reader of Wordsworth's major lyrics, none is more central to interpretation or difficult to solve than that of defining the self of the speaker. Despite the long-familiar dictum inherited from the New Criticism that the speaker of a lyric is a persona, a fictional representation not to be confused with the poet, the solution to the problem preferred by most Wordsworth critics identifies the speaker with the poet himself. So favored has it been, Don Bialostosky has observed, that in Wordsworth criticism "the 'intentional fallacy' has rarely been considered a fallacy."[1] The reasons for favoring it are well known. No major poet before or since has insisted so much on the autobiographical experience behind his poetry. Throughout his letters, prefaces, essays, and recorded comments, Wordsworth identifies himself as the speaker of his poems. Indeed, he repeatedly authorizes an authorial definition of the speaker or the "I" with the use of the phrase "the poet in his own person."

In the 1800 Preface to *Lyrical Ballads*, for example, he draws a distinction between those occasions in poetry ("those parts of composition") "where the Poet speaks through the mouths of his characters" and those where he "speaks to us in his own person and character."[2] As at other times when he uses the phrase, he wants to distinguish the speaker of

---

1. Bialostosky, *Making Tales*, 20.
2. *The Prose Works of William Wordsworth*, ed. W. J. B. Owen and Jane Worthington Smyser, 1:142. Quotations from Wordsworth's prefaces and essays are taken from this edition and are hereafter given in the text. The context from which the quotation is drawn requires a word of explanation. It is part of Wordsworth's general discussion of style (including the quotation and brief discussion of Gray's sonnet) and his more specific argument against the use of "poetic diction." In the second of the sentences I quote from he is temporarily conceding that "it may be proper and necessary [to employ a particular language or use poetic diction] where the Poet speaks to us in his own person," only then to insist that, given the description of the Poet he has already set forth ("He is a man

a poem such as "Tintern Abbey" from characters or narrators in other poems. He had used a similar phrase in the Advertisement to *Lyrical Ballads* (1798) in his remark that "The poem of the Thorn, as the reader will soon discover, is not supposed to be spoken in the author's own person: the character of the loquacious narrator will sufficiently shew itself in the course of the story" (*Prose*, 1:117). Years later, in the 1814 Preface to *The Excursion*, he continues to make such a distinction when he says that "the first and third parts of the Recluse will consist chiefly of meditations in the Author's own person; and . . . in the intermediate part (The Excursion) the intervention of characters speaking is employed, and something of a dramatic form adopted" (*Prose*, 3:6). Although *The Recluse* remains unfinished and we therefore cannot be certain of the contrast Wordsworth is developing between the first and third parts, on one hand, and *The Excursion*, on the other, we have some idea from "Home at Grasmere" ("Book First, Part First of *The Recluse*") of what he means by "meditations in the Author's own person" and how they differ from those parts of *The Excursion* where "something of a dramatic form is adopted" and the Poet, the Wanderer, the Solitary, and the Pastor engage in an extended dialogue. Wordsworth uses the notion of the poet speaking in his own person again in the 1815 "Essay, Supplementary to the Preface" in a remark about Shakespeare: "There is extant a small Volume of miscellaneous poems, in which Shakspeare expresses his own feelings in his own person" (*Prose*, 3:69). The "miscellaneous" poems are,

---

speaking to men. . . ."), the use of poetic diction or of "language differ[ing] in any material degree from that of all other men" would not be possible. The reason, of course, is that the thoughts and feelings the Poet expresses are the "general passions and thoughts and feelings of men," not just "his [own] feelings for his own gratification." Although this statement might seem to raise questions about whether Wordsworth would ever think of himself as a "Poet who speaks to us in his own person," it does not imply that because a poet draws on the same language as other men ("How, then, can his language differ in any material degree from that of all other men who feel vividly and see clearly?") he is incapable of speaking in his own person. Wordsworth's general point is that a poet, whether in the dramatic parts of composition or in those parts where he is speaking in his own person, should use "the language of men" rather than "a diction of the Poet's own, either peculiar to him as an individual Poet or belonging simply to Poets in general."

of course, Shakespeare's sonnets.³ Coleridge held a different view of the Shakespearean "I," and the difference underscores the autobiographical emphasis Wordsworth gives the phrase "in his own person." Shakespeare "shaped his characters out of the Nature within," Coleridge writes, but not "out of *his own* Nature, as an *individual person*—No! . . . Shakespeare in composing had no *I* but the I representative."⁴ Coleridge universalizes Shakespeare, makes him representative man. Wordsworth does not surrender the potential of Shakespeare (or himself) to be representative of a universal human nature, but he insists that Shakespeare "expresses his own feelings in his own person," and in this way makes him into a Wordsworthian poet of sincerity.

By his repeated use of the phrase "in his own person," Wordsworth calls attention to a defining characteristic of his poetry: that he is its subject in two senses of the word, as speaker and theme. His remarks about individual poems often emphasize that his subject is his own subjectivity. In a June 14, 1802, letter to Sara Hutchinson, for example, he not only identifies himself as the speaker of the poem that would eventually be titled "Resolution and Independence" but also offers a supplement to the depiction of his subjectivity in the poem: "I describe myself as having been exalted to the highest pitch of delight by the joyousness and beauty of Nature and then as depressed, even in the midst of those beautiful objects, to the lowest dejection and despair." He repeats this emphasis on his subjectivity many years later in his remarks to Isabella Fenwick ("I was in the state of feeling described in the beginning of the poem, while crossing over Barton Fell from Mr. Clarkson's at the foot of Ulswater").⁵ Similar evidence from Wordsworth's letters and notes relates the speakers of the other major lyrics, as well as the speakers of numerous shorter lyrics (for example, "Nutting," the Matthew poems, and "A Narrow Girdle of Rough Stones"), to the autobiographical Wordsworth.

---

3. Wordsworth is referring to *Shakespeares Sonnets Never before Imprinted*, iv. See *Prose*, 3:90.

4. Samuel Taylor Coleridge, *Lectures, 1808–1819: On Literature*, 1:149.

5. William Wordsworth and Dorothy Wordsworth, *The Early Years, 1787–1805*, 366 (hereafter cited as *Letters: The Early Years*). For the note to Isabella Fenwick, see *The Fenwick Notes of William Wordsworth*, 14.

Yet the notion of a poet speaking "in his own person" is one that a nineteenth-century writer such as Wordsworth could rely on with a good deal more confidence than a twenty-first-century reader can. To define the "I" of the major lyrics and the phrase "the poet in his own person" as "Wordsworth" begs the question of how we should define and understand the "I" (and the subjectivity to which it gives expression) by substituting the proper noun for the speaker. Since the implicit definition and function of the name of an author in a particular critical discussion will vary with an individual critic's selection and emphasis of certain biographical and historical facts, anecdotes, images, quotations from the poetry, and autobiographical comments from letters, prefaces, and notes (not to mention the critic's theoretical orientation and the problem under investigation), the referentiality suggested by the name, as Foucault has made clear, is far more complicated and elusive than it appears to be in practice.[6] Further, since Wordsworth's is a poetry where speakers are shown to be in a process of making discoveries about themselves, and developing and changing in some fundamental way, the proper noun *Wordsworth* or the phrase "in his own person" implies a stability of identity contradicted by the representation in the poems of feelings and thoughts in flux and process. This is especially true of the major lyrics, where speakers represent themselves as having experienced a powerful moment of recognition or new awareness that has radically changed them in some way.

An identification of the speaker with the poet also tends to overlook the fact that the autobiographical "I" presented in a poem has been imaginatively transformed. He is not, Robert Langbaum remarked many years ago, "the man his friends knew and his biographers write about." The "I" is "a character in a dramatic action, a character . . . endowed by the poet with the qualities necessary to make the poem happen to him." Wordsworth himself is in part responsible for the tendency to confuse the poet with his speakers because, as Don Bialostosky has pointed out, when he says "the Poet speaks to us in his own person and character" he is describing the poet as "'speaking,' not as representing or composing fictive speech-acts." Yet Coleridge, in his account of how *Lyrical Ballads* came to be written, appears to make the distinction that

---

6. I am drawing here, in a general way, on a number of important distinctions developed by Michel Foucault in his essay "What Is an Author?"

Langbaum, Bialostosky, and others have in mind when he differentiates the friend he knew so well from the character of the genius found in Wordsworth's poetry: "Mr. Wordsworth added two or three poems written in his own character, in the impassioned, lofty, and sustained diction, which is characteristic of his genius."[7] Although the phrase "in his own character" appears to mean something close to the phrase "in his own person" (and was at times used thus synonymously by Wordsworth), Coleridge's emphasis on Wordsworth's "genius" and particularly on his "impassioned, lofty, and sustained diction" implies a distinction between the lyrical presence he found in the poetry and the individual he knew. In this way Coleridge seems to anticipate a distinction that would become a central postulate of the New Criticism.

In the first half of the twentieth century a consensus developed that the speaker is never the poet in his own person. This consensus, as Donald Davie pointed out, "had taken the idea of the *persona* from Ezra Pound, and the closely related idea of the *mask* from W. B. Yeats; and it had taken from T. S. Eliot the ideas that the structure of a poem was inherently a *dramatic* structure, and that the effect of poetry was an impersonal effect. It had elaborated on these hints to formulate a rule, the rule that the 'I' in a poem is *never* immediately and directly the poet; that the-poet-in-his-poem is always distinct from, and must never be confounded with, the-poet-outside-his-poem, the poet as historically recorded between birthdate and date of death."[8] But there are good reasons to question the use of *persona* to refer to Wordsworth's speakers. For one thing, its use assumes a clear distinction that in recent years has become difficult to maintain, a difficulty foreshadowed by the fact that both *person* and *persona* share the same etymology, from the Latin *persona*, meaning "a mask used by a player, a character or personage acted" (OED). Can the actual or real person ever be fully distinguished from the many roles or masks or identifications he or she assumes in the course of being (or attempting to become) the person he or she is (or wants

---

7. Langbaum, *Poetry of Experience*, 52; Bialostosky, *Making Tales*, 19; Coleridge, *Biographia Literaria*, 2:8.

8. Donald Davie, "On Sincerity: From Wordsworth to Ginsberg," 62. Harry Berger identifies "the dissociation of the text and its speaker or 'point of view' from the author" as one of six postulates of the old New Criticism in his "Reconstructing the Old New Criticism," 10–11.

to be)? One need not work out full deconstructions of *persona* and the phrase "the poet in his own person" to see that they posit distinctions and a differentiation from each other that can never be fully established. Even Wordsworth does not posit such a differentiation in comments that he made about Burns and that seem to have special relevance for Wordsworth himself. In his "Letter to a Friend of Robert Burns," he remarks that Burns "avail[s] himself of his own character and situation in society, to construct out of them a poetic self—introduced as a *dramatic personage*," but he then goes on to say, in a brief discussion of "Death and Dr. Hornbook," that Burns could not have written "with such pathetic force" except by *"speaking in his own voice"* and "from the text of his own errors" (*Prose*, 3:125, emphasis added).

Another problem is that, at the practical level of reading the poetry, a critic's use of *persona* implies a greater distinction between the poet and the speaker than the strongly autobiographical nature of Wordsworth's poetry warrants. Few readers would confuse the degree of imaginative self-representation in Wordsworth's speakers in his major lyrics with the fictional license Tennyson and Browning take in developing dramatic characters such as Ulysses and Rabbi Ben Ezra, even though most would acknowledge that both Tennyson and Browning, while fictionalizing their characters, have also drawn on their own experience and convictions in creating these characters, and to some extent have projected themselves into them. Yet the use of *persona* to refer to the speaker in "Tintern Abbey" or "Resolution and Independence" is misleading. It appears to represent a middle ground between "poet in his own person" and "dramatic character," but in fact it radically distorts the relationship of the speaker to Wordsworth's inner life, and it represents him as a largely fictional character. It sets up an artificial boundary between life and art, one that is particularly inappropriate for Wordsworth. As Keats knew, Wordsworth is not a "camelion Poet," a Shakespearean ideal of a poet without "Identity," one who is "continually in for[ming?]—and filling some other Body" and who "has as much delight in conceiving an Iago as an Imogen," but is rather a poet of the egotistical sublime.[9]

---

9. *The Letters of John Keats, 1814–1821*, 1:386–87. Keats's notion of himself as a "camelion Poet" who has "no Identity" provides a valuable insight into the sympathetic character of the poetic imagination, but it should not be taken to mean that he consistently thought poets like Shakespeare and himself had no

Wordsworth's speakers in the major lyrics are self-representations with his identity unmistakably stamped on them.

As problematic as the phrase "the poet in his own person" is, it has the merit of reminding us that the poetry, especially the major lyrics and *The Prelude*, is strongly autobiographical. Wordsworth possessed an instinctive confidence that he could speak in his own person and imbue his verse with autobiographical life. Nor did he doubt that there is a self. At times he speaks of "my true self" or "the human creature's absolute self" (*Prelude*, 11.342, 8.123), at other times of an "inner" or "inward self" ("Guilt and Sorrow," l. 439; *Excursion*, 8.57).[10] In the first of his "Essays upon Epitaphs" he wrote that "every man has a character of his own, to the eye that has skill to perceive it" (*Prose*, 2:56). Although the word *character* cannot be taken as synonymous with *self*, and is haunted by problems of definition similar to those surrounding the word *person*, its use again calls attention to Wordsworth's conviction that there is something essential in the makeup of the individual that differentiates it from other selves and gives it identity.

It is more characteristic of Wordsworth to set forth a conception of self in poetic form, however, than to engage in a prose discussion of the problems of identifying or knowing the self. In *The Prelude* he proceeds cautiously, doubting whether it will be possible "To understand myself" (1.628) and sometimes, as in the Blind Beggar episode, not only seeing in "The face of everyone / That passes by me . . . a mystery" but suggesting that there is very little we can know "of ourselves" (7.628–29, 644–46). Yet he repeatedly returned to the poem on his own life because, he said, "Here at least I hoped that to a certain degree I should be sure of succeeding, as I had nothing to do but describe what I had felt and thought, therefore could not easily be bewildered."[11] Although one can hear undertones of doubt in this effort at self-assurance ("Here at least,"

---

identity. For more on this subject, see my *Keats and the Silent Work of Imagination*, 33–34, 187–89.

10. Quotations from Wordsworth's poetry (except for *The Prelude*) and from his notes are taken from *The Poetical Works of William Wordsworth*, ed. Ernest de Selincourt and Helen Darbishire, with references given in parentheses. Quotations from *The Prelude* are taken from the 1850 version, unless otherwise noted, in *The Prelude: 1799, 1805, 1850*, ed. Jonathan Wordsworth, M. H. Abrams, and Stephen Gill.

11. *Letters: The Early Years*, 586.

"hoped . . . to a certain degree," the possibility of being "bewildered"), suggesting that the self-assurance is defensive, and although Wordsworth often acknowledges the difficulties or seeming impossibility of knowing the self, the entire project of *The Prelude* is based on the intertwined assumptions that there is a self and that it is possible to know it, at least to some extent. Even in moments when he experiences a profound sense of self-division, as when he says, "often do I seem / Two consciousnesses, conscious of myself / And of some other Being" (2.31–33), the observation is made with an awareness of the surprise and contradiction that the idea of *two* registers on *one* consciousness. By the end of the poem, in his reflections on the experience of having ascended Mount Snowdon, Wordsworth holds out the possibility that "higher minds" can achieve "the highest bliss / That flesh can know . . . the consciousness / Of Whom they are" (14.90, 113–15).

His confidence in the possibility of achieving such a consciousness, and implicitly in the idea of an authentic self, appears to be brought into serious question by the countless revisions he made to *The Prelude* over a forty-year period. They reveal numerous reconstructions of himself, as several critics have demonstrated.[12] The varying self-representations in "Tintern Abbey" and the other major lyrics I shall discuss may be thought of as additional evidence in a long record of self-revision, though less for the comparatively minor revisions of each poem in later versions (only "Resolution and Independence," originally "The Leech Gatherer," underwent the kind of substantial revision after the first complete version that *The Prelude* underwent) than for the repeated effort at self-reconstruction each poem represents. Yet many if not all the uncertainties about the self evident in Wordsworth's revisions and reconstructions, I would argue, result more from the difficulties of trying to know and represent the self in the course of experiencing continual change and development over a lifetime than from questions about its existence.[13] This is not to say that Wordsworth never entertained

---

12. Among a number of excellent studies of Wordsworth's revisions and self-revisions in *The Prelude*, see especially Richard J. Onorato, *The Character of the Poet: Wordsworth in "The Prelude"*; Peter J. Manning, "Reading Wordsworth's Revisions: Othello and the Drowned Man," in *Reading Romantics: Texts and Contexts*, 100–132; Susan J. Wolfson, "Revision as Form: Wordsworth"; and Jack Stillinger, "Multiple Consciousnesses in Wordsworth's *Prelude*."

13. For a recent study arguing that Wordsworth's revisions reflect a continuity of self, see Zachary Leader, "Wordsworth, Revision, and Personal Identity."

doubts about the existence of a continuous self and personal identity. His persistence in revising *The Prelude* over many years may well have been an unconscious defense against such doubts that refused to be put by but could not be faced. It may also have been defensive in the sense that revision, as Susan Wolfson has explained, "coincides with life, the energy that postpones death and quickens the mind, and writing, with a hope for limitless adventure."[14] At the same time, if revision was a defense against doubt and death, it was also part of an unending effort to know the self, and it therefore necessarily involved the question of whether, and to what extent, knowing the self is possible. Wordsworth leaves the question open in the positive sense of believing that some can achieve a consciousness "Of Whom they are." For to have claimed certain knowledge of himself would have risked a figurative death of the self, a foreknowledge of its end and final shape, and therefore an end of hope and expectation. He would have been surrendering an ideal of self essential to the very definition and continued life of the self. He naturally hesitated to claim such a certainty, and no doubt this figured into his refusal to publish *The Prelude* in his lifetime.[15]

If, then, Wordsworth's poetry is so undeniably autobiographical, with the "I" of the major lyrics never a purely invented or wholly separable speaker or persona, and yet the speaker never simply "Wordsworth" (or one of the versions of the historical and biographical person that the proper noun denotes), how is a reader to think of the "I" of a particular poem, how define and conceptualize that presence and the subjectivity it represents?

I

Wordsworth's claim that he speaks "in his own person" is difficult to reconcile with the lyrical, dramatic, rhetorical, and other strategies

---

14. Wolfson, "Revision as Form," 131.

15. There were other, more practical reasons for not publishing it, of course, primary among them the risk to his reputation that a disclosure of his republican sympathies would have run. The risk was at its greatest a few years after the poem's completion in 1805, for by then, as Johnston points out, "the 'fit audience' he sought was gone," and if it had appeared he might well "have awakened to find himself [in contrast to Byron on the appearance of *Childe Harold's Pilgrimage* in 1812] infamous" (*Hidden Wordsworth*, 827, 835).

the "I" relies upon in the act of self-representation. In his 1800 Preface to *Lyrical Ballads* he blurs a distinction in the course of trying to establish it that would be essential to a clear understanding of what is meant by the notion of a poet speaking "in his own person." He wants to distinguish between "the Poet [who] speaks through the mouths of his characters" (in "those parts of composition" he calls "dramatic") and "the Poet [who] speaks to us in his own person and character" (*Prose*, 1:142). The blurring occurs when he says that the poet speaking in his own person is expected to employ certain dramatic devices. The "Poet," who is described as "a man speaking to men," is said to possess "an ability of conjuring up in himself passions, which are indeed far from being the same as those produced by real events, yet . . . do more nearly resemble the passions produced by real events" (*Prose*, 1:138). Wordsworth's allowance for a "selection" of the language "really used by men" and for the idea of "conjuring," however, indicates that even when he claims to be speaking in his own person he assumes the license to imitate, fabricate, and dramatize (*Prose*, 1:123, 138).

In his Preface to the edition of 1815 he further blurs the distinction in some remarks concerning poems "essentially lyrical" and how they should be read. He reminds his reader that "All poets, except the dramatic, have been in the practice of feigning that their works were composed to the music of the harp or lyre." He will not "violate probability so far, or . . . make such a large demand upon the Reader's charity." Nevertheless, he points out, "Some of these pieces are essentially lyrical; and, therefore, cannot have their due force without a supposed musical accompaniment." As a "substitute for the classic lyre or harp," or for the supposed accompaniment, he requires of his reader "nothing more than an animated or impassioned recitation, adapted to the subject" (*Prose*, 3:29). While appearing to ask for "nothing more" than an "animated or impassioned recitation," however, he is in fact asking for something more than the kind of simple identification suggested by the notion that a reader must "read with the feelings of the Author," as he had remarked in his June 14, 1802, response to Sara Hutchinson's criticisms of a draft of "The Leech Gatherer." He is asking for a performance. Although his requirement that a reader give his lyric poems an animated or impassioned recitation does not necessarily mean that at the time of composition he consciously thought of his speakers as dramatized, the fact that the major lyrics rely on such dramatic features as apostrophe, the staged return or encounter, interaction between the speaker and a character or silent auditor (or apostrophized other), and the reenacted moment of new awareness suggests that Wordsworth conceived of these lyrical utterances as dramatic in fundamental ways.

Wordsworth's emphasis on the dramatic nature of the lyric was, not surprisingly, part of a general conception of lyric form taking shape during the Romantic period. The first generation of English Romantics, as Stuart Curran has explained, "evolved, or reinforced, a recognizable conception of the ode as an inherently dramatic form."[16] In their hands the ode became a highly dramatic and self-reflexive form that would eventually serve as a model for self-representation in other forms. In a note he appended to 1800–1805 editions of *Lyrical Ballads*, Wordsworth remarked that he had had the ode in mind when he composed "Tintern Abbey": "I have not ventured to call this Poem an Ode; but it was written with a hope that in the transitions, and the impassioned music of the versification, would be found the principal requisites of that species of composition" (*Poetical Works*, 2:517). Certainly one of the principal "requisites" was that a poem be dramatic. Not only the two features Wordsworth mentions here (transitions and impassioned music) but also the others I have noted above are part of the self-dramatizing that is characteristic of the Romantic lyric. In the speaker's representation of his subjectivity, he tends to adopt a dramatic mode and to transform into that mode whatever in his lyrical voice is declarative, descriptive, narrative, interrogative, or meditative. This tendency to appropriate other modes of poetic discourse for the dramatic is a characteristic of the "I" of the major lyrics that I shall emphasize throughout this study.

How, then, is one to reconcile this self-dramatizing character of the speaker of the major lyrics to Wordsworth's claim that he is speaking in his own person? To be more precise: Is the self-dramatizing strategy merely an aesthetic device, designed to enhance the autobiographical voice of the speaker, or is it an essential part of the voice and character of the poet speaking in his own person? Several of Wordsworth's statements in various notes and essays suggest that he believes it is the latter, and his belief seems to make it more difficult to distinguish between the poet and the lyric speaker. In his 1800 Note to "The Thorn," in the course of justifying his view that "repetition and apparent tautology are

---

16. Stuart Curran, *Poetic Form and British Romanticism*, 78.

frequently beauties of the highest kind," he gives as the chief reason "the interest which the mind attaches to words, not only as symbols of the passion, but as *things,* active and efficient, which are of themselves part of the passion" (*Poetical Works,* 2:513).[17] Just before this passage he remarked that "Words, a Poet's words more particularly, ought to be weighed in the balance of feeling. . . . For the Reader cannot be too often reminded that Poetry is passion." Now he is saying that the mind, because of its interest in words, often treats them not only as "symbols" of the passion but as "part" of the passion. He seems to anticipate Coleridge's remark in *The Statesman's Manual* on the nature of the symbol: "It always partakes of the Reality which it renders intelligible; and while it enunciates the whole, abides itself as a living part in that Unity, of which it is the representative."[18] His comment in the Note is confined to one aspect of the poet's art, namely, his choice of words, but it expresses a strongly held conviction that a poet's words, in the moment of communicating impassioned feelings, seem to become part of the passion.

This idea is taken up again in the third of his "Essays upon Epitaphs," particularly in the well-known incarnation passage. The immediate context for the passage is the recent history of epitaphs and how they have been "tainted by the artifices which have overrun our writings in metre since the days of Dryden and Pope" (*Prose,* 2:84). But the larger context is the integral relationship between language and feeling. For Wordsworth, the expressive language of poetry is not merely dress for thought but an incarnation of thought. He argues that if words were only clothing, they would be "an ill gift; such a one as those poisoned vestments, read of in the stories of superstitious times, which had power to consume and to alienate from his right mind the victim who put them on." Language would be "a counter-spirit, unremittingly and noiselessly at work to derange, to subvert, to lay waste, to vitiate, and to dissolve." Against such a possibility he insists—and from "deep conviction"— that words and expressions are essential parts of thought itself, not mere representations: "Energy, stillness, grandeur, tenderness, those feelings

---

17. Cf. Wordsworth's remark in an 1829 letter to William Rowan Hamilton that, "to speak a little metaphysically, words are not a mere *vehicle,* but they are *powers* either to kill or to animate." William Wordsworth and Dorothy Wordsworth, *The Later Years,* 2:185.

18. Samuel Taylor Coleridge, *The Statesman's Manual,* 30.

which are the pure emanations of nature, those thoughts which have the infinitude of truth, and those expressions which are not what the garb is to the body but what the body is to the soul, [are] themselves a *constituent part and power* or function in the thought" (*Prose*, 2:84–85, emphasis added). Here, too, as in the Note to "The Thorn," the idea that words and expressions in poetry are part of the passion, part of the thing being thought and expressed ("The Reader cannot be too often reminded that Poetry is passion"), is corollary to the idea that a representation in poetry is part of the thing represented.[19]

Wordsworth's comments about language and representation bear directly on his ideas of self-representation and the notion of the poet speaking in his own person. If a representation in language is not merely clothing to the body but rather "what the body is to the soul," and therefore an essential part of the thing represented, then a self-representation in poetry is a "constituent part and power" of the self. This premise underlies the poetics of self-representation in Wordsworth's lyrics and indicates that the dramatic and performative nature of self-representation does not contradict the notion of a poet speaking in his own person or the traditional notion of lyric poetry as expressive (though it does appear to contradict John Stuart Mill's notion that lyric poetry is "overheard," since that notion equates the speaker with the poet in an unqualified way).[20] On the contrary, the act

---

19. In an important deconstructive reading, Frances Ferguson has revealed that language and death are in "a complex dialectic" in the incarnation passage and that Wordsworth's belief that language is an incarnation of thought (and not the counterspirit he fears) gets subverted (see *Wordsworth: Language as Counter-Spirit*, 30–34). In emphasizing his belief that language in poetry is an incarnation of thought, my purpose is not to dispute Ferguson's reading but to call attention to the continuing importance in Wordsworth's ideas about language in poetry that it is part of the passion being represented, as well as to the corollary idea that a self-representation is part of the self.

20. In his essay "What Is Poetry?" John Stuart Mill says that "eloquence is *heard*; poetry is *over*heard. Eloquence supposes an audience. The peculiarity of poetry appears to us to lie in the poet's utter unconsciousness of a listener" (*Norton Anthology*, 1143). See Helen Vendler, "'Tintern Abbey': Two Assaults" for the view that only the speaker of a dramatic monologue of the kind Browning wrote can be said to be "overheard" (184). See also Herbert Tucker, "Dramatic Monologue and the Overhearing of Lyric."

of self-representation is a means of constituting the self and for this reason the resulting self-representation, the "I" of the poem, would be, according to Wordsworth, both the poet in his own person and the self in the act of reconstituting itself.

2

To summarize briefly, if the poet who speaks in his own person is a representation, and yet this self-representation is also in certain ways the actual or "real" self or subjectivity of the poet, then we need a definition and a way of conceptualizing the "I" that can describe its psychological complexity and explain the paradox by which an invented, idealized, and performing "I" can at the same time be the self of the poet speaking in his own person.

One might begin to develop such a definition by taking the self-dramatizing character of the "I" of the major lyrics as an essential and self-defining quality.[21] Such a definition would differentiate it from Wordsworth's other self-representations in prose, though never completely, of course, since self-dramatizing can appear in prose. It would also differentiate the "I" of the major lyrics from the speakers in other—often shorter—poems by the extent and depth of the self-dramatization. It would prove to be of little value, however, if it did no more than identify and differentiate. We need a definition that will enable us both to conceptualize the self of the speaker (with the dynamics of its various tendencies, conflicts, strategies, and intrapsychic workings) and to understand its developmental role in the life of the poet. When we consider the relation between the "I" of a poem and the poet's life, we usually think only of the ways in which the life contributed to the makeup of the "I." We think of the early death of Wordsworth's mother

---

21. In *Art of the "Lyrical Ballads,"* Parrish has shown how the speakers in poems such as "The Thorn" are dramatic characters rather than Wordsworthian personas. His concern, however, is with the speakers in the ballads, not with those in the major lyrics or *The Prelude*. In *Revolutionary "I,"* Nichols emphasizes the dramatic makeup of Wordsworth's "I" in *The Prelude*, calling it a "dramatized projection," and says that it "presents a dramatized cultural self rather than an authentic self-biographer." (29). In this emphasis, however, Nichols separates the "I" from the autobiographical self and defines it in historical and cultural rather than psychological terms.

and how it may have contributed to the maternal image of Nature that the speaker of "Tintern Abbey" idealizes, or of Wordsworth's experience in France and of how it may have contributed to his sense of himself in 1793, on his earlier visit to the Wye valley, as "more like a man / Flying from something that he dreads than one / Who sought the thing he loved" (70–72). Or we may think of the ways in which the death of John shaped the questioning consciousness of the speaker of "Elegiac Stanzas." From either a biographical or a critical point of view, however, it is also important to consider the ways in which the "I" contributed to the ongoing life and development of the poet.

As a first step toward a definition, I want to suggest that the speaker or "I" of a major lyric is a dramatized, transitional self of the poet that enables him to experience a special mode of being in which he can explore certain potentialities of self and attempt a transformation of self. The experience typically takes place in the presence of an important addressee or object (or Other), establishing a distinctly dramatic context for the speaker's utterance. The utterance itself has a dramatic structure, possessing not only a beginning, middle, and end, but also a climactic moment of new awareness that the speaker is at some pains to highlight or dramatize, usually in a tone markedly different from that used elsewhere in the poem. The content of the new awareness or the succeeding reflection upon it tends to emphasize the speaker's sense of having undergone a profound transformation as a result of the dramatized experience. Yet the whole experience is transitional, not simply in the sense of being transient or passing, lasting only as long as the poem does, but in the sense of being a crucial stage in a movement from one moment or period of development to another.

Let me now explore and expand this notion of transitional experience and of a transitional self that I am using to define Wordsworth's lyrical speaker. Freud discusses it in two of his papers on technique, "The Dynamics of Transference" and "Observations on Transference Love." In the transference an analysand commonly exhibits a form of behavior, often referred to as the *transference neurosis*, that is not typical of his or her ordinary—or ordinarily neurotic—life, nor is it representative of the healthy condition being sought. In another important paper, "Remembering, Repeating, and Working-Through," Freud says that the transference "creates an intermediate region between illness and real life through which the transition from the one to the other is made." It arises in treatment as a result of the special relationship between analysand and analyst, a relationship that eventually revives infantile imagos, old conflicts, and unconscious impulses in the analysand. Since the behavior takes place in an intermediate region in the psychological life of the analysand, it has an "artificial" or fictional character about it. At the same time, Freud insists, it is "a piece of real experience," although "of a provisional nature."[22] Indeed, it is also a part of normative experience and a "universal characteristic" of human nature to transfer old conflicts and impulses onto current relationships. In that way, Freud reminds us, transference is a part of the psychopathology of everyday life.[23]

The intermediate region in which the transference takes place can be likened to the "potential space" in which, D. W. Winnicott has argued, much of an infant's early life takes place. The potential space is the psychological area "between the individual and the environment (originally the object)." In it the infant plays, pretends, and forms a close relationship with a "transitional object" such as a teddy bear or favorite blanket. The transitional object has an important developmental function. It facilitates the infant's "journey of progress towards experiencing" and through a particular stage of life. Despite the fact that Winnicott calls the object transitional, he emphasizes that "It is not the object, of course, that is transitional." The object rather represents the infant's transition from one state of being to another ("from a state of being merged with the mother to a state of being in relation to the mother as something outside and separate").[24] It is the experiencing self that is transitional.

Although Freud's conception of an intermediate region and Winnicott's of a potential space are drawn from quite different kinds of

---

22. Freud, "Remembering, Repeating, and Working-Through," in *Standard Edition*, 12:154. See also Freud, "The Dynamics of Transference," in *Standard Edition*, 12:99–108.

23. See Freud, *Introductory Lectures on Psycho-Analysis*, in *Standard Edition*, 16:446. In his postscript to the case of Dora ("Fragment of an Analysis of a Case of Hysteria," in *Standard Edition*, 7:3–122), Freud observes that "Psycho-analytic treatment does not *create* transferences, it merely brings them to light, like so many other hidden psychical factors" (7:117). Peter L. Rudnytsky has shown in *Freud and Oedipus* how a series of transferences haunted Freud's own life, particularly his relationships with figures such as Fliess, Adler, and Jung.

24. Donald W. Winnicott, *Playing and Reality*, 100, 6, 14. For the discussion of transitional objects and phenomena, see 1–25.

human experience (adult analysis and infant playing), both conceptions posit a transitional self for their respective experiences and both insist on the paradox of an experience that can be simultaneously artificial and real. Winnicott, in fact, goes further and enlarges the conception of potential space to include all cultural experience. The "intermediate area of experience" of playing and pretending "constitutes the greater part of the infant's experience," he writes, "and throughout life is retained in the intense experiencing that belongs to the arts and to religion and to imaginative living, and to creative scientific work." Both conceptions have also been used by literary critics as a model for understanding the relationship between the reader and the text. Murray Schwartz proposed Winnicott's idea of potential space as a model for understanding the psychological space between subjective and objective worlds that a reader enters into when he reads a work of literature. More recently Peter Brooks, relying on Freud's papers on transference, has proposed a "transferential model" that "illuminates the difficult and productive encounter of the speaker and the listener, the text and the reader, and how their exchange takes place in an 'artificial' space—a symbolic and semiotic medium—that is nonetheless the place of real investments of desire from both sides of the dialogue."[25]

I want to suggest that if the intermediate region of the transference can serve as a model for the artificial space in which an exchange takes place between reader and text, as Brooks argues, it can also provide a model for the relationship between the writer and the self he creates and portrays in that text. The writer, after all, transfers attitudes to and invests strong feelings in the "I" of a lyric in the course of projecting himself into it. In the act of doing so, he becomes a transitional self in the sense that I have suggested.

25. Winnicott, *Playing and Reality*, 14 (see also "The Location of Cultural Experience" in the same work [95–103]); Murray Schwartz, "Where Is Literature?"; Peter Brooks, "The Idea of a Psychoanalytic Literary Criticism," 344. In a book that I discovered after completing the present study, Jonathan Lear extends the ideas of Freud and Winnicott in a chapter entitled "An Interpretation of Transference." He suggests that "In the transference, the psyche is engaged in its characteristic activity of trying to create a meaningful world in which to live" (*Open Minded: Working Out the Logic of the Soul*, 66) and goes on to say that "transference is an attempt to make the world over—in phantasy and actings out—according to an image of what would gratify basic wishes, under certain conditions of conflict" (132).

Like the self presented in the intermediate region of the transference, the lyrical "I" existing in the potential space and transitional experience of a poem is always shown to be constituted through an intersubjective relationship with an Other or an intrapsychic relationship with an aspect or image of the self, or both. For Wordsworth, the Other may be an anthropomorphized and gendered Nature, as in "Tintern Abbey," or an idealized Leech-gatherer, or it may be an idealized image of the self, one that had a preexistence, as in the Intimations Ode, or one that is associated with a hypothetical, ideal painting, as in "Elegiac Stanzas." However the Other is depicted in the poem, and with whatever social and cultural determinants that shape its outward appearance, it is always representative of an internal object in the poet's mind drawn from his early history, and it can never completely escape being recast as a version of that "original" in the psyche of the poet. The Other that the "I" sees, imagines, or encounters may appear to be like a transitional object, external and unique ("The oldest man he seemed that ever wore grey hairs," the speaker says of the Leech-gatherer [56]), but it is always representative or symbolic of an internal object that is "immortal" in the sense that the self cannot end its relationship with it.[26] The self can only imagine or experience certain changes in the representation of it or in the relationship with it. The Other can function in a variety of ways—at times as symbolic of an ideal to be restored, reinstated, or identified with, at other times as an opposing figure or rival to be questioned or defied or overcome. However it may be depicted, the Other that the "I" imagines or encounters, addresses or reflects upon, and transfers feelings and attitudes toward plays an important role in an intersubjective or intrapsychic relationship in which the "I" attempts to construct its subjectivity.

To take the analogy with the transference a step further, the lyrical "I" is not only a transitional self that achieves temporarily a special mode of being in an intersubjective relationship with a chosen addressee, but one that reenacts old conflicts, anxieties, and aspirations in the poet's psychic history. For Freud, the reenactment is a conspicuous feature of the transference. He calls it a form of repetition. The patient "does not *remember* anything of what he has forgotten and repressed, but *acts*

---

26. I am drawing here on Roy Schafer's "The Fates of the Immortal Object," in *Aspects of Internalization*, 220–36.

it out. He reproduces it not as a memory but as an action; he *repeats* it, without, of course, knowing that he is repeating it." For example, "the patient does not say that he remembers that he used to be defiant and critical towards his parents' authority; instead, he behaves in that way to the doctor." This behavior is thought to have an artificial character to it, as we have already seen, but to be at the same time a piece of real experience.[27] Similarly, the experience of the "I" of a poem is not purely fictional or illusory, but rather a piece of the poet's real life. It is a transitional experience in a potential space and the "I" acts out certain potentialities of the poet's self in a theater of the poet's mind.

The concept of reenactment or acting out in a transference, however, poses two important problems when applied to a literary text that I want to address briefly. The first concerns the extent to which self-dramatizing in a poem may be, like acting out in transference, a form of unconscious repetition. Since transferring feelings and attitudes from old to new relationships is not limited to the analytic situation, however, and is thought by Freud to be a universal characteristic, it is to be expected that some unconscious acting out would be a part of the self-dramatizing in a poem. The possibility that in "Tintern Abbey" Wordsworth transferred feelings to Nature that were originally experienced in his relationship with his mother or that he transferred feelings to Dorothy that he had experienced in his relationship with Annette Vallon may serve as an example not only of acting out a transference but of unconscious repetition.[28]

The second problem is more difficult. It concerns the question of whether the self-dramatizing in a poem is a form of resistance, as Freud maintained the transference is. And, if so, is it only resistance? On one hand, self-dramatizing in a poem can be resistance in the sense that a poem or any creative work may construct a fantasy world, a moral or philosophical position, or a conclusion that attempts to resist or defend against painful truths or experiences. A poem can be a "lie against solitude," as Susan Hawk Brisman and Leslie Brisman have shown in their Lacanian discussion of Coleridge, or a denial of social and economic

---

27. Freud, "Remembering, Repeating, and Working-Through," 12:150, 154.
28. For discussions of these two forms of transference in "Tintern Abbey," see, respectively, Onorato, *Character of the Poet*, 29–87, and Johnston, *Hidden Wordsworth*, 399–400.

reality, as several New Historicists have argued. On the other hand, the transference is never only resistance. It can also be an important mode of advance. Freud called it the patient's "most powerful motive" to make progress in the treatment, where progress is defined as the ability to change, to transform the self.[29] Similarly, the self-dramatization in a poem is never only a form of resistance or unconscious repetition or self-deception, but rather a part of a larger effort at self-transformation.

One further aspect of the analogy with transference that needs to be explored has to do with motivation and goal. In analysis, of course, the goal is cure, which necessarily involves some transformation of the self. The self-transformation is sought through a process that attempts, with the intervention of the analyst, to convert the unconscious repetition of acting out into remembering. Freud believed that remembering and new awareness would bring release from unending repetition. Where unconscious repetition is, there should memory and new awareness be. But in literature the goal is not "cure," at least not in any conventional sense, though a work may have some cathartic or therapeutic aims, as when Wordsworth recommends the "healing thoughts" of "Tintern Abbey" to Dorothy in the last verse paragraph of the poem, or Coleridge struggles against a profound, unknown grief that is "void, dark, and drear" in "Dejection: An Ode," or Keats thinks of the poet as a "physician to all men" in "The Fall of Hyperion." The analogy with transference can be taken only so far. Still, the greater Romantic lyric is a crisis poem, and in it a speaker typically tries to resolve the most serious moral, psychological, and philosophical problems.[30] In doing so, he also tries to achieve a self-transformation through a process of self-dramatization that attempts to convert the real/artificial experience of the poem and distill its essence into memory and new awareness. In the last verse paragraph of "Tintern Abbey" the speaker urges his sister to "remember" him "And these my exhortations!" (145–46). In the last two lines of "Resolution and Independence" the speaker concludes with a resolution

---

29. See Susan Hawk Brisman and Leslie Brisman, "Lies against Solitude: Symbolic, Imaginary, Real"; Freud, "Fragment of an Analysis," 7:117; Freud, *Introductory Lectures*, 16:443.

30. See M. H. Abrams, "Structure and Style in the Greater Romantic Lyric," and, more generally, Abrams, *Natural Supernaturalism: Tradition and Revolution in Romantic Literature*.

to remember: "'God,' said I, 'be my help and stay secure; / I'll think of the Leech-gatherer on the lonely moor!'" For both Wordsworth and Freud, the goal of self-transformation can be reached only through a process that converts a reenactment of old longings and anxieties into remembering and new awareness.

Beyond the goal of self-transformation lies the more distant and unattainable ideal of self-realization that is well known to be inherent in Romantic thought, though it appears to be more characteristic of what Anne Mellor has called masculine Romanticism. It may be traced to the Romantic assumption that change in human experience is growth that leads, if not inevitably at least potentially, to self-realization. "Every individual human being, one may say," Schiller wrote in his *Aesthetic Education of Man*, "carries within him, potentially and prescriptively, an ideal man, the archetype of a human being, and it is his life's task to be, through all his changing manifestations, in harmony with the unchanging unity of this ideal."[31] However illusory the ideal may be, it is the one that, more than any other, drives the psyche of the Romantic poet forward. Few premises are as central to Romantic thought as the ideal of self-realization, and few have been as central to scholarship on the Romantics.[32] Self-realization is the ideal that the "I" of the Romantic lyric strives to achieve. The fully realized self is, in the words of Geoffrey Hartman, "the [ideal] 'I' toward which that 'I' [of the lyric] reaches."[33]

---

31. See Mellor, *Romanticism and Gender*, especially chapter 7, "Writing the Self/Self-Writing: William Wordsworth's *Prelude*/Dorothy Wordsworth's *Journals*," 144–69; Friedrich Schiller, *On the Aesthetic Education of Man*, 17.

32. For studies that reflect the centrality of this theme and also take Wordsworth as their primary subject or as an exemplary figure, see Langbaum, *Poetry of Experience*; Langbaum, "Wordsworth: The Self as Process"; Abrams, *Natural Supernaturalism*; Onorato, *Character of the Poet*; Mary Jacobus, *Tradition and Experiment in Wordsworth's Lyrical Ballads (1798)*; and Paul Jay, *Being in the Text: Self-Representation from Wordsworth to Barthes*, 13–91.

33. Geoffrey Hartman, "Romanticism and 'Anti-Self-Consciousness,'" 52. In the next sentence Hartman offers the illuminating suggestion that "The very confusion in modern literary theory concerning the fictive 'I,' whether it represents the writer as person or as persona, may reflect a dialectic inherent in poetry between the relatively self-conscious self, and that self within the self which resembles Blake's 'emanation' and Shelley's 'epipsyche'" (52). The dialectic Hartman identifies is a

What still needs to be explored in any effort to understand the "I" of Wordsworth's major lyrics is the dynamics of the self-dramatizing process by which the lyrical "I" strives toward self-realization. At the heart of that process is the climactic moment of new awareness. No strategy that the "I" employs in its striving toward a realization of an ideal self is more characteristic of its nature or essential to its efforts than its staging of such a moment. In that moment the self-dramatizing "I" comes closest to giving true voice to the subjectivity it represents and being the poet speaking in his own person, and it is to that moment that I shall now turn.

3

The moment is always represented as an achievement of new awareness that becomes a turning point in the life of the "I," a move from ignorance to knowledge or understanding. The speaker makes a revelatory discovery about himself, his past, Nature, or human existence. In such a moment, Wordsworth says in "Tintern Abbey," "We see into the life of things" (49). Inherent in the moment is a sense of self-realization: in a "serene and blessed mood" one "become[s] a living soul" (41, 46). One experiences a sense of having reached a moment of self-fulfillment, of having brought to realization the self that one has aspired to be, no matter how momentary and illusory the experience may be. The recurrence of moments like this in Wordsworth's poetry, it is no exaggeration to say, constitutes both a structural principle and a principle of being, of psychological life, for the "I" of the major lyrics.[34]

---

crucial part of the subject of this study, though I define it in psychoanalytic and formalistic terms and see it in the speaker's problematic act of self-representation.

34. Surprisingly little attention has been given to the psychology of these moments. Langbaum, in *Poetry of Experience*, borrowing from Joyce, appropriates the term "epiphany" for them but does not explore their content or psychological dynamics, asserting only that the new awareness is more of a gain "in the intensity of understanding than in what is understood" (46; see also Langbaum, "The Epiphanic Mode in Wordsworth and Modern Literature"). Hartman makes such moments central to his readings in *Wordsworth's Poetry*, but his interest is more in the apocalyptic character of the experience than in the psychological dynamics of the moments and their relation to the speaker's self. Abrams calls attention in

Moments of new awareness or recognition occur as part of the plot or dramatic structure of a poem and the Aristotelian concepts of recognition and reversal that have been applied to drama are also relevant for the Romantic lyric. In Romantic poetry moments of recognition tend to occur at or near the ends of poems. In "Nutting" the last line proclaims that "there is a spirit in the woods." In Coleridge's "This Lime-Tree Bower My Prison" the speaker is quite explicit about the recognition in the last verse paragraph: "Henceforth I shall know / That Nature ne'er deserts the wise and pure" (59–60). The last two lines of Keats's "Ode on a Grecian Urn"—"'Beauty is truth, truth beauty,'—that is all / Ye know on earth, and all ye need to know"—have been the subject of unending debate, but no one can doubt that they are intended by the poet to announce a new understanding of sufficient power to conclude the poem, even if for a reader (T. S. Eliot, for example) they may raise more questions than they answer. Some moments, however, are situated in the middle of a poem, others at the beginning. In *Prometheus Unbound*, Shelley's hero comes to a new understanding early in act I ("I wish no living thing to suffer pain" [305]) and from this moment unfolds all the subsequent action of the play.[35] In "The Rime of the Ancient Mariner," on the other hand, the moment of new awareness and turning point in the Mariner's fate comes in the middle of the poem when he blesses the water snakes. In *The Prelude* Wordsworth depicts numerous moments or "spots of time" when the poet is shown achieving a new awareness, but the two principal ones occur at the middle and end of the poem, in

---

Natural Supernaturalism to their preeminent role in Romantic experience, referring to them as sublime moments and treating them as secular versions of the Augustinian moment of revelation. His concern is more with intellectual history, however, than with the psychology of self-representation. Ashton Nichols valuably traces the modern epiphany to the Romantic poets, especially Wordsworth, in his *The Poetics of Epiphany: Nineteenth-Century Origins of the Modern Literary Moment*, but does not deal with the crucial psychological issues posed by these moments. Terence Cave's authoritative *Recognitions: A Study in Poetics* explores its subject in depth, from the Greeks to the moderns, but is concerned with drama and fiction, not lyric poetry, and does not consider Wordsworth and the other Romantic poets.

35. Quotations of Coleridge's poetry are taken from *The Complete Poetical Works of Samuel Taylor Coleridge*, ed. E. H. Coleridge, unless otherwise noted; of Keats's poetry from *The Poems of John Keats*, ed. Jack Stillinger; and of Shelley's poetry from *Shelley's Poetry and Prose*, ed. Donald H. Reiman and Sharon B. Powers.

the crossing of the Alps episode in book 6 and the Mount Snowdon episode in book 14.

The similarities of such moments in the work of an individual poet raise difficult critical questions. Wordsworth dramatizes a recognition of a presence in Nature in "Tintern Abbey," "Nutting," various episodes of *The Prelude*, and numerous other poems. While no moment of recognition is ever an exact repetition of a previous one, or of its psychological, philosophical, moral, or other content, there is enough similarity in the recognitions to undermine the claim that they are discoveries. If, as Freud maintains, repetition is a form of remembering, what kind of discovery or recognition requires repeated remembering? The repetition suggests that the poet, somewhere in the depths of his soul, does not accept the discovery as authentic or conclusive. He then invents another situation in which another "I" achieves a similar "new" awareness. If we were to think of a poet's entire work as a single text with a narrative design, we might take the repetition as indicating the shape of a masterplot in which a composite "I" repeatedly achieves a similar new awareness.[36] Keats, for example, early in his poetic career leads Endymion to a recognition that there should be "no more of dreaming" (4.669), yet the wish that dreams could come true remains irrepressible, and for the rest of his short writing life Keats continues to invent situations in which this recognition (and the proposition it attempts to deny: "What the Imagination seizes as Beauty must be truth—whether it existed before or not")[37] may be tested and attitudes toward it developed. He does this most memorably, perhaps, in "The Eve of St. Agnes," "Ode to a Nightingale," "Ode on a Grecian Urn," and "Lamia."

We expect a certain amount of repetition in the work of any writer, of course, and we often refer to its object as a preoccupation. Taken together, the preoccupations of a Keats or a Wordsworth may be seen to form a strong continuity in his thought and development, and the basis for some definition or notion of identity. But underneath them and their expression in poetic form lies an apparent compulsion to repeat. One is tempted to say of the repetition in Romantic poetry what Freud said of recurrent dreams in traumatic neuroses: "This astonishes

---

36. I am drawing here on Peter Brooks, *Reading for the Plot: Design and Intention in Narrative*, especially chapter 4 ("Freud's Masterplot: A Model for Narrative").

37. *Letters of John Keats*, 1:184.

people far too little."[38] Repetition does not belie the poet's claim of discovery, his conviction that, as Wordsworth wrote in his 1815 "Essay, Supplementary to the Preface," he introduces "a new element into the intellectual universe," but it does complicate things a great deal (*Prose*, 3:82). How, after all, can we take a moment of awareness as new when we know that it is a repetition? How can a moment of new awareness result from a process of repetition? What purpose does the repetition serve in the poet's dramatization of the life of the self?

One may begin to answer these questions by recalling that traditional recognition scenes are based on repetition. The word carries this meaning in its Latin root, *recognitio*, to recall, to know something or someone and to experience a recollection. A form of repetition also lies at the heart of the classical notion of a recognition scene. In *The Poetics* Aristotle identifies five kinds of recognition: by sign, announcement, memory, reasoning, and, best of all, incidents natural to the development of the plot. Examples include the scene in which the old nurse, Eurycleia, recognizes the returned Odysseus by a scar she sees while bathing him, and the scene in which Electra reasons that Orestes has returned to Argos after she has spotted a strand of hair and his footprints at the tomb of Agamemnon. Recognitions in Romantic poetry do not typically depict a return of a person, but they tend to involve a return of the repressed. If one seeks comparisons outside of Romantic literature, one thinks of works where a radical change of consciousness takes place— for example, when Oedipus comes to understand who he is in the course of questioning the herdsman, or when Hamlet comprehends Claudius's villainy in the revelatory meeting with the ghost on the ramparts. These discoveries also, it is well to note, do not come as a complete surprise: Oedipus's recognition of who he is is the fulfillment of a prophecy he knew all too well but sought to avoid, and Hamlet's discovery is followed by the exclamation "Oh, my prophetic soul!"

To account for the repetition in moments of new awareness, we need a psychology of new awareness. Freud was from the beginning fascinated by such moments. In his 1895 *Project for a Scientific Psychology* he tried to explain the new awareness that results from traumatic experience. In many of his later, famous works he continued to use the notion of a new awareness—for example, in the case histories, especially that of

---

38. Freud, *Beyond the Pleasure Principle*, in *Standard Edition*, 18:13.

the "Wolf Man" ("From the History of an Infantile Neurosis"), where the idea of the primal scene is explored, and in papers such as "The Uncanny" and "On the Medusa's Head." His analysis of the *fort/da* game of little Ernst in *Beyond the Pleasure Principle* not only deals with a continually reenacted moment of awareness, but represents it as coming into existence in relation to an imagined but potentially traumatic loss (the temporary disappearance of Ernst's mother), with the aim of mastering the anxiety caused by the anticipation of loss. Moments of new awareness continue to hold a place of unique importance in psychoanalytic theory because the promise of a talking cure assumes that they will result in a new understanding of the self, which, in turn, will result in a transformation of the self, even though Freud's emphasis on repetition, as Terence Cave has observed, "makes the possibility of a definitive ending—a full recognition and a consequent cure—more remote and problematic."[39]

To address the problem of repetition in Wordsworth's major lyrics and how it figures in the life of the "I," I want to propose two kinds of psychological events as prototypes for the moments of new awareness: (1) the identity-making event when the individual first discovers himself or herself in the mirror of an Other's eye and (2) the traumatic moment when the significance of a present, remembered, or imagined event presses itself forcefully on consciousness. The poetic moment conflates and repeats these two events.

Of the first of these psychological events, Winnicott has written, "the precursor of the mirror is the mother's face." Such a mirroring function of a maternal figure is now widely acknowledged to be crucial for establishing the basis on which the earliest sense of self or identity will be built,[40] but it was also known to Coleridge in the form of

---

39. Cave, *Recognitions*, 170.

40. Winnicott, *Playing and Reality*, 111. In addition to Winnicott, Heinz Lichtenstein, Edith Jacobson, Margaret Mahler, and Heinz Kohut have all emphasized the formative importance of the mirroring function. Here, for example, is Mahler: "the mother conveys—in innumerable ways—a kind of 'mirroring frame of reference,' to which the primitive self of the infant automatically adjusts. . . . The primary method of identity formation consists of mutual reflection during the symbiotic phase. This narcissistic, mutual libidinal mirroring reinforces the delineation of identity" (*On Human Symbiosis and the Vicissitudes of Individuation*, 19).

what Thomas McFarland calls a remarkable "pre-Freudian insight." The baby's first sense of its humanity breaks forth in

> the Eye that connects the Mother's face with the warmth of the mother's bosom, the support of the mother's Arms. A thousand tender kisses excite a finer life in its lips & there first language is imitated from the mother's smiles. Ere yet a conscious self exists the love begins & the first love is love to another. The Babe acknowledges a self in the Mother's form, years before it can recognize a self in its own.[41]

One first discovers oneself as an "I" in the response to oneself by a significant Other. Rather than an independent being emerging from its own physiological and mental capacities into a state of psychological and social autonomy, the self has an existence and a self-image that are mediated by and dependent upon an Other. It is in part the creation of an Other and his or her own needs. Lacan goes so far as to say that the "first object [aim] of desire is to be recognized by the other." For this reason, the self, or its agency the ego, is strongly situated in a "fictional direction."[42]

The self-image that one sees in a moment of self-recognition, therefore, has emerged from a symbiotic relationship with another person and is perpetuated in part through an imaginative re-creation of that relationship with various real or imaginary others. In Wordsworth's poetry that relationship is reproduced with Nature in "Tintern Abbey," with the Leech-gatherer in "Resolution and Independence," and with an image of a prior (and preexistent) self in the Intimations Ode. The self is never established in any final shape, but it is continually revised and adapted to changing inner demands and outer circumstances. It unfolds from a never-ending dialectic with various representations of an Other that is always partly fictional, and the self re-creates, revises, and affirms its existence in this dialectic. These two characteristics of inner life—the birth of the self in the presence of a mirroring Other and the self's continuing dependence on substitutes—provide a psychological basis for understanding the male Romantic poet's preference for self-Other,

---

41. MS of the *Opus Maximum*, cited in Thomas McFarland, *Romanticism and the Forms of Ruin: Wordsworth, Coleridge, and Modalities of Fragmentation*, 150.

42. Jacques Lacan, "The Function and Field of Speech and Language in Psychoanalysis," 58, and "The Mirror Stage as Formative of the Function of the I as Revealed in Psychoanalytic Experience," 2 (both essays in *Écrits: A Selection*).

I-thou lyrical structures and his predisposition to encounters with figures or symbols in whose presence he seeks to redefine and affirm the self.

Yet an essential feature of the moments of new awareness in Wordsworth's major lyrics would remain unexplained by this self-Other psychology. How would we account for the fact that the new awareness always appears to emerge out of a crisis? That Nature in "Tintern Abbey" is "felt" as a powerful "presence" because of an acute sense of the "burthen of the mystery," or that resolution and independence, if achieved at all, follow thoughts about despondency and madness, and a poet who committed suicide? What is the relation between the crisis and the new awareness? To what extent does the former determine the content of the latter? These and other, related questions require an explanation not only of self-Other relationships but of special moments of consciousness, visionary experience, and affective intensity.

Freud's early theory of trauma provides a basis for such an explanation. There is nothing new, of course, in suggesting that traumatic experience may have figured in the conception of, or may be represented in, a literary work. The idea is nowadays a critical commonplace. Biographers and critics of the Romantic poets have often used a theory of traumatic experience to explain preoccupations, recurrent imagery, and other aspects of a poet's work.[43] What has not been done is to use the premise of traumatic experience in attempting to understand the self-dramatizing moments of new awareness in the Romantic lyric.

---

43. In Aileen Ward's *John Keats: The Making of a Poet*, for example, the disappearance, return, and subsequent death of Keats's mother is seen as a determining event in Keats's personal and intellectual development. In the words of Robert Gittings, Keats's mother was "the ultimate enigma" of his early years, and his "complete silence about her suggests some shattering knowledge, with which, at various times in his life, he can be seen dimly struggling to come to terms" (*John Keats*, 30). In Onorato's *Character of the Poet*, the death of Wordsworth's mother when he was almost eight is seen as having undone his normative development up to that point, leaving him in later life "obsessed by a vital relationship with Nature" that had "come to stand unconsciously for the lost mother" (64). In G. Kim Blank's *Wordsworth and Feeling: The Poetry of an Adult Child*, the traumatic events of Wordsworth's childhood, particularly the loss of both parents, are seen as accounting for important aspects of his behavior (72, 218). Similar examples could be cited from the biographical and critical literature on other writers, starting with Edmund Wilson's *The Wound and the Bow: Seven Studies in Literature*.

In his *Project for a Scientific Psychology*, Freud defined psychological trauma as "deferred action." Briefly summarized, his argument is that a traumatic event is a delayed and anxiety-ridden recognition of the significance of a (memory of a) prior event that, at the time, was not seen as threatening. The event or the memory of it becomes traumatic afterwards.[44] The recognitions in Wordsworth's poetry are also deferred reactions to an earlier event or memory charged with traumatic potential. The poet represents them as moments of unexpected discovery, but the dynamics of repetition, of maintaining a sense of self in relation to an Other, and of traumatic experience indicate that they are always revisionary afterthoughts. Wordsworth characteristically represents them as sudden illuminations, yet he is also aware that they are second thoughts. When recalling that in his boyhood Nature spoke "Rememberable things" to him, he says that they "were doomed to

    44. Freud cites the case of a young girl, age eight, who had twice gone into a shop to buy sweets and become the object of a sexual advance by the shopkeeper. She quit going there and had no further reaction to the experience until four years later when, at twelve, she went into another shop in which she saw two assistants standing together and laughing. She rushed out in fright, clearly linking the two scenes, using one to interpret the other. After this, and at the time Freud was treating her, she suffered from a phobia of entering shops alone. What made the memory of the earlier event traumatic now, Freud said, was the onset of puberty, which "had made possible a different understanding of what was remembered" (*Project for a Scientific Psychology*, in *Standard Edition*, 1:356). See also Freud's reference to deferred action in the case of the "Wolf Man" (*Standard Edition*, 17:45n), as well as the article on it in Jean Laplanche and J.-B. Pontalis, *The Language of Psycho-Analysis*, 111–14. In another work, Laplanche has argued that it is impossible to "fix the traumatic event historically" as either the first event (the sexual advance) or the second (when the two assistants' laughter revived the memory of the first event). The trauma exists in the relation between the two (see *Life and Death in Psychoanalysis*, 41–42). See also Cynthia Chase's careful reading of Freud's account of Emma in her "Oedipal Textuality: Reading Freud's Reading of *Oedipus*," 179–80. Cathy Caruth, in *Unclaimed Experience: Trauma, Narrative, and History*, has recently explored the notion of deferred or belated awareness and emphasized that the narrative of a trauma attempts "to tell us of a reality or truth that is not otherwise available" and that "it is only in and through its inherent forgetting [the forgetting of the experience of a trauma] that it is first experienced at all" (4, 17). What I wish to emphasize here is the continuing importance of the idea of "deferred action" in psychoanalytic understandings of traumatic experience.

sleep / Until maturer seasons called them forth / To impregnate and to elevate the mind" (*Prelude*, 1.588–96). The "spots of time" are thought to be carried in some dark corner of one's mind, in "the hiding-places of man's power" (12.279), until experience and maturity bring them forth. When in Paris in 1792 he viewed the place of the September massacres, "where so late had lain / The dead, upon the dying heaped, and gazed/ On this and other spots," he did so "as doth a man / Upon a volume whose contents he knows / Are memorable, but from him locked up, / Being written in a tongue he cannot read" (10.56–61). But later that night in his room he felt "most deeply in what world I was," felt "the fear gone by" pressing upon him "almost like a fear to come," thought about "those September massacres" (10.64–73), and came to a new awareness of the tragic history unfolding in France. In the short period of a few hours Wordsworth experiences the delayed reaction of a traumatic new awareness. The fear aroused by his viewing the place where the massacres had taken place, the fear that for a few brief hours that night had seemed "gone by," eventually pressed on him like "a fear to come," and made it impossible to sleep.

Now, many years later, writing about the traumatic experience of seeing the place where the bodies had been piled, as he had once seen the place "where in former times / A murderer had been hung in iron chains" (12.235–37), he uses it to illustrate the way the mind stores certain experiences until one is ready to deal with them and then returns to them:

>   no star
> Of wildest course but treads back his own steps;
> For the spent hurricane the air provides
> As fierce a successor; the tide retreats
> But to return out of its hiding place
> In the great deep; all things have second birth;
> The earthquake is not satisfied at once. (10.79–86)

Wordsworth rarely refers to the more threatening events in nature (making "Tintern Abbey" stand in marked contrast to Shelley's "Mont Blanc," with its "frozen floods," "Earthquake-daemon," and mountain domes, pyramids, and pinnacles that seem to compose "A city of death" [64, 72, 104–5]), but here he uses the hurricane and the earthquake to illustrate the forceful impact of a new awareness on the mind in a powerful moment of recognition. It is "frequently true of second words as of second thoughts," he wrote, "that they are the best."[45]

But moments of new awareness in Romantic poetry differ in a crucial way from those in traumatic experience: They typically do not result in flight, phobia, inhibition of thought, or paralysis of action, but rather result in a presentation of a self-dramatizing and wish-fulfilling variation on a traumatic theme. Even when recognitions appear to result in a contraction or chastening of the self, they usually contain a defensive, anxiety-mastering, self-sustaining content, as the self-admonishment in the recognition concluding "Resolution and Independence" suggests. In the Intimations Ode the speaker's sense of loss and of a contraction of self is to some extent reversed in stanza 9 when, older and far inland, he looks back to the immortal sea to rediscover a nearly lost sense of infinitude in the soul. Moments of new awareness in Romantic poetry, therefore, though deferred reactions, try to solve a crisis or present a consolation. Rather than register painful insights into the self, as in traumatic recognitions, they try to offer a defensive, countertraumatic sense of resolution. As James Heffernan has pointed out in his consideration of the revisions of the 1799 version of the spots of time episodes, the "original story of traumatic separation and loss" comes close to being assimilated "into a story of reunion and re-integration." "What is obvious in the design of both later versions of *The Prelude* is Wordsworth's desire to convert the memory of separation into the memory of union and re-union."[46]

In the moment of new awareness the speaker brings to a climax all his self-dramatizing efforts to achieve a realization of self. The "I" is shown to be, in the self-defining language of *The Prelude*, "a mind sustained / By recognitions" (14.74–75). Recognition becomes "re-cognition" in the sense that the speaker attempts to reconceive and refashion the self in ways that, however defensive and illusory they may be, appear for the moment to master anxiety and bring the self closer to a fulfillment of its aspirations.

45. William Wordsworth and Dorothy Wordsworth, *The Middle Years*, 2:179 (hereafter cited as *Letters: The Middle Years*).
46. James A. W. Heffernan, "The Presence of the Absent Mother in *The Prelude*," 266, 267.

4

What is needed in critical considerations of the identity and role of the "I" in Wordsworth's major lyrics, I have been arguing, is a way of conceptualizing it and the subjectivity it represents that gives due recognition to its autobiographical dimensions without equating it with "Wordsworth" (or one of the critical versions of the empirical self of the poet) and to its fictional dimensions without reducing it to the notion of a persona. Borrowing from Freud's notion of the intermediate region of the transference and from Winnicott's idea of the potential space between the individual and the environment, I suggest that the lyrical "I" or speaker is a transitional self of the poet that, in the suspended moment and cultural space of lyrical form, presents through his utterance a self-dramatization of what is both an artificial and real experience in an attempt to perform and achieve a transformation of self. While transformation is the immediate aim of the self-dramatization, self-realization is the ultimate (if unachievable) aim. I am aware that such a definition does not provide the kind of handy term or easy label that "Wordsworth" or "persona" or even "poet in his own person" does, but it is truer than those terms, I believe, to the dramatics and psychology of self-representation in the major lyrics.

The self-dramatizing character of Wordsworth's lyrical "I," more than any other aspect of its real/artificial being, provides a basis for developing a conceptualization of the speaker's subjectivity. By observing and analyzing the self-dramatizing strategies used by the speakers of "Tintern Abbey," "Resolution and Independence," the Intimations Ode, and "Elegiac Stanzas," I hope both to reveal the dramatic art Wordsworth devotes to his self-representations and to develop an understanding of the "I" as a transitional self of the poet. Despite the many differences in the self-representations, the similarities in them and the continuities from one poem to another suggest that the "I" of the major lyrics, while never the same as the poet speaking "in his own person," represented for Wordsworth an ideal of self in its repeated attempt to achieve a self-transformation. To what extent, if any, the ideal was ever experienced as achieved by Wordsworth is not a question I address, and is perhaps unanswerable, though it is worth recalling that in his comments in his Note to "The Thorn" and in the third of his "Essays upon Epitaphs" he implies that a self-representation is a constituent part and power of the self.

2 ✦ The Dramatics of Self-Representation in "Tintern Abbey"

More than any other major lyric, "Tintern Abbey" appears to exemplify the autobiographical nature of Wordsworth's poetry. It seems to be an almost perfect illustration of the notion of the poet speaking "in his own person," suggesting an identification of the speaker with the twenty-eight-year-old poet who toured the Wye valley with his sister in July 1798, who had a volume of poems in press (to which "Tintern Abbey" would be added, almost at the last minute), and who, as Wordsworth would tell Isabella Fenwick many years later, began the poem "upon leaving Tintern, after crossing the Wye, and concluded it just as I was entering Bristol in the evening, after a ramble of 4 or 5 days, with my sister."[1] The long title identifying a moment in Wordsworth's life, the opening lines specifying "Five years . . . five summers, with the length / Of five long winters" since the 1793 visit, the memory of the "absence" as a time often spent "in lonely rooms, and 'mid the din / Of towns and cities" (25–26), the retrospective meditation on the three stages of his life in the fourth verse paragraph, and the address to his sister in the fifth all seem to identify the speaker as the autobiographical Wordsworth.

In the last two decades and more, however, this traditional definition of autobiography as it relates to "Tintern Abbey," dependent on information and a perspective provided by Wordsworth, has been challenged in several ways and as a consequence the autobiographical character of the speaker has been redefined. Psychoanalytic readings of the poem have deepened the definition of the poet's psyche to include, among other dynamics, a traumatically determined unconscious attachment to his lost mother, represented in the figure of Nature. New Historicist readings have broadened the definition of the poet's consciousness by including his awareness of the economic and social conditions in the Wye

---

1. *Fenwick Notes*, 15.

valley in 1798, particularly the presence of the ironworks, the houses in ruin, the numerous vagrants, and the general poverty mentioned by William Gilpin in his *Observations on the River Wye* (1782), though this awareness, as well as that of the threatening political reality created by the French Revolution, is repressed in the poem as part of an effort to escape into an inner world of consolation and transcendence. Intertextualist, dialogic, and psychobiographical readings have extended the range of autobiographical referentiality in the poem to include the echoes of and allusions to other voices in the poem, particularly those of Coleridge.[2]

Although these redefinitions have deepened and broadened our understanding of the poet-speaker's consciousness, they have also tended, by equating the speaker with the historical or biographical Wordsworth, to overlook the extent to which the speaker's utterance is an act of self-dramatization. I am aware that the distinction between the speaker as the poet and the speaker as a self-representation of him is not easy to maintain in discussions of Wordsworth's poetry, and that too little attention to the biographical and historical Wordsworth as the speaker of the poem, or too much insistence on the speaker as a self-dramatization, separated from the biographical and historical matrix in which he took shape and assumed an appearance of being in the text, can lead to a false sense of the speaker as a disembodied voice and unsouled presence, and obscure the autobiographical characteristics of his utterance. But to understand the character of the lyric speaker in "Tintern Abbey" as a transitional self of the poet it is necessary, I believe, to emphasize the self-dramatizing features of his utterance. Only in this way will it be clear to what extent Wordsworth is involved in using the "I" of the poem to act out a transformation of self, as well as to what extent this "I" represents a subjectivity defined more by a sense of something evermore about to be than by any achieved sense of what it is.

2. Of the various psychoanalytic readings of the poem, I would cite Wallace W. Douglas, *Wordsworth: The Construction of a Personality*, 133–36, and Onorato, *Character of the Poet*, 29–87. For New Historicist readings, see McGann, *Romantic Ideology*, 85–88, and Levinson, *Wordsworth's Great Period Poems*, 14–57. For intertextualist and psychobiographical readings, see, respectively, Magnuson, *Coleridge and Wordsworth*, 163–76, and Matlak, *Poetry of Relationship*, 119–37. For a new biographical reading that emphasizes the historical and political context in which the poem was composed while remaining sensitive to issues raised in psychological and intertextualist studies, see Johnston, *Hidden Wordsworth*, 397–400, 590–98.

I

In Wordsworth's notes and letters, as well as his comments to Isabella Fenwick, he says a number of things about "Tintern Abbey" that call attention to both the expressivist and dramatic elements in the speaker's utterance, suggesting a complex relationship between them. In recalling for Isabella Fenwick the events at the time of composition, he emphasizes the expressivist character of the utterance by insisting on the spontaneity and authenticity of the moment that the poem seems to capture ("Not a line of it was altered, and not any part of it written down till I reached Bristol").³ But in a note to the 1800–1805 editions of *Lyrical Ballads* he is much less clear. He remarks that "I have not ventured to call this Poem an Ode; but it was written with a hope that in the transitions, and the impassioned music of the versification, would be found the principal requisites of that species of composition" (*Poetical Works*, 2:517). The "impassioned music" seems to emphasize the expressivist character of "Tintern Abbey," but the sudden transitions and the mention of the ode as a model for the poem suggest that the utterance is dramatic. The ode was an inherently dramatic form. Whether he has in mind the Pindaric ode, with its emphasis on the performative voice, or the Horatian, with its stress on the contemplative and self-reflexive qualities in the voice of the speaker, the suggestion is that the speaker is engaged in an animated, self-dramatizing expression. The "sudden, sharp, [and] self-advertising" transitions of "Tintern Abbey," as Stuart Curran has observed, indicate the dramatic nature of the poem.⁴

In a letter to R. P. Gillies in June 1817 Wordsworth criticizes a stanza on solitude in *Childe Harold's Pilgrimage* because "the sentiment by being expressed in an *antithetical* manner, is taken out of the Region of high and imaginative feeling, to be place[d] in that of point and epigram," and then goes on to illustrate an expression of "the same sentiment" by quoting lines from "Tintern Abbey," specifically "How often has my spirit turned to thee" (57) and "Nor greetings where no kindness is, nor all / The dreary intercourse of daily life" (130–31). In Byron, Wordsworth says, the sentiment is expressed "formally," whereas in "Tintern Abbey" it is "ejaculated as it were [fortuit]ously in the

---

3. *Fenwick Notes*, 15.
4. Curran, *Poetic Form and British Romanticism*, 77.

musical succession [of preconceiv]ed feeling." If he appears to emphasize the expressivist character of the lines from "Tintern Abbey" by noting the spontaneity, music, and feeling in them, his characterization of his "Thanksgiving Ode" as a "dramatised ejaculation" in a letter to Robert Southey just a year before the one to Gillies indicates that he believes that such a sudden and strong expression of feeling as the one in "Tintern Abbey" may also be dramatized.[5]

The dramatic nature of "Tintern Abbey" is again emphasized in a letter to Catherine Clarkson in January 1815 when Wordsworth defends himself against the charge (made by a female friend of Mrs. Clarkson) that he is a pantheist. He notes that the friend "talks of my being a worshipper of Nature," then characterizes the phrase, perhaps too defensively, as "a passionate expression uttered incautiously in the Poem upon the Wye," which (he goes on to say) has led Mrs. Clarkson's friend "into this mistake, she reading in cold-heartedness and substituting the letter for the spirit." Alone this statement seems to call attention to a lyrical and expressivist rather than a dramatic context, but it is immediately followed by Wordsworth's mention of a similar passage from *The Excursion*, book 4, and by his remark that "the intelligent reader will easily see the *dramatic* propriety of the Passage."[6]

Wordsworth's comments indicate his awareness of how the expressive impulses of the lyric may seek realization in a dramatic context, and they fit well with our sense of the Romantic lyric as dramatic. His major lyrics, however, are not just dramatic. They are self-dramatizing in the sense that the speaker, representing a transitional self of the poet, as I suggested in Chapter 1, attempts to act out and achieve a self-transformation. The lyrical mode is in this sense not only intertwined with but given direction and enhancement by the dramatic.

When we turn to "Tintern Abbey," we observe a number of features that mark it as a dramatic utterance, features that both highlight the

---

5. *Letters: The Middle Years*, 2:385, 324.

6. *Letters: The Middle Years*, 2:188. The passage in *The Excursion* concerning the boy and the shell that Wordsworth refers to is addressed by the Wanderer to the Solitary, and begins at 4.1132. In it the Wanderer compares the shell that "A curious child" might hold near his ear to the universe: "Even such a shell the universe itself / Is to the ear of Faith; and there are times, / I doubt not, when to you it doth impart / Authentic tidings of invisible things. . . . Here you stand, / Adore, and worship, when you know it not" (1141–48).

expressive and meditative tenor of the speaker's thoughts and attempt to transform them into a climactic moment in his life. From the beginning, the "I" of the poem is characterized by the dramatic situation in which he is placed. Unlike Wordsworth himself, who, according to his comments to Isabella Fenwick, composed the poem while leaving Tintern, crossing the Wye, and walking to Bristol, the speaker is on the scene. He is represented as observing it rather than remembering it. In a reading of the poem alert to its dramatic structure and style, Paul Sheats observes that the poem "reenacts" Wordsworth's return to a beloved landscape.[7] Taking the point a step further, one can see that the speaker's utterance is actually a dramatic reenactment of Wordsworth's 1798, not his 1793, visit. From the speaker's point of view, of course, it is not a reenactment, though it is a repetition of (or variation on) the 1793 visit referred to in the opening lines. But from the point of view of a reader who is aware that Wordsworth represents the experience as taking place in the present even though he told Isabella Fenwick he began composing the poem after leaving Tintern, the speaker's utterance has to be seen as a reenactment.

Wordsworth's decision to place the speaker at the scene suggests both the liberties he is willing to take with the notion of the poet speaking "in his own person" and the extent to which he wants to dramatize rather than simply recollect the experience and meditate on it. The first verse paragraph reflects his concern to dramatize the moment. The speaker's opening words, rather than beginning a meditation, announce a return:

> Five years have past; five summers, with the length
> Of five long winters! and again I hear
> These waters, rolling from their mountain-springs
> With a soft inland murmur.

Wordsworth's use of the present tense and the pronoun *I* in these lines and the rest of the first verse paragraph—"I hear," "I behold," "I see"—foregrounds the speaker's presence and focuses attention on his thoughts as the central action in the scene. Many eighteenth-century poems employ the revisit formula and, like Gray's "Elegy Written in a Country Churchyard," begin in the present tense ("The curfew tolls the

---

7. Paul Sheats, *The Making of Wordsworth's Poetry, 1785–1798,* 230.

knell of parting day, / The lowing herd wind slowly o'er the lea"). But they do not figure the speaker's presence in such a prominent way. As Mary Jacobus has pointed out, "Wordsworth's opening description of the Wye valley builds on these earlier passages [from eighteenth-century topographical poetry by Thomson, Cowper, and Lyttleton]. But now landscape evokes inner life, and imaginative re-creation has taken over from the faithful cataloguing of detail in *The Seasons* and *The Task*. It is not so much the scene that stands out as the poet's presence in it."[8]

That presence, unlike the wise passiveness recommended in the credal poems, becomes an active, strong intervention into the scene. The use of the word *behold*, as Carl Woodring has suggested, represents an act of possession: "The poet revisiting the banks of the Wye says, 'once again, / Do I behold these steep and lofty cliffs.' I *behold*. By contemplation (as the derivation of *behold* implies) I make them mine to keep. By contemplation I make them *mind*." In addition to this act of possession and internalization, Wordsworth's use of "behold," with its biblical and Miltonic echoes, suggests a form of what Keats called Miltonic "stationing." Keats, in a marginal comment on *Paradise Lost*, 7.420–23, wrote that Milton "is not content with simple description, he must station,—thus here, we not only see how the Birds '*with clang despised the ground*,' but we see them '*under a cloud in prospect*.' So we see Adam '*Fair indeed and tall—under a plantane*'—and so we see Satan '*disfigured— on the Assyrian Mount*.'"[9] In "Tintern Abbey," a dramatic lyric set in a

---

8. Jacobus, *Tradition and Experiment*, 109.

9. Carl Woodring, "The New Sublimity in 'Tintern Abbey,'" 90; *The Poetical Works and Other Writings of John Keats*, 8:303–4. As Beth Lau points out in her recent study of Keats's reading of *Paradise Lost*, the concept of stationing at the time Keats was underlining passages in Milton's great poem and writing comments in the margins was associated by Hazlitt, Hunt, and others with static composition and sculpture, something that helps to account for "Keats's tendency to focus in his reading on sculpturesque images and descriptive passages to the neglect of dialogue, character development, and action" (*Keats's "Paradise Lost,"* 43). It can also help to account for Keats's use of stationing in some of his poems—the stationing of the hero of "Hyperion," for example, "standing fierce beneath" the "great main cupola," where he "stampt his foot, / And from the basements deep to the high towers / Jarr'd his own golden region" ("Hyperion," 1:221–24). Such a concept of stationing seems to fit better with a narrative mode of poetry than a dramatic. Yet there are obviously ways in which a poem may be dramatic without the use

picturesque landscape rather than an epic poem set in the grandeur of a mythological scene, Wordsworth stations the speaker in a position to "behold these steep and lofty cliffs," to "repose / Here, under this dark sycamore," to "view / These plots of cottage-ground," and "see / These hedge-rows" (5, 9–11, 14–15). The stationing here is not as striking as that of his statuesque representation of the shepherd in book 8 of *The Prelude* ("In size a giant . . . A solitary object and sublime, / Above all height! like an aerial cross / *Stationed* alone upon a spiry rock / Of the Chartreuse" [266–75, emphasis added]), but it does foreground the speaker's presence in the scene and in this way it enhances the self-dramatizing character of his utterance. The moment of arrival at the Wye valley announced in the opening lines, along with the beholding of the scene in succeeding lines, is not unlike that moment in the first verse paragraph of *The Prelude* where, in another return dramatized in the present tense, the autobiographical speaker says, "The earth is all before me" (1.14), echoing Milton in his momentary stationing of Adam and Eve before the wide world after their expulsion from paradise (12.646).[10]

In several blank verse fragments dating from the time when Wordsworth was working on "The Ruined Cottage" and "The Pedlar," and therefore several months before he composed "Tintern Abbey," he uses language that underscores the importance of stationing the observer in nature and prefigures the self-dramatizing impulse not only in "Tintern Abbey" but in much of the great poetry to follow:

---

of dialogue and interaction between characters. "One of Keats's innovations in his famous odes," as Lau observes, "is the development of a debate between the speaker and a central symbol, a confrontation that is charged with dramatic tension, climax, and resolution" (47). Stationing in a poem is therefore not necessarily limited to a scene that is static or sculpturesque to the exclusion of the dramatic. In a larger understanding of what can be dramatic in a lyric poem, it can be seen in "Tintern Abbey" as an outer manifestation of the inner drama of the speaker's interaction with the scene before him. It gives prominence to the speaker's presence in the scene and it becomes a part of the effort to affirm his renewal of his relationship with Nature and the presence that he divines in it, and in these ways it forms a part of his dialogue with himself and that presence. Stationing is thus an important part of the speaker's act of self-dramatization.

10. Quotations of and references to Milton's poetry are taken from *The Poems of John Milton*, ed. John Carey and Alastair Fowler.

> Yet once again do I behold the forms
> Of these huge mountains, and yet once again
> *Standing* beneath these elms. . . .
>
>   there would he *stand*
> In the still covert of some [?lonesome] rock
> Or gaze upon the moon. . . .
>
>   There was a spot,
> My favorite *station* when the winds were up,
> Three knots of fir-trees, small and circular,
> Which with smooth space of open plain between
> Stood single, for the delicate eye of taste
> Too formally arranged. Right opposite
> The central clump I loved to *stand*. . . .
>   (*Poetical Works*, 5:340–42, emphasis added)

Whatever else they may reveal, these fragments suggest that the stationing of a speaker is not an indication of passiveness but rather of activity. Physical motion is arrested, it is true, but for the purpose of emphasizing the internal motions of mind and desire.

    The dramatic presence of the speaker is enhanced, however, not only in Wordsworth's use of an announced return, the present tense, and the device of stationing, but in his use of repetition. Certain words and phrases ("Five years," "five summers," "five long winters"; "secluded scene," "deep seclusion"; "again," "Once again"; "these plots," "these orchard tufts," "these hedge-rows, hardly hedge-rows") support the thematic content of the speaker's thoughts (the past, the return, the solitary consciousness, nature observed in its particularity), but their repetition functions to enhance the dramatic character of the moment. Repetition forms a part of the idiom, rhythm, and spontaneity of the spoken word, representing the mood and feelings of the speaker. In his "Note to 'The Thorn,'" Wordsworth, as part of his justification for the use of repetition, remarked that because of the interest the mind attaches to words they are "part of the passion" and that "the mind luxuriates in the repetition of words which appear successfully to communicate its feelings" (*Poetical Works*, 2:513). Repetition creates an intensification of the acts of seeing, hearing, and feeling, emphasizes the passion and spontaneity of the moment, and enhances the dramatic illusion of the speaker's voice while at the banks of the Wye. We observe a subtle form of spontaneity in the second-thought qualification of the hedge-rows as "hardly hedge-rows," as if the speaker takes sudden delight in the particularity of them, as well as in the further refinement, "little lines / Of sportive wood run wild" (15–16). Still another kind of spontaneity may be seen in the use of "Or," as if the speaker is still thinking his way through the scene and suddenly entertaining the possibility of alternative accounts of the "wreaths of smoke," which may come from "vagrant dwellers in the houseless woods," *or* from "some Hermit's cave, where by his fire / The Hermit sits alone" (17, 20–22).

More important, repetition also contributes to the pacing of the speaker's thoughts. At times it slows him down, as in the use of spondees ("Five years have past"), the three variations on time past (years, summers, winters), and the recurrence of the notion of dreary waiting in "the length / Of five long winters," making the speaker's long absence from the Wye valley, despite the mention of summers, seem more like a winter. "How like a winter hath my absence been, from thee," he seems to say. Yet at other times, as in the repetition of "again" and "Once again" and in the seemingly sudden impulse to qualify the hedge-rows as "hardly hedge-rows," we can hear the tempo pick up and sense the rise and fall of the speaker's feelings, the alterations in his mood, and the movement of his thoughts.

The most conspicuous feature of the dramatic situation is of course the presence of a silent auditor, the "dear, dear Sister" (121) to whom the last third of the poem is addressed. The whole matter of an addressee, however, is more complicated than it appears. We do not learn that there is an addressee until the final verse paragraph, specifically lines 114–15 ("For thou art with me here upon the banks / Of this fair river; thou my dearest Friend"), or that it is the speaker's sister until line 121. As a result, on a first reading of the poem (or on subsequent readings in which we imaginatively re-create the sense of hearing the speaker for the first time) we are not aware of the auditor until near the end of the poem. Once aware, it is not clear how much of what has been said prior to line 111 has been shaped by her presence.[11] Yet the fact that she is not addressed until the last verse paragraph suggests she is a nominal rather than an

---

11. For the view that the poem is an argumentative response to Dorothy and that it has been shaped by her presence, see Matlak, *Poetry of Relationship,*

actual addressee in the sense that, as Geoffrey Jackson has explained, a nominal addressee is someone whose real or imagined existence or presence "provides a pretext for the utterance," in contrast to an actual addressee of a letter or other communication.[12] Sara Hutchinson appears to be the actual addressee in the verse letter that was the earliest version of Coleridge's "Dejection: An Ode," but in the versions of July 1802, October 1802, August 1803, and 1817 she is replaced by Wordsworth, then Edmund, then William, and finally an unnamed "Lady," all of whom become increasingly nominal as the most specific and potentially embarrassing autobiographical references are removed in the succeeding versions. "The reason that Coleridge could carry out these shifts of address without writing many fresh lines," Stephen Parrish points out, "was, of course, that the original poem was more about Coleridge than about Sara—as much a psychological self-analysis as a love letter."[13] It becomes an interesting question whether any of Coleridge's auditors in the conversation poems are actual addressees. Sara Coleridge in "The Eolian Harp," "gentle-hearted Charles" in "This Lime-Tree Bower," and Hartley in "Frost at Midnight" all appear to be nominal in the sense

---

119–37. She is the poem's "overt" auditor, Coleridge its "implied" auditor. Wordsworth is thought to be responding to and arguing with each—for example, correcting "Dorothy's preference . . . for earthly rather than celestial landscapes" and redefining Coleridge's representation of Nature in "Frost at Midnight" (*Poetry of Relationship*, 131–32). For a different view of Coleridge as the implicit auditor and of the poem as Wordsworth's response to "Frost at Midnight," see Magnuson, *Coleridge and Wordsworth*, 163–76. " 'Tintern Abbey' was not inspired primarily by Wordsworth's visit to the Wye, or Dorothy's presence, or even his own anxiety about his ability to continue to write. It originates in the poetic dialogue with Coleridge" (*Coleridge and Wordsworth*, 170). Matlak and Magnuson both employ intertextualist analysis, but Matlak's critical context is psychobiographical, Magnuson's dialogic. Both are persuasive in the terms of their respective critical contexts and methods. But if the speaker of "Tintern Abbey" is seen as a self-representation by the poet, as I am arguing he should be, then the addressee, whether Coleridge or Dorothy Wordsworth, is more nominal than actual and important primarily for his/her role in the speaker's act of self-representation. For a discussion of Dorothy's role, see section 4 of this chapter.

12. Geoffrey Jackson, "Nominal and Actual Audiences: Some Strategies of Communication in Wordsworth's Poetry," 227.

13. Parrish, *Coleridge's "Dejection": The Earliest Manuscripts and the Earliest Printings*, 17–18.

that the poems are more about Coleridge than about the addressees and in the sense that the speakers' effusions are addressed to these auditors less as individuals than as silent figures presumed to be sympathetic. In a very real sense, even Coleridge is a nominal addressee in *The Prelude*, despite the numerous occasions when he is addressed and the crucial role he played in urging Wordsworth to write a philosophical poem, for which *The Prelude* was to be the preparation. The most important auditor in the poem is Wordsworth himself. Referring to the "glad preamble" at the beginning of the poem, he says

> My own voice cheered me, and, far more, the mind's
> Internal echo of the imperfect sound;
> To both I listened, drawing from them both
> A cheerful confidence in things to come. (I.55–58)

Although these lines indicate a doubling of the speaker's consciousness in the split between his actual voice and the mind's "Internal echo," as Mary Jacobus has argued, they also reveal Wordsworth's awareness of himself as an auditor and, implicitly, his awareness of his own voice as a self-dramatization.[14] In listening to his own voice, in being cheered "far more" by "the mind's / Internal echo of the imperfect sound," presumably because it leads him toward a more perfect expression and sense of being, and in deriving from both a sense of being positively transformed ("drawing from them both / A cheerful confidence"), he becomes a self-dramatizing witness to his own efforts at self-transformation.

None of this is to say that Dorothy is unimportant in the development of the speaker's thoughts in "Tintern Abbey," only that she is not represented as the immediate reason for their expression. Her function as a nominal addressee and her appearance near the end of the poem not only allow the speaker in the first two-thirds of the poem to develop his thoughts in a more expressive, abstract, and speculative vein than would be possible if they were addressed as a communication to her, but enable him to dramatize his thoughts and feelings. The absence of any mention of her until the last verse paragraph, as Lawrence Kramer

---

14. For Mary Jacobus's illuminating reading of the lines in intertextualist and intersubjective terms, see *Romanticism, Writing, and Sexual Difference: Essays on "The Prelude,"* 168–70.

has remarked, is part of a "deliberately sustained illusion that the poet is a solitary figure in the landscape."[15] The illusion is essential to the speaker's self-representation as wiser than his sister, possessed of greater experience and knowledge, before turning to address her in the final verse paragraph. The plot of his utterance (or design in the unfolding of his thoughts) and the dramatic action it represents require that he have the experience of being disturbed with "elevated thoughts" and "a sense sublime" and achieving a new awareness before delivering his "exhortations" to her.

A less conspicuous but more important feature of the dramatic situation is the presence of Nature. The apostrophe to the Wye, which appears to be limited to lines 55–57 ("How oft, in spirit, have I turned to thee, / O sylvan Wye! thou wanderer thro' the woods, / How often has my spirit turned to thee!") but actually includes lines 49–57, indicates that there is more than one nominal addressee in the poem. The sylvan Wye is both nominal and pronominal, both pretext for the utterance and referent for (or representative of) another named and important presence in the poem. Though the speaker does not specifically address the figure of Nature ("the nurse, / The guide, the guardian of my heart, and soul / Of all my moral being," that "never did betray / The heart that loved her" [109–11, 122–23]), it is clear that his relationship to her, as well as to the presence evoked in her midst ("something far more deeply interfused"), however it may be defined, is what has drawn him back to the Wye as "A worshipper of Nature . . . Unwearied in that service" (152–53). Wordsworth stages the central dramatic action of the poem, the speaker's experience of a crisis and its resolution, in her presence.

Nature's presence further complicates the matter of addressees, the dramatic situation, and the whole question of how to conceptualize the subjectivity of the "I" of the poem. Her prominent role in the speaker's thoughts indicates that she is something more than a nominal presence. When he says "And I have felt / A presence that disturbs me with the joy / Of elevated thoughts; a sense sublime / Of something far more deeply interfused" (93–96), it becomes clear that Nature is a necessary condition—or "presence"—for his utterance. The speaker's relationship with Nature derives its depth of course from the Wordsworth who, through the speaker, is staging a reenactment of his visit to the Wye valley

---

15. Lawrence Kramer, "Victorian Sexuality and 'Tintern Abbey,'" 401.

and it largely defines his subjectivity. Because Nature is characterized not only as feminine but as maternal, and because we are aware that the presence the speaker intuits as he looks on Nature is metonymically related to that "one dear Presence" in the "Blest the infant Babe" passage in book 2 of *The Prelude*, and ultimately to the lost presence of Wordsworth's "honoured Mother, she who was the heart / And hinge of all our learnings and our loves" (5.257–58), the speaker's thoughts appear to contain an internalized drama of object relations, where the true, silent auditor in the poem is the reconstituted image of the maternal presence in the speaker's mind.[16] It is this image—represented as a nurse and guide, experienced as a sense sublime—that is the subliminal presence, if not actual addressee, in the speaker's thoughts. Nature, or the image of Nature in the speaker's mind, is the other silent auditor in the poem, and it is in her presence that the speaker expresses his thoughts and feelings and acts out a self-transformation (specifically, the intellectual development depicted in the move from the second to the third stage in the relationship with Nature).

In addition to these means of enhancing the dramatic effect of the speaker's utterance (the revisit formula, the stationing of the speaker, the present tense, the various verbal, phrasal, and syntactical forms of repetition, apostrophe, the presence of Dorothy, and the evocation of a subliminal presence in Nature), Wordsworth's structuring of the speaker's utterance needs to be considered. Of the several accounts of the structure in the criticism, the triadic is the one that best represents the self-dramatizing nature of the speaker's utterance.[17] In the first part of the poem (1–22), as we have already seen, Wordsworth uses several dramatic

---

16. The most thorough discussion of Nature as a maternal figure in Wordsworth's poetry remains the one in the second chapter of Onorato's *Character of the Poet*, 29–87. But see also Douglas, *Wordsworth*, 133–36; Homans, *Women Writers and Poetic Identity*, 13–22; Barbara Schapiro, *The Romantic Mother: Narcissistic Patterns in Romantic Poetry*, 93–129; Heffernan, "Presence of the Absent Mother"; and Duncan Wu, "Wordsworth and Helvellyn's Womb," 6–25.

17. For Albert Gerard, the structure is dyadic, with the poem "built on a pattern of ascent and descent which is repeated twice: ascent toward the loftiest heights of mystical speculation, descent toward the firm ground of ascertained fact" (*English Romantic Poetry: Ethos, Structure, and Symbol in Coleridge, Wordsworth, Shelley, and Keats*, 105); for Vendler, the structure is triadic: "a description of a landscape invested with memory; a narrative autobiography; and an address to a female

strategies in placing the speaker on the scene and having him describe the landscape. In the second (23–111), the speaker presents a narrative history of his relationship with Nature as a progress from a naive form of physical interaction with it to a state of intense awareness of it as a powerful and ubiquitous spirit. This second, autobiographical part is set forth in two movements, the first (23–49) showing how the relationship has been maintained in absence, culminating in a moment of profound understanding ("We see into the life of things"), the second (49–111) explaining how it developed through three stages, moving from a lesser to a greater consciousness of Nature's presence, culminating in a climactic moment of new awareness ("And I have felt / A presence that disturbs me with the joy" [93–94]). In the third part, he addresses his sister as a way of concluding but also of ensuring that the moment and its significance will be preserved and extended into the future. This three-part structure, despite the fact that it contains narrative sections (the longest being the history of the relationship with Nature [49–111]), is designed to give prominence to the two climactic moments in the speaker's utterance when he represents a self-transformation taking place.

2

Wordsworth uses several strategies in the representation of a movement in the speaker's thoughts toward a climactic self-transformation in both moments. In the first (23–49) he represents a movement into the consciousness of the speaker. There had been a hint of such an inward movement in the image of the cliffs that can "impress / Thoughts

---

companion" ("'Tintern Abbey': Two Assaults," 179); for Levinson, the poem has a four-part structure, a repetition of strophe and antistrophe: (1) "Lines 1–22 form a strophic unity; here the narrator invokes and describes his divine subject . . . a landscape"; (2) "In lines 22–48, the antistrophe, the speaker withdraws from the enthrallments of vision"; (3) "Lines 49–111 develop a second strophe, emergence from reverie into self-knowledge"; and (4) "Lines 112 to the conclusion develop the consolidation and farewell that mark this section's odal epode" (*Wordsworth's Great Period Poems*, 47–48); and for Richard Matlak the poem follows the Ciceronian pattern of argumentation, with five functional parts, the *exordium*, the *propositio*, the *narratio*, the *argumentatio*, and the *peroratio*, as well as a sixth part, an appeal to emotion, included in the peroration ("Classical Argument and Romantic Persuasion in 'Tintern Abbey'").

of more deep seclusion" (6–7), but now the scene and its "beauteous forms" are not observed but remembered. The direction of thought is away from the external scene observed in the first verse paragraph and toward the landscape of memory.[18] In the next few lines there is a suggestion of a movement inward, toward what Isobel Armstrong has aptly called "the multiple possibility of 'in-ness,'" first into memory, with a supporting emphasis on inwardness in the image of being "in lonely rooms" and in the use of prepositions ("*'mid* the din / Of towns and cities" and "*In* hours of weariness"), then in the image of "sensations sweet," with the continuing movement "Felt *in* the blood, and felt along the heart," until "passing even *into* my purer mind" (25–29, emphasis added).[19] The use of the comparative-intensive adjective in "my purer mind," like the use of comparative-intensive adjectives and adverbs in the "more deep seclusion" of line 7, the "more sublime" of 37, and the "far more deeply interfused" of 96, reinforces the sense of progressive inwardness.[20] The progression is toward "that blessed mood" and the climactic moment in which the speaker claims to "see into the life of things" (49).

Another strategy is sentence elongation, which Wordsworth often uses to suggest passion and elevated thoughts. The paragraph is composed of only two sentences, suggesting a continuous flow of thought that complements the way the "sensations sweet" and the "motion of our human blood" are felt to move "along the heart" (27–28, 44) toward a supreme moment of new awareness. Various phrasal and syntactic repetitions ("Felt in the blood, and felt along the heart" [28], "that blessed mood . . . that serene and blessed mood" [37, 41], "In which the burthen . . . In which the heavy and the weary weight . . . In which the affections" [38–39, 42]) evoke a sense of increasing tension and accelerated movement toward the moment. The approach is not that of a straight trajectory but of a movement artfully delayed and halted, at one point, by an additional thought ("feelings too / Of unremembered pleasure" [30–31]), at another by an explanation ("such, perhaps, / As . . ." [31–32]), and at still another by a second beginning ("Nor less,

---

18. In using this phrase, I refer to Christopher Salvesen's fine study.
19. Isobel Armstrong, "'Tintern Abbey': From Augustan to Romantic," 271.
20. For a discussion of Wordsworth's uncompleted comparatives, see Robert M. Maniquis, "Comparison, Intensity, and Time in 'Tintern Abbey.'"

I trust, / To them I may have owed another gift" [35–36]), all suggesting the flux and reflux, the ebb and flow, of the speaker's thoughts.[21] Still, the forward motion continues, strengthened at the crucial moment by a shift in tense from the more general present perfect ("These beauteous forms . . . have not been," "I have owed" [22–23, 26]) to the more immediate present ("the heavy and the weary weight . . . Is lightened," "the affections gently lead us on," "we are laid asleep . . . and become a living soul," "We see" [39–49]).

These and other strategies are evident in the crucial second half of the paragraph where Wordsworth represents the speaker achieving a transformation of self in a moment of new awareness or recognition.

> Nor less, I trust,
> To them I may have owed another gift,
> Of aspect more sublime; that blessed mood,
> In which the burthen of the mystery,
> In which the heavy and the weary weight
> Of all this unintelligible world,
> Is lightened:—that serene and blessed mood,
> In which the affections gently lead us on,—
> Until, the breath of this corporeal frame
> And even the motion of our human blood
> Almost suspended, we are laid asleep
> In body, and become a living soul:
> While with an eye made quiet by the power
> Of harmony, and the deep power of joy,
> We see into the life of things. (35–49)

The fact that this moment does not come from a specific event in Wordsworth's personal history, as do the moments in the boat-stealing,

---

21. Geoffrey Hartman has observed "in the opening verses of 'Tintern Abbey,' as well as in other sections . . . a *wave effect* of rhythm whose characteristic is that while there is internal acceleration, the feeling of climax is avoided" (*Wordsworth's Poetry*, 26–29). In *The Prelude* Wordsworth uses the simile of a river that "Turns and will measure back his course—far back, / Towards the very regions which he crossed" in his acknowledgment of the "motions retrograde" in the narrative of the poem (*1805* 9.5–9), or, as he refers to it in *1850*, the "intricate delay" (*1850* 9.8). See Paul Sheats, "Wordsworth's Retrogrades and the Shaping of *The Prelude*."

Mount Snowdon, and other episodes in *The Prelude*, but is rather a representation of a composite moment, a kind of experience rather than a particular experience, calls attention to its fictional and, I would argue, staged quality. The staging begins somewhat hesitantly with the first words of the second sentence ("Nor less, I trust . . ."), a gesture of tentativeness characteristic of the beginning of Wordsworth's dramatized moments of recognition, one that establishes credibility for the elevated language and rhetoric of the succeeding lines. But the tentativeness is quickly overcome when the speaker suddenly introduces the unexpected "aspect more sublime," bringing with it an odelike abruptness in transition from the quotidian world of "lonely rooms," "hours of weariness," and "little, nameless, unremembered acts / Of kindness and of love," and breaking into the lofty mood and sustained rhythm of the remainder of the paragraph. The use of anaphora in the "In which" phrases and the repetition of "blessed mood," with the amplification in the appositive "that serene and blessed mood," the use of the verbs "lead" and "become," and the positioning of the preposition "Until" just before the supreme moment, with the qualifying dependent clause ("the breath of this corporeal frame / And even the motion of our human blood / Almost suspended") introduced to delay and thereby enhance the climax, all contribute to the staging of this dramatic moment, as if an irresistible passionate feeling, after various vicissitudes of thought and expression have been overcome, has finally broken through. To heighten the effect of a climactic moment, Wordsworth uses imagery of arrested motion ("Almost suspended," "laid asleep / In body," "eye made quiet") to convey a sense, after so much effort to suggest movement and direction, of having reached a point of equilibrium and conclusion. The use of another dependent clause at the end, beginning with "While," extends the moment further and, with language that again emphasizes the inward movement of the entire paragraph (the outward gazing eye is closed, "made quiet" like that of the blind man, to turn inward), and with repetition that sustains the rhythm and passion of the moment, provides an articulation of the new awareness with forceful understatement: "We see into the life of things."

The shift toward the end from first-person singular to first-person plural ("our human blood," "we are laid asleep," "We see"), indicating a change from a highly personal to a public voice, moves away from an identification of the speaker with the biographical and historical

"Wordsworth" and toward a notion of the speaker as "the I-representative," to use Coleridge's phrase. The shift to a representative "I," not only here but at later points in the poem, as well as in the other major lyrics and *The Prelude*, enables Wordsworth to attribute to his lyric speaker experiences that every human being can be thought to have some knowledge of. We recall that Tennyson remarked of *In Memoriam* that the " 'I' is not always the author speaking of himself, but the voice of the human race speaking thro' him."[22] Without questioning that the "I" of an autobiographical poem such as "Tintern Abbey," *The Prelude*, or *In Memoriam* can assume an authoritative public voice in order to make its appeal as broadly representative of human experience, we know that the assumption of a public voice can have multiple functions in a speaker's act of self-representation. One of its functions here is to support the speaker's representation of a change in himself. The use of "living soul" and other echoes shows how he identifies with a scriptural and prophetic voice and how, in doing so, he represents a transformation of the experience-bound "I" recalled at the beginning of the paragraph (living "in lonely rooms, and 'mid the din / Of towns and cities") into a universal "I." The identification is one of the strategies of self-representation by which the speaker attempts to achieve a sense of self-transformation.

3

The new awareness or recognition in the great passage that begins "And I have felt / A presence that disturbs me with the joy / Of elevated thoughts" (93–95) is accompanied by a kind of Aristotelian reversal or self-transformation that is largely dependent upon the strategy of splitting. Other self-dramatizing strategies are of course employed. The speaker stations himself in the scene with some self-consciousness—"here I stand" (62)—before the "presence" of Nature. While he never addresses Nature or the "presence" directly, it is clear that what he says is in response to it. He also structures his memories, thoughts, and reflections in a way that is dramatic in design. By dividing his history into three successive stages, culminating in the moment of new awareness beginning at line 93, he gives the meditative content and lyrical context

---

22. Hallam Tennyson, *Alfred, Lord Tennyson: A Memoir*, 1:305.

of his utterance a developmental structure and a sense of progression toward a turning point. But splitting is the crucial strategy. It became explicit in the second verse paragraph (where the self is divided between the isolated figure "in lonely rooms" and the present self that possesses the "gift / Of aspect more sublime" [25, 36–37]), but it is now extended and given elaborate support in the narrative of his personal history.

Since in my use of the term *splitting* I mean something more general than is usually found in psychoanalytic theory, as well as something more specific than the division of self represented by then/now and earlier/later situations that are part of the structure of many lyrics, from the Romantic period to the present, a word of explanation is called for.[23] By "splitting" I want to suggest a strategy both defensive and dramatic—defensive in the sense that a deep ambivalence divides attitudes toward the self into a present self and a past self, enabling the speaker to isolate one from the other and to attribute anxieties, limitations, and immature notions to one and to endow (and to some extent idealize) the other with control, hope, and a potential for growth; dramatic in the sense that it builds into the poem a tension between the two selves (or two images in the speaker's self-representation) that requires resolution, privileges the speaker's present self, and directs attention to his utterance and the resolution it seeks. More often than not in Wordsworth's poetry, it is a past self rather than the present one that is burdened or fearful or naive, though the Intimations Ode is a striking exception.

Although the speaker in "Tintern Abbey" recounts his life in terms of his relationship to Nature by dividing it into three stages, for all practical purposes he divides it into two since the first stage is dismissed in a parenthetical aside ("the coarser pleasures of my boyish days, / And their glad animal movements all gone by" [73–74]). This splitting of the self calls attention to several differences between the early self and the present. For one thing, the early is characterized by ceaseless activity, the present by arrested motion. The early "came among these hills," "bounded o'er the mountains, by the sides / Of the deep rivers, and the lonely streams," and went "Wherever nature led: more like a man /

23. For discussions of the term, see Freud, "Splitting of the Ego in the Process of Defence," in *Standard Edition*, 23:275–78; Melanie Klein, "Mourning and Its Relation to Manic-Depressive States"; and Laplanche and Pontalis, *Language of Psychoanalysis*, 427–30.

Flying from something that he dreads than one / Who sought the thing he loved" (67–72). The present, on the other hand, is stationed in the natural scene before the "presence" that he sees in it. His is a mood of observation, recollection, and reflection, and instead of the verbs of action used before to characterize the earlier self ("came," "bounded," "led") we have verbs of perception and inner experience ("felt," "behold," "pleased to recognise" [93, 104, 107]), and of being ("Therefore am I" [102]). For another, the early self is characterized by its relationship to a highly particularized nature (the deep rivers, the lonely streams, the tall rock, and so on), while the present self is characterized by its awareness of the presence in Nature defined in terms of geographical and spatial immensity ("Whose dwelling is the light of setting suns, / And the round ocean and the living air, / And the blue sky" [97–99]). Still another difference is that the early self is defined by external experience and physical pleasure ("aching joys," "dizzy raptures" [84–85]), the present self by inner experience and profound thought ("The still, sad music of humanity"; "elevated thoughts; a sense sublime" [91, 94]).

These differences, it is important to remember, are part of the speaker's self-representation and are designed to support his claim that he has undergone a transformation. His repeated emphasis on the present moment ("And now," "While here I stand," "in this moment," "Therefore am I still" [58, 62, 64, 102]), his use of various phrases to mark the differences between times past and present ("though changed . . . from what I was when first / I came among these hills," "For nature then," "boyish days," "I cannot paint / What then I was," "That time is past," and "thoughtless youth" [66–67, 72, 73, 75–76, 83, 90]), and his reliance upon connectives ("For," "And," "Therefore")—all contribute to his representation of himself as approaching a turning point and transformation of self.

Even the speaker's grammar and syntax are features of the act of self-representation, and are used in lines 85–93 to enhance the tension just before the moment of new awareness:

>   Not for this
> Faint I, nor mourn nor murmur; other gifts
> Have followed; for such loss, I would believe,
> Abundant recompense. For I have learned
> To look on nature, not as in the hour

> Of thoughtless youth; but hearing oftentimes
> The still, sad music of humanity,
> Nor harsh nor grating, though of ample power
> To chasten and subdue.

These seven lines (and two half-lines) contain three halting sentences, in contrast to the following eighteen lines with their two flowing sentences. The breaks in grammar and thought brake the forward momentum and create suspense. The conditional "I would believe" qualifies the most important assertion in these lines, "for such loss . . . Abundant recompense." Other qualifiers slow the movement even more: "Not for this," "nor mourn nor murmur," "not as in the hour," "nor harsh nor grating," "though of ample power." Wordsworth often uses such phrases beginning with "not," "nor," or "though" just prior to a climactic moment to enhance the sense of breakthrough that follows. In stanza 5 of the Intimations Ode, for example, two negative constructions, "Not in entire forgetfulness, / And not in utter nakedness," immediately precede and prepare the way for the strongly affirmative "trailing clouds of glory do we come / From God, who is our home" (62–65). Again, in stanza 9 two similar constructions ("not indeed / For that which is most worthy to be blest" and "Not for these I raise / The song of thanks and praise" [135–36, 140–41]) prepare the way for the affirmations that follow ("But for those obstinate questionings / Of sense and outward things . . ." [142ff]).

The artful nature of the speaker's self-representation, reflected particularly in the strategies of stationing, structuring, and splitting, as well as in some grammatical and syntactical features of his utterance, contributes to our sense of the climactic moment reached in line 93:

> And I have felt
> A presence that disturbs me with the joy
> Of elevated thoughts; a sense sublime
> Of something far more deeply interfused,
> Whose dwelling is the light of setting suns,
> And the round ocean and the living air,
> And the blue sky, and in the mind of man:
> A motion and a spirit, that impels
> All thinking things, all objects of all thought,
> And rolls through all things. (93–102)

The plot of the poem—the trajectory of the speaker's thoughts—has all along been leading to this moment. The return, the recollection of the long absence, and the narrative of the three stages have now culminated in it. The stationing of the speaker in the natural setting of the Wye valley has for the first time become a dramatic encounter with Nature. Prior to now—earlier in this verse paragraph, as well as in the poem—Nature has been either a physical setting or a memory. But now Nature is defined as a "presence," a "motion," and a "spirit," and in this guise makes a first appearance, the effects of which are suggested by the use of the word *disturbs* in line 94 and by the great outpouring of thought and feeling that follows.

The grammar, syntax, diction, and imagery of the two sentences that conclude this verse paragraph are all essential to the dramatization of the moment. No conditional or qualifying clauses beginning with "if," "though," "but," or "not for this" interrupt the flow of thought. Instead Wordsworth begins the first sentence with the connective "And," going on then to employ it six more times, and begins the second with "Therefore," employing "and" an additional seven times. The power of the passage, as Thomas McFarland has observed, consists in "the sense of inevitability" that it creates: "The movement of the passage is so sure and deep that its statement seems ineluctible; it seems, that is, to constitute a steady current of certainty, an irresistible flow of feeling."[24] The repeated use of enjambment to create a sense of an overflow of powerful feeling is supplemented by the use of appositional phrasing ("A presence that disturbs . . . a sense sublime . . . a motion and a spirit"), and a series of "and" phrases to describe the ubiquity of the presence ("And the round ocean and the living air, / And the blue sky, and in the

---

24. Thomas McFarland, *William Wordsworth: Intensity and Achievement*, 51. McFarland's observations about lines 93–102 are part of a larger argument dealing with "The Infrashape of the Longer Romantic Lyric" (the subtitle of chapter 2). "The ideas of progression, of unboundedness, and of flow," he writes, "combined to produce the subliminally visual infrashape of the longer Romantic lyric" (38). The stream, as a recurrent metaphor and image in Wordsworth and other Romantic poets, epitomizes it. At the same time, I would argue, the streaming or flowing character of lines 93–102 is an essential part of the self-dramatization in the speaker's utterance. The spontaneity, expressiveness, and inevitability in the lines are part of the speaker's effort to represent himself as having reached a climactic moment in his development.

mind of man . . . And rolls through all things") is used to suggest the rush of an impassioned moment and to help the speaker dramatize his sense of having reached a turning point. While he remains stationary, his thoughts accelerate, as if to represent the increased momentum of passionate feeling. The presence is also portrayed as continually active—it "disturbs," it is "a motion and a spirit," it "impels" and "rolls through all things." The speaker's representation of movement toward a sense of completion and fullness is further supported by the imagery of geographical and spatial immensity ("setting suns," "round ocean," "blue sky") and by the repetition of the word *all* four times in only two lines (101–2).

Wordsworth employs the imagery of immensity in this passage to evoke a Burkean sense of magnitude and infinity associated with an experience of the sublime that is central to the art and psychology of the speaker's act of self-representation. The speaker uses the word *sublime* twice, each time to mark one of the moments of new awareness. In the first he characterizes the "blessed mood" in which "the burthen of the mystery . . . Is lightened" and "We see into the life of things" (37–41, 49) as possessing an "aspect more sublime" (37) and in the second he says that the awareness of the "presence" or spirit of Nature brings with it "a sense sublime" (95). Both call attention to the speaker's effort to dramatize an experience of the sublime as support for his representation that a new awareness or understanding has been achieved and that a reversal—a transformation of self—takes place, and in that order.

In his essay-fragment "The Sublime and the Beautiful," it is not clear whether Wordsworth thinks new understanding precedes an experience of the sublime, follows it, or occurs simultaneously. But in his representation of the two sublime moments in "Tintern Abbey" the fact that the second, more important moment comes in the third stage of the speaker's development, and as a climax to it, suggests that new understanding precedes the experience of "a sense sublime" and that the latter occurs as a result of new understanding. It is also worth noting that the speaker says he has "learned / To look on nature" (88–89) in a different way prior to his attempt to define his "sense sublime / Of something far more deeply interfused" (95–96) in the beautiful sentence that follows, again suggesting that an experience of the sublime results from new understanding. In Thomas Weiskel's three-phase model of the sublime moment, although the astonishment that signals an experience of the sublime occurs in the second phase at the moment that the "habitual relation of mind and object suddenly breaks down" and persists into the third phase when the mind "recovers the balance of outer and inner by constituting a fresh relation between itself and the object," the fact that the sublime moment would cease if there were "a reversion to habitual perception" indicates the extent to which sublime moments are dependent upon and result from new understanding.[25] In the first sublime moment in "Tintern Abbey," too, the "burthen of the mystery . . . and the weary weight / Of all this unintelligible world" appear to be lightened (if not entirely lifted) and better understood before one experiences being "Almost suspended" and "laid asleep / In body" to "become a living soul." The structure of the poem also needs to be taken into account. The placement of the two moments in the unfolding of the speaker's thoughts suggests that an experience of the sublime follows new understanding, for the first moment emphasizes the struggle to understand ("mystery," "unintelligible world," "see into the life of things"), while the second emphasizes the participation in power (the "presence . . . disturbs . . . with the joy / Of elevated thoughts" and its power is felt "in the mind of man"). None of this is to say, however, that new understanding can be fully separated from an experience of the sublime. In the first moment it is clear that new understanding penetrates the experience of the sublime, for the "eye made quiet by the power / Of harmony" reflects the new understanding of seeing "into the life of things" (47–49), and in the second moment the "sense sublime" includes an awareness of "something far more deeply interfused" (95–96). It is only to recognize a general pattern in the dramatization of these moments.

The speaker's dramatization of the second moment (93–102) represents it as an experience of such great intensity, with the verbs "disturbs," "elevated," and "interfused" all functioning as intensifiers (creating what Wordsworth called in his essay-fragment on the sublime "the sensation [of] intense unity" [*Prose*, 2:354]), that whatever gain there is in perception may seem to be only in the intensity of understanding rather than in what is understood.[26] Yet if the emotional and ideational

---

25. Thomas Weiskel, *The Romantic Sublime: Studies in the Structure and Psychology of Transcendence*, 23–24.
26. For an articulation of this view, see Langbaum, *Poetry of Experience*, 46.

content of the moment of intensity appears to be left vague, with nothing so defining as the details of narrative history and character development that typically precede the anagnorisis and peripeteia in drama and fiction, "Tintern Abbey" nevertheless does provide indications of the psychological content of the intensity and these need to be specified in order to understand the transformation of self that the speaker is representing.

One indication is the anxiety over absence, a kind of separation anxiety, that motivated the return and now gives shape to the speaker's self-representation. The poem begins with memories of "a long absence" and the potential of "a vain belief." The anxiety continues to be evident in the opposition of the language of emptiness and meaninglessness associated with absence ("lonely rooms," "hours of weariness," "burthen of the mystery," "unintelligible world," "the many shapes / Of joyless daylight," "the fretful stir / Unprofitable, and the fever of the world" [25–53]) to the language of fullness associated with presence ("Abundant recompense," "presence," "something far more deeply interfused," "all" [88–105]). Another indication of the psychological content of the intensity is the figuring of Nature as maternal, "the nurse, / The guide, the guardian of my heart, and soul / Of all my moral being," and as a presence that "never did betray / The heart that loved her" (109–11, 122–23). When the speaker is identified with the biographical Wordsworth, his defensive insistence that "Nature never did betray" and his anxiety over absence can be traced to Wordsworth's traumatic loss of his mother at age eight, as Richard Onorato has proposed, or possibly to some still earlier disturbance in their relationship.[27] Yet even without considering the biographical origins of this recurrent anxiety in Wordsworth's poetry it is clear that the psychological content of the intensity of the supreme moment in "Tintern Abbey" is defined not simply in terms of a recompense for loss but in terms of a substitution (or "tranquil restoration" [30]) of a maternally figured presence for the earlier sense of emptiness, weariness, and meaninglessness experienced in a state of separation and absence. In addition, this presence is associated with power—it is "A motion and a spirit, that impels / All thinking

---

27. See Onorato on the death of Wordsworth's mother as a traumatic event in his early life in *Character of the Poet*, 66–68. For the suggestion of a preoedipal potential for trauma in Wordsworth's relationship with his mother, see Douglas, *Wordsworth*, 133–35, as well as Schapiro, *Romantic Mother*, 94.

things" (100–101). In discussing the experience of the sublime in his essay-fragment "The Sublime and the Beautiful," Wordsworth says that when "Power awakens the sublime . . . it rouses us to a sympathetic energy & calls upon the mind to grasp at something towards which it can make approaches but which it is incapable of attaining—yet so that it participates [in the] force which is acting upon it" (*Prose*, 2:354). The notion of participating in the force in the essay-fragment and the notion of an interfusion of the presence or power of Nature and "the mind of man" (99) are complementary, suggesting that the speaker in "Tintern Abbey" experiences—or rather represents himself as experiencing—an identification with the presence.

In these ways, the psychological content of the intensity of the sublime moment in lines 93–111 that the speaker represents himself as experiencing is given some definition. The moment of intensity is brought about by the speaker's new awareness of the "presence" in Nature and by a resulting countertraumatic sense of resolution, however temporary or illusory, of his anxiety over absence. But the new awareness involves more than conscious knowledge; it involves identifying with—or, to use Wordsworth's phrase, "participating [in the] force [of]"—the presence. Whatever transformation of self the speaker experiences is due to his representation of himself as having recovered a lost maternal presence and achieved an accompanying sense of meaning essential to his sense of self.

4

The self-transformation that the speaker represents himself as having achieved is dramatized in a special way in the last verse paragraph through his address to his sister. Although Dorothy Wordsworth made the tour of the Wye valley with her brother in July 1798, she did not have to be brought into the poem. Just two years later (October 1800) they would encounter the old man who would become the Leech-gatherer in "Resolution and Independence," but she was not made a part of that poem. She is brought into "Tintern Abbey" for the purpose of enhancing the self-representation of the speaker that he has been at such pains to develop. Had Wordsworth introduced her as an addressee earlier in the poem, her presence would have been a disruptive intrusion into the speaker's solitary experience. Sublime moments in Wordsworth's poems are experienced only by individual speakers, not by their companions or addressees, as we know from the Crossing of the Alps, Mount Snowdon, and other episodes in *The Prelude.* When others are present, they are excluded from this solitary experience, their presence eclipsed or suppressed by the speaker's narration or reflections, though of course he may at some point use *we* to include his addressee, as the speaker does here when he says "We stood together" (151), or use a more public "we" to generalize about and broaden the implications of his experience, as in the first sublime moment in "Tintern Abbey" when he says "we are laid asleep / In body, and become a living soul . . . We see into the life of things" (45–49). Wordsworth does not let the speaker acknowledge the presence of his sister in the first two-thirds of the poem in order to preserve and enhance the interiority and intensity of the speaker's experience and its potential sublimity.

But when she is finally introduced in the last verse paragraph, it is for the purpose of confirming and dramatizing the speaker's achievement of a self-transformation. She is in some ways a double or second self, as Wordsworth imagined in "Michael" that "youthful Poets . . . among these hills / Will be my second self when I am gone" (38–39), and she is used by the speaker to represent a continuation of himself in her memories and thoughts when he imagines his own death ("If I should be where I no more can hear / Thy voice" [147–48]). Lawrence Kramer has observed that "Dorothy's image in the text is . . . invested with a powerful current of Wordsworth's narcissism." The all-too-familiar character of that narcissism is illuminated, I believe, by Virginia Woolf's incisive remark that "Women have served all these centuries as looking-glasses possessing the magic and delicious power of reflecting the figure of man at twice its natural size."[28]

No doubt both the masculine bias in the culture and Wordsworth's special relationship with his sister contributed to the selection of her as the auditor. It would have seemed only natural to him to appropriate the feminine for the purposes of enhancing the role of authority of a masculine speaker.[29] It is true that he could have chosen a different

---

28. Kramer, "Victorian Sexuality and 'Tintern Abbey,' " 402; Virginia Woolf, *A Room of One's Own,* 38.

29. For discussions of the masculine bias and the appropriation of the feminine, see Marlon B. Ross, "Naturalizing Gender," and Ross, *Contours of Masculine Desire,* as well as Judith W. Page, *Wordsworth and the Cultivation of Women.*

auditor to serve much the same purpose. Coleridge's diverse choices of auditors in "The Eolian Harp," "This Lime-Tree Bower," and "Frost at Midnight" suggest that a poet determined to do so can appropriate the presence of anyone he chooses. "My pensive Sara," "gentle-hearted Charles," and the "Dear Babe" who is Hartley are all predictably silent, absent, or asleep, allowing the speakers to go on at length about their wider experience and greater wisdom and making the auditors serve in the role of enhancing the self-image of the speaker. But Dorothy, a year and a half younger, with far less education and experience of the world, and with a great, idealizing love of her brother, was the natural and inevitable choice for Wordsworth. It is not surprising in "To a Highland Girl" that, of the possible relationships the speaker imagines he might have with her, he mentions those of "elder Brother" and "Father" (60–61).

Yet the presence of the speaker's sister in "Tintern Abbey" has to be understood in the context of his efforts at self-representation. She becomes the means at the end of the poem of dramatizing the authority and maturity that he wants to represent himself as having achieved. When he says to her, "in thy voice I catch / The language of my former heart, and read / My former pleasures," and then exclaims, "Oh! yet a little while / May I behold in thee what I was once" (116–20), he casts her in the role of a younger, more innocent version of himself, and casts himself in the role of her mentor, someone now possessed with sufficient wisdom to be able to speak with authority on Nature, human nature, memory, and the future. She becomes the enlarging mirror Woolf had in mind, enabling the speaker to adopt a confident tone designed to confirm his greater moral and intellectual stature in the relationship. His tone is more authoritative and his voice takes on, as Richard Matlak has observed, "the language and rhythm of benediction" ("Therefore let the moon / Shine on thee . . . let the misty mountain-winds . . . blow against thee," "thy mind / Shall be a mansion . . . Thy memory . . . a dwelling-place" [134–41]).[30]

Although he employs the first-person singular throughout the paragraph and personalizes his exhortations to his "dear, dear Sister!" (121), he shifts to the plural at a crucial point early in the paragraph, after delivering the aphorism that "Nature never did betray / The heart that loved her," and while claiming that "she can so inform / The mind that

30. Matlak, *Poetry of Relationship*, 135.

is within us" that none of the evils he lists—including "evil tongues," "Rash judgments," and "The dreary intercourse of daily life"—"Shall e'er prevail against us, or disturb / Our cheerful faith, that all which we behold / Is full of blessings" (122–34).[31] (An exception to this more public sense of the speaker's use of the first-person plural comes at a moment when he is thinking only of himself and his sister, and says she will not forget "That on the banks of this delightful stream / We stood together" [150–51]). The use of aphoristic statement, the shift to first-person plural, and the whole benediction-like character of his speech indicate that in the course of his utterance he changes from the personal voice to his sister to a public and representative voice for a larger audience. This use of a public voice in the last verse paragraph, as elsewhere in the poem, is also designed to confirm the speaker's representation of having achieved a transformation of self, which is further supported by the use of argumentative connectives ("for," "Therefore" [125, 134]) and repeated imperatives ("Nor . . . wilt thou then forget" [146–49, 155]), strengthening the sense of a conclusion.

The range of the speaker's voice when addressing his sister is remarkable. It goes from a tone of deep, personal sincerity ("Oh! yet a little while / May I behold in thee what I was once, / My dear, dear Sister! and this prayer I make") to one of lofty thought and philosophical assertiveness ("Nature never did betray / The heart that loved her") to benedictory comfort and consolation ("Therefore, let the moon / Shine on thee") to self-elegizing reflection ("Nor, perchance— / If I should

---

31. The verbal parallel between "Nature never did betray / The heart that loved her" and "Henceforth I shall know / That Nature ne'er deserts the wise and pure" in Coleridge's 1797 "This Lime-Tree Bower" (59–60) is, as Magnuson has shown, so close that it can be seen, along with other parallels in structure, diction, and thought to Coleridge's conversation poems, as evidence that Wordsworth is responding to Coleridge and that, by implication, the speaker's voice and subjectivity are not entirely his own. See Magnuson, *Coleridge and Wordsworth*, 168–70. It is also true, however, that no voice or subjectivity is entirely free of such appropriations and influences. Their presence in "Tintern Abbey," important though it is for an understanding of the relationship between the two poets, also needs to be considered in the self-dramatizing context of the speaker's utterance that has been my concern in this chapter. In that context, they take on meanings that are largely determined by the speaker's effort to represent that he has achieved a self-transformation.

be where I no more can hear / Thy voice"). The range testifies to the artistry in the speaker's act of self-representation. Despite whatever doubts we may have about the affirmation represented here (because of the ambiguous phrasing, perhaps, suggesting a fear of betrayal as much as a confidence that Nature won't betray, or because of the speaker's apparent need to appropriate and use his sister's presence, or because of hidden or repressed historical references to Wordsworth's life that raise questions about or deconstruct the affirmation in the speaker's address), we remain aware of a certain confidence in the tone of the speaker's address, as well as the artful representation of it.

When we come to "Resolution and Independence" we find a very different kind of speaker, and I want to mention a few of the differences here as a way of highlighting the character of the speaker of "Tintern Abbey." The speaker who encounters the Leech-gatherer is a more deeply troubled figure. While the speaker who returns to the Wye valley with his sister reflects on his personal experience of depression "in lonely rooms . . .'mid the din / Of towns and cities," as well as on the general human experience of "the burthen of the mystery" and the "still, sad music of humanity," he does so in relatively abstract, philosophical terms. The speaker of "Resolution and Independence," on the other hand, experiences radical changes of mood, remembers poets who commit suicide or die early, and must deal with "the fear that kills," a "hope that is unwilling to be fed," and the thought of "mighty Poets in their misery dead." The speaker of "Tintern Abbey" represents himself as achieving a profound new understanding; he sees into the life of things and he experiences "a sense sublime / Of something far more deeply interfused." On the basis of this self-representation he assumes a superior role in his relationship with his sister and exhorts her to follow in his footsteps. The speaker of "Resolution and Independence," in contrast, achieves no such grand understanding. At best he hopes to offer counsel to himself in the future. He will "think" of the Leech-gatherer on the lonely moors. He is much more of a figure in crisis, and "Resolution and Independence" is in certain ways a poem in which Wordsworth takes greater risks. The speakers in both poems act out self-representations designed to reconstitute the self, but the results are quite different.

3 ❖ *In the Mind's Eye/"I"*
"Resolution and Independence"

Like "Tintern Abbey," "Resolution and Independence" is very much an autobiographical lyric. Mary Moorman goes so far as to say that in it "we see more of Wordsworth than in any other single poem." And like "Tintern Abbey," it is based on an actual experience that Wordsworth shared with his sister. As we know from her *Grasmere Journals*, the two of them encountered an old man who gathered leeches on September 26, 1800, though Dorothy Wordsworth did not write her description of the encounter until October 3. In it she recalls that "When Wm & I returned from accompanying [Robert] Jones [partway to Keswick] we met an old man almost double, he had on a coat thrown over his shoulders above his waistcoat & coat.... [H]is trade was to gather leeches but now leeches are scarce & he ... was making his way to Carlisle where he should buy a few godly books to sell." Some of the details she noted reappear in revised form either in an early version of the poem ("coat thrown over his shoulders" became "a Cloak") or in *Poems, in Two Volumes*, as well as later editions ("an old man almost double" became "His body was bent double" and "now leeches are scarce" became "they have dwindled long by slow decay"). Wordsworth himself emphasizes the autobiographical nature of the poem when, in his comments to Mary and Sara Hutchinson in his June 14, 1802, letter, only a month after he began writing it, he identifies himself as the speaker: "I speak as having been much impressed ... by the sight of the old man," "I describe myself," "I think of this till I am so deeply impressed by it," and so on. Many years later he would tell Isabella Fenwick that he met "this Old Man ... a few hundred yards from my cottage at Town-End, Grasmere; & the account of him is taken from his own mouth. I was in the state of feeling described in the beginning of the poem, while crossing over Barton Fell."[1]

1. Mary Moorman, *William Wordsworth: A Biography*, 1:538; Dorothy Wordsworth, *The Grasmere Journals*, 23–24; *Poems, in Two Volumes, and Other Poems, 1800–1807*, 126 (line 73), 126n (line 85), and 129n (line 132); *Letters: The Early Years*, 364–67; *Fenwick Notes*, 14.

Yet there are good reasons not to equate the speaker of the poem with either the Wordsworth who encountered the old man in September 1800 or the Wordsworth who wrote the poem in the spring of 1802. For one thing, Wordsworth represents himself in "Resolution and Independence," as he had in "Tintern Abbey," as someone who, prior to the experience dramatized in the poem, has been carefree. In "Tintern Abbey" he represents himself as having been a "thoughtless youth" in 1793 "when first / I came among these hills," and as bounding "o'er the mountains" with "a feeling and a love, / That had no need of a remoter charm / By thought supplied" (90, 66–68, 80–82). And now in "Resolution and Independence" he represents himself in a similar way: "My whole life I have lived in pleasant thought, / As if life's business were a summer mood" (36–37). But both self-representations are contradicted by his experiences in France and London. By 1793 he not only had lost his political innocence and acquired strong republican sympathies, but had lost his personal innocence as well, having fathered a daughter with Annette Vallon without the means or will (or both) of assuming the responsibilities of husband and father.[2]

Another problem with a strict autobiographical reading is that several of the events and states of feeling originally connected with the encounter of the old man have been rearranged for dramatic effect, as has been often done in *The Prelude*.[3] The state of feeling that Wordsworth describes himself as having been in at the beginning of the poem is one that he would have experienced at the time of writing it in the spring of 1802 rather than in late September 1800 at the time of the encounter. As William Heath has argued, "though Wordsworth remembers the poem as having been written in 1807, the circumstances involved with his 'state of feeling' seem to have survived more vividly in his mind than the date. The most obvious time for him to have been crossing Barton Fell must have been the visit he and Dorothy paid to the Clarksons at Eusemere in April 1802. . . . And the most likely occasion during that

---

2. For the most thorough account of Wordsworth's experiences in France and London in the years 1790–1792, see Johnston, *Hidden Wordsworth*, 188–328 (chapters 9–13).

3. The best-known instance, perhaps, is the "glad preamble" in book I, in which Wordsworth conflates experiences from Goslar and London. See *1805*, I.1–51 and note 2.

visit was the day William left for Middleham to see Mary—April 7th, his thirty-second birthday." Heath speculates that Wordsworth, "going to meet the woman he had promised to marry, [and] about to cross through or near the estate of Lord Lonsdale, the man who had been responsible for his own financial distress, might well have thought of the anxious prospects facing a poet."[4] Still another reason not to take the speaker as Wordsworth, and perhaps the most important (if also the most obvious), is that Wordsworth has employed the endowing and modifying, shaping and creating, powers of imagination, as he described them in the Preface of 1815, not only in his representation of the encounter and the Leech-gatherer but in his representation of himself.

A special complication in that self-representation lies in the imaginative act of splitting the self. Wordsworth represents himself as essentially two different selves, the one before meeting the Leech-gatherer and the one after. In "Tintern Abbey," as we have seen, as well as in the Intimations Ode, "Elegiac Stanzas," and many other poems, Wordsworth represents the self of the speaker as similarly divided. Such a self-representation is central to the dramatic structure of these poems, designed to reinforce the idea that a fundamental change in the self results from the speaker's experience and the new awareness it brings. The division of self in "Resolution and Independence" is represented in terms of time (the early self and the later), vision and reality (the self that idealizes the Leech-gatherer versus the self that recognizes him as a decrepit old man), and subject and object (the reflective self versus the experiencing self that encountered the Leech-gatherer). Yet the self-division is only the speaker's way of representing himself and not necessarily the experiential or psychological fact that he represents it as being. Although we accept it while reading the poem, we should not accept it uncritically. I do not mean to suggest that his splitting of the self is merely a representation, merely a fiction or fantasy, but rather that it is a self-representation so fundamental to his sense of being himself that it must be analyzed for what it reveals about the self. To understand the speaker one must understand the function of the splitting in his representation of himself. The splitting calls attention to an important dimension of his experience that we must take into

---

4. William Heath, *Wordsworth and Coleridge: A Study of Their Literary Relations in 1801–1802*, 123.

account in reading and interpreting the poem: that his achievement of resolution and independence, real or apparent, is built on a mode of self-representation.

An obvious purpose that the splitting serves is to reinforce the notion, central to the speaker's claim in the last two stanzas, that he has undergone the radical change the title announces and that his self-representation attempts to achieve. Yet the very use of such a strategy raises questions about whether resolution and independence have been achieved. It suggests that the speaker's present sense of himself is dependent upon a certain representation of himself to himself, one that attempts, with the use of the defensive strategy of splitting, to keep a self associated with fears, doubts, and despondency sharply distinguished from the so-called new self that the speaker wants to link to the model of perseverance and strength that he saw in the Leech-gatherer, and continues to see in what Geoffrey Hartman calls the "after-image" of him ("In my mind's eye I seemed to see him pace / About the weary moors continually, / Wandering about alone and silently" [129–31]).[5] Nor is splitting the only strategy that the speaker employs in representing himself in the poem. At different times he employs idealization, internalization, and identification, as well as various complementary dramatic and rhetorical strategies (dialogue, self-quotation, the staging of the encounter as sudden and providential, extended similes, and the making of interior images of the Leech-gatherer while talking to him). In calling attention to the strategies in his self-representation I do not wish to deny his implicit claim in the last stanza (and explicit in the title) that he has achieved resolution and independence, though the claim is part of his effort at self-dramatization and therefore deserves to be questioned. My purpose is rather to look closely at the whole act of self-representation for what it might reveal about the self responsible for it. What do these strategies reveal about the speaker? How do they affect the way he sees the Leech-gatherer? What can they tell us about his representation of himself, and what can be perceived about the speaker's self through—or despite—the mode of representation? How do the strategies qualify the content of the recognition in the last two stanzas, and redefine the real or apparent achievement of resolution and independence?

5. Hartman, *Wordsworth's Poetry*, 269.

I

The splitting in the speaker's representation of himself begins early, persists throughout the poem, and functions crucially in the effort at resolution (in both senses of the word). Although he does not actually appear in the first two stanzas, he begins his act of self-representation in them.

> There was a roaring in the wind all night;
> The rain came heavily and fell in floods;
> But now the sun is rising calm and bright;
> The birds are singing in the distant woods;
> Over his own sweet voice the Stock-dove broods;
> The Jay makes answer as the Magpie chatters;
> And all the air is filled with pleasant noise of waters.
>
> All things that love the sun are out of doors;
> The sky rejoices in the morning's birth;
> The grass is bright with rain-drops;—on the moors
> The hare is running races in her mirth;
> And with her feet she from the plashy earth
> Raises a mist; that, glittering in the sun,
> Runs with her all the way, wherever she doth run.

The mode of these two stanzas is more dramatic than narrative. The speaker is not just representing but dramatizing an experience in the present tense that he had in the recent past. We learn that the stanzas are a dramatization only when we reach the first line of stanza 3 ("I was a Traveller then upon the moor" [15]), which, in suddenly replacing the "now" of line 3 with "then," in effect announces that in the first two stanzas the speaker was representing himself as he had been (in a state of relative innocence), and not as he is in the "now" of the remainder of the poem (in a state of greater awareness and reflectiveness). The strategy here is similar to the one in the "glad preamble" at the beginning of *The Prelude*, where Wordsworth dramatizes an experience in the present tense, his escape from city life and his joyful return to Nature (1–45), that he will reveal in the third verse paragraph (46–58) took place in the recent past, thus transforming a dramatic "now" to a narrative "then." As Don Bialostosky has pointed out, the "glad preamble" "takes the form of an extended prosopopeia or self-impersonation, which is revealed as such only at the end when he declares that he has been recording his own previous spontaneous utterance."[6]

The function of the self-impersonation at the beginning of "Resolution and Independence" is to dramatize the sense of a division in the self that the speaker wants—chooses—to emphasize in his representation of himself. He uses the present tense and the description of a pleasant scene ("All things that love the sun are out of doors; / The sky rejoices in the morning's birth . . . The hare is running races in her mirth" [8–11]) to set the stage for his sudden arrival in stanza 3, which is announced in three "I"-asserting sentences—"I was a Traveller," "I saw the hare," "I heard the woods" (15–17). The speaker's staging of his arrival is not unlike his staging of the Leech-gatherer's appearance in stanza 8. In stanzas 1–2 he makes something of the radical changes in the weather to set the stage for his arrival in 3, and they are paralleled by the extreme changes in mood that set the stage for the Leech-gatherer's appearance in 8. The speaker represents both appearances as sudden and dramatic.

In stanzas 3 through 7 he represents himself as having been in a state of passive longing. Although the longing is not explicitly referred to until after he has met and spoken to the Leech-gatherer ("Perplexed, and longing to be comforted" [117]), the speaker's thoughts and behavior are clearly those of one waiting passively for something to happen. Even his role as an observer of Nature is involuntary: "I heard the woods and distant waters roar; / Or heard them not, as happy as a boy" (17–18). In comparing himself to a boy who can be happy with or without hearing the roar of the woods and waters, he represents his former state of happiness as a given, requiring no act of will. The "pleasant season" acts upon him ("did my heart employ") and his "old remembrances" (of "all the ways of men, so vain and melancholy" [19–21]) went from him wholly, again requiring no act of will. He is more acted upon than acting. There is a parallel in his mind between the behavior of nature and his states of consciousness that is central to his representation of himself. He represents his thoughts and changes in mood as not only involving no act of will but also beyond its control. His old remembrances went from him wholly, but soon "fears and fancies thick upon me came" (27).

---

6. Don H. Bialostosky, *Wordsworth, Dialogics, and the Practice of Criticism*, 210.

This characterization of the self as subject to sudden, involuntary changes of mood appears to be foreshadowed in the first two stanzas. In the opening lines the speaker situates himself in a natural setting that emphasizes nature's familiar but unexpected and seemingly inexplicable changes of weather: "There was a roaring in the wind all night; / The rain came heavily and fell in floods; / But now the sun is rising calm and bright." Wordsworth's real interest is not in the fluxes and refluxes of the weather, of course, but in those of the mind, and the first two stanzas show the speaker establishing a precedent in nature for the radical changes in his own mood, a precedent that early in the poem prepares a defense against the extremes of despondency and madness that he will shortly reveal he fears. He makes a choice in his positive representation of the direction of change, from night to day, and storm to sunny morning, that appears designed to accord with, if not actually predict, a similarly fortunate change in his mind later in the poem.

His reference to the stock-dove brooding ("Over his own sweet voice the Stock-dove broods" [5]) is self-referential in a doubly auspicious way. Wordsworth would comment on this line in his Preface of 1815 that "by the intervention of the metaphor *broods*, the affections are called in by the imagination to assist in marking the manner in which the bird reiterates and prolongs her soft note, as if herself delighting to listen to it, and participating of a still and quiet satisfaction, like that which may be supposed inseparable from the continuous process of incubation" (*Prose*, 3:32). Although this comment is specifically concerned with the operations of the imagination, the notion that the stock-dove, in brooding over her own voice, broods over a process leading to a birth has implications for the poet-speaker's own brooding thoughts, not simply about "the morning's birth" but about the new self that will emerge from the brooding that is the poem itself. In his characterization of the stock-dove's brooding the speaker implicitly represents himself as someone presiding over a meditative process leading to a birth of a new self. Yet if Wordsworth at the time of writing this line recalled the Spirit in *Paradise Lost* that "with mighty wings outspread / Dove-like sat'st brooding on the vast abyss / And madest it pregnant" (1.20–22), his own representation of the speaker's self is notably different, making him more of an observer waiting for a birth to happen than a spirit or power making it happen.

Wordsworth's silent change of the stock-dove's masculine gender in the line of the poem he is discussing ("Over *his* own sweet voice the Stock-dove broods" [emphasis added]) to feminine in the Preface ("the bird reiterates and prolongs *her* soft note" [emphasis added]) is a noteworthy slip, pointing to a tendency to gender "soul" and "mind" as feminine, as he repeatedly does in the 1850 *Prelude*. One might account for his gendering of "soul" by recalling that in classical mythology Psyche (soul) is traditionally feminine, but in the work of a poet where Nature is not only feminine but maternal and where the mind's workings are so often emblematized by Nature's workings, as in the passage from the Mount Snowdon episode where, in another echo of Milton, the human mind "broods / Over the dark abyss" (14.71–72), the gendering suggests an identification of the creative self with the feminine and an appropriation of the feminine for the creative potential of the mind. Wordsworth characterizes himself as similarly brooding early in *The Prelude* when he says that "The poet, gentle creature as he is, / Hath like the lover his unruly times," and then calls the mind, "The meditative mind, best pleased perhaps / While she as duteous as the mother dove / Sits brooding" (*1805*, 1.145–46, 150–52). Again, in the Fenwick note on the Intimations Ode he associates brooding with an involuntary rebirth: "I used to brood over the stories of Enoch & Elijah & almost to persuade myself that whatever might become of others I s[houl]d be translated in something of the same way to heaven."[7]

The speaker's emphasis on passive waiting and involuntary change in his representation of himself becomes especially marked in stanza 4. The lines "As high as we have mounted in delight / In our dejection do we sink as low" (24–25) indicate his sense of an inexplicable reversal of mood over which he had no control. The verb phrases underscore his sense of having been overcome: "To me that morning *did it happen so;* / And fears and fancies thick *upon me came*" (26–27, emphasis added). The notion of "blind thoughts" confirms his sense of having been paralyzed. The use of the word "chanceth" in the opening line ("But, as it sometimes chanceth, from the might / Of joy in minds that can no further go" [22–23]) is especially interesting in this context. A. W. Thomson has suggested that it contains the "faintest reminiscence" of *Hamlet*, 1.4.23.[8] Faint though the reminiscence may be, it has a profound resonance for

---

7. *Fenwick Notes*, 61.
8. A. W. Thomson, "Resolution and Independence," 182n.

the poem, I believe, and for that reason the relevant section of Hamlet's soliloquy deserves to be quoted in full:

> So, oft it chances in particular men,
> That for some vicious mole of nature in them,
> As in their birth, wherein they are not guilty
> (Since nature cannot choose his origin),
> By the o'ergrowth of some complexion
> Oft breaking down the pales and forts of reason,
> Or by some habit that too much o'er-leavens
> The form of plausive manners—that these men,
> Carrying, I say, the stamp of one defect,
> Being nature's livery, or fortune's star,
> His virtues else, be they as pure as grace,
> As infinite as man may undergo,
> Shall in the general censure take corruption
> From that particular fault: the dram of [ev'l]
> Doth all the noble substance of a doubt
> To his own scandal.[9]

Several parallels are striking. Hamlet waits on the ramparts for the ghost of his father to appear; the speaker, wandering on the lonely moor and, as he will shortly reveal, experiencing a "longing to be comforted" (117), waits, though without being consciously aware that he is doing so, for the appearance of an old man who is in several respects a father figure. Hamlet mentions "particular men," among whom he himself must be included, and the speaker reflects on Chatterton and Burns, with both of whom he soon acknowledges a sense of identification. The speaker is concerned with the same sense of fate in the lives of particular men that Hamlet is, yet he also retains, as does Hamlet, a sense that these men are somehow responsible for their fate. Hamlet's identification of "one defect" and "vicious mole of nature" in these men and his accusation against himself, later in the play, for failing to act, may be compared to the speaker's charge against himself and the other poets for failure to take heed for themselves. Most important, the intellectual melancholy

---

9. Quotations from Shakespeare are taken from *The Riverside Shakespeare*, ed. G. Blakemore Evans.

so characteristic of Hamlet, resulting in his hesitation, puzzled will, and thoughts of suicide, is the state of mind the speaker represents himself as being in in stanzas 4–7.

In the speaker's representation of himself in the first seven stanzas, therefore, we see not only a self that is dejected, passive, heedless of the future, given to fears, fancies, and blind thoughts, subject to chance, and afraid of despondency and madness, but also a self that harbors notions with the potential to reverse his situation. His characterization of change in the weather as fortunate, with promise inherent in the rising sun and the morning's birth, his use of the image of the stock-dove brooding over its own voice, with the potential for creative change inherent in his use of "brooding," and his allusion to Hamlet, with the implicit parallel in his waiting for the appearance of the ghost of his father, all suggest not only that his representation of himself is split between an earlier and a later self, but also that the earlier and more despondent self is itself split between despondency and hope. This splitting in the depiction of the earlier self in the first seven stanzas serves a function similar to that of the more prominent splitting in the poem between the earlier self and the later, defending the speaker's wish for the birth of a new self against extreme despondency by preserving the possibility of a sudden, longed-for, fortunate change.

Yet his representation of himself at the end of the poem as having achieved resolution and independence appears to be undermined by his narration of the way he achieved it. He is blind to the irony of his narrating a self-history that is designed to demonstrate a release from passive longing and dependence but that actually underscores his continued dependence. In stanza 6 he condemns himself for assuming that "all needful things would come unsought" (38) and for failing to take heed for himself, yet he represents himself in stanza 8 as believing that the appearance of the Leech-gatherer came to him not only unsought but providentially, "by peculiar grace, / A leading from above, a something given" (50–51). The resolution and independence that he claims in the last line, involving an act of will ("I'll think of the Leech-gatherer on the lonely moor!"), is here represented as having come to him in the shape of the Leech-gatherer without his willing it, just as the weather is earlier said to have changed for the better in order to be used as a precedent for the idea that fortunate change may occur without human will or effort. The speaker desires to represent himself as having overcome a crisis and achieved resolution and independence, but in the act of representing such an achievement he shows that he is still dependent on something happening to him, on the whole notion of "it sometimes chanceth" and "it befel."

Hence there is a difference between the way the speaker wants to represent himself (as seeking independence) and the way he does represent himself (as ambivalent, seeking independence yet still conceiving of it as given to him rather than seized by his own initiative). He represents his prior self as subject to mood changes (like the changes in the weather), as passive, and as deserving to be chastised, all for the purpose of attempting to reinforce the notion that that weaker self is in the past. At the same time, he is blind to the fact that his present telling of the story of how that earlier self received its independence as a gift, through peculiar grace, undermines the later claim of independence.

Yet the paradox at the heart of the speaker's situation is that if he possesses any independence from the various forces, both internal (the chances that cause the mind to go from delight to dejection, the "fears and fancies that thick upon me came" [22–27]) and external ("peculiar grace, / A leading from above, a something given" [50–51]) that he imagines control his fate, he possesses it in his capacity for self-representation. That capacity is the most important thing we know about him. He must first imagine and represent himself as being the person he would become. Whatever resolution and independence he may be thought to achieve is not finally the result of the encounter with the Leech-gatherer but rather of a mode of self-representation. His independence, to the extent that he possesses any at all, resides in his imagination, in his capacity to create an enabling fiction about himself and the Leech-gatherer. This act of imagination is an attempt to free him from fears, despondency, and an unstable self that he prefers to represent as a thing of the past.

2

At the heart of this fiction is the dramatization of the encounter with the Leech-gatherer, standing in marked contrast to the matter-of-fact record of it in Dorothy Wordsworth's journal entry on October 3, 1800. It occupies a central place in the speaker's mind and present sense of himself. The memory of it at the end of the poem ("I'll think of the

Leech-gatherer") rather than the God on whom he calls is the actual help and stay secure on which he now relies. Yet the encounter exists in his mind as much more than a memory. His telling of it now, his use of rhetorical, narrative, and dramatic strategies to bring it to life, and his representation of it as a revelatory moment, a turning point in his life, all indicate a present need to revive and maintain the significance he imagines it has. However we may wish to define that significance, a crucial antecedent question must be, why does Wordsworth return to the encounter now and make it the central event in the speaker's life? The question is all the more intriguing because of the two-year hiatus between the encounter and the composition of the poem. Paul Magnuson has argued that "Resolution and Independence" originates in Wordsworth's lyrical dialogue with Coleridge on the subject of dejection, stemming from Coleridge's "Dejection: An Ode." Parallels such as the changeability of mood from joy to depression ("As high as we have mounted in delight / In our dejection do we sink as low" [24–25]) and echoes in words such as "dejection" suggest that Wordsworth was responding to Coleridge. The fact that he composed "The Leech-Gatherer" shortly after hearing Coleridge read the first version of "Dejection," the verse-letter to Sara Hutchinson, and then sent a copy to Coleridge on May 10, 1802, only a month after Coleridge composed the verse-letter, points both to a lyrical dialogue and to an effort by Wordsworth to free himself from a dependence on Coleridge's poetry.[10] But it can also be argued that the dejection dialogue is less the originating event than a screen event, that in writing a poem about problems of independence Wordsworth was reaching beyond the relationship with Coleridge and far back into his personal history to the fate of orphans, and that it is this anxiety that drives him repeatedly toward new efforts at self-representation and self-construction.

 The encounter screens a complex dynamic underlying the speaker's first image as well as recollected afterimage of the old man: an anxiety over the absence of a father that is joined with a corollary, irrepressible wish for a rescuing father figure. The wish seizes upon the accidental

---

10. Magnuson, *Coleridge and Wordsworth*, 308–17. Two others who see "Resolution and Independence" as a response to Coleridge's "Dejection: An Ode" are George Wilbur Meyer, *"Resolution and Independence: Wordsworth's Answer to Coleridge's Dejection: An Ode,"* and Ruoff, *Wordsworth and Coleridge*, 104–66.

encounter with the Leech-gatherer and swells it into a fiction that would reverse the experience of loss and, through this self-healing imaginative act, realize an ideal image of the self. In his discussion of Wordsworth's relationship to the Leech-gatherer as that of a son to a father, Peter Manning interprets the poem as representing Wordsworth's "passage from an image of himself as a child protected by maternal nature . . . to the solitary condition of identity in a world of men of which the Leech-gatherer is the emblem." He suggests that the death of Sir James Lowther in May 1802, which brought Wordsworth hope that the long-standing debt to his father would be paid, may have been a factor in the revision of the poem in July because it would have "revived [the] memory of the loss of his father, thereby contributing to his self-presentation in *Resolution and Independence* as a 'happy child' confronted by an old man."[11] Manning's suggestion that the death of Lowther may have been an oedipal catalyst in the revision of the poem contains within it another possibility I want to explore: that Wordsworth's memory of the death of his father figured in the original composition of the poem. In other words, the sense of loss revived at the time of Lowther's death would have been an ever-present though often unconscious sense not only of his father's death but of his continuing absence.

Freud, recalling the death of his father, said in the preface to the second edition of *The Interpretation of Dreams* that the death of the father is "the most important event, the most poignant loss, in a man's life."[12] However we may respond to this claim, perhaps by qualifying it as a general truth or one that applies to Wordsworth, perhaps by rejecting it, we must acknowledge that there is a good deal of evidence of an anxiety about losing a father in Wordsworth's poetry. Prior to "Resolution and Independence," Wordsworth wrote several poems dealing with

11. Peter J. Manning, " 'My Former Thoughts Returned': Wordsworth's *Resolution and Independence*," 400.

12. Freud, *The Interpretation of Dreams*, in *Standard Edition*, 4:xxvi. Freud's remark was prompted by his delayed recognition that the book had, as he states, a "subjective significance . . . which I only grasped after I had completed it. It was, I found, a portion of my own self-analysis, my reaction to my father's death" (xxvi). Similarly, in his remarks on *Hamlet* he assumes that it was composed "immediately after the death of Shakespeare's father (in 1601), that is, under the immediate impact of his bereavement, and, as we may well assume, while his childhood feelings about his father had been freshly revived" (4:265).

father-son relationships and four represent an anticipated, actual, or figurative experience of loss through death or departure. "Old Man Travelling" was the earliest (1797) and, in the first published version in the 1798 *Lyrical Ballads*, the old man replies at the end of the poem to a question from the narrator, " 'Sir! I am going many miles to take / A last leave of my son, a mariner, / Who from a sea-fight has been brought to Falmouth, / And there is dying in an hospital.' "[13] A distinguishing feature of the other three poems, "The Two April Mornings," "The Fountain," and "Michael," all published in the 1800 *Lyrical Ballads*, is that while the manifest concern of the encounter or story told by the speaker or narrator is also with a father's rather than a son's experience of loss, the underlying preoccupation of the speaker is with his own sense of loss. The loss at the center of "The Two April Mornings," the death of Emma, is framed by the speaker's consciousness of his loss of Matthew, who, as the speaker reveals in the last stanza, is "in his grave" (57). In "The Fountain," Matthew's loss of several children is again framed by the speaker's relationship with Matthew—"I'll be a son to thee!" (62). Although Matthew does not die at the end of this poem, his insistence that the speaker cannot replace the loss he has had to suffer ("Alas! that cannot be" [64]) is itself a denial of the speaker-son's wish for a father, and in this way represents a figurative loss of a father. Wordsworth represents himself in these poems in search of a father.

In "Michael" the case is more complicated, but the story of Michael's loss of Luke is motivated by the narrator's own sense of loss and framed by the elegiac mood with which he mourns the absence of Michael through the poignant description of the lost cottage ("the ploughshare has been through the ground / On which it stood") and the "unfinished Sheep-fold" (477–78, 481). In addition, there is the speaker's awareness of his own mortality in his concern for the "youthful Poets, who among these hills / Will be my second self when I am gone" (38–39) and in his implicit attempt to be the son to Michael that Luke was not, substituting the perpetuation of Michael's story through the poem for the lost inheritance, and himself for the lost Luke.

---

13. *Poetical Works*, 4:247n. The original title, "Old Man Travelling; Animal Tranquillity and Decay, *A Sketch*," became "Animal Tranquillity and Decay" in 1845 and after. Lines 15–20, including the four I quote (17–20), were dropped after 1805.

A narrative called the "Matron's Tale," originally written for "Michael" but later included in the 1805 *Prelude*, book 8, should also be mentioned. Although the story is of a threatened rather than an actual death, and of a son rather than a father, it is the son's fears that Wordsworth concentrates on. The son becomes separated from his father in pursuit of a lost lamb, which had found its way to an island in a brook. When the son leapt to the island, the sheep "sprang forward to the further shore / And was borne headlong by the roaring flood," and "At this the boy looked round him, and his heart / Fainted with fear" (*1805*, 8.281–84). The boy has become "A prisoner on the island, not without / More than one thought of death and his last hour" (288–89). His loss of the sheep vividly represents the danger he is exposed to and prefigures the possibility of his father's loss of him. Although Wordsworth has the father eventually rescue the boy, and places him "safe within his father's arms," he emphasizes the "distress and fear" the father felt (311, 308). Both "Michael" and the "Matron's Tale" recount stories of sons who, taking independent courses of action and in effect straying from the protective presence of their fathers, fail.

The twin themes of the loss of fathers and the vulnerability of sons link these two stories with the "spots of time" passages in book 12 of *The Prelude* and, ultimately, to "Resolution and Independence." The two episodes were composed in 1799 and included in *The Two-Part Prelude*. Both deal with a boy's experience of separation, loss, and death in the context of a father-son relationship. The second episode deals explicitly with the death of Wordsworth's father and is therefore more relevant to my argument. It is worth noting, however, that the first spot of time contains elements of a similar oedipal configuration emphasizing separation, loss, and death: the boy with a father-substitute, "honest James . . . my encourager and guide" (*1799*, 1.303–4); the separation from him and the consequent experience of "fear" (305); and the transformation of the fear into a threat of death in the sudden encounter of a gibbet-mast where a murderer had been hanged many years before.

The episode in the second spot of time deals with the events just prior to and right after the death of Wordsworth's father. It recounts Wordsworth's feelings and thoughts as a boy waiting for his father's servant and three horses to take him and his two brothers home for Christmas, as well as his reaction to the experience of waiting after his father's death. Wordsworth's recollection and recasting of this experience bears a striking resemblance, especially in its psychological character, to the speaker's situation in "Resolution and Independence." The boy is "impatient for the sight" of the three horses expected from his father (*1799*, I.333) and he waits in "an anxiety of hope" (*1799*, I.357); the speaker of "Resolution and Independence" is in a state of anxiety, waiting for something to happen, and "longing to be comforted" (117).¹⁴ The boy waits on the crag by himself, while his two brothers wait elsewhere; the speaker describes himself as waiting in a larger sense, "As if all needful things would come unsought / To genial faith, still rich in genial good" (38–39), and in relation to two brother poets, Chatterton and Burns. The boy experienced a sense of "chastisement" (*1799*, I.355); the speaker an "apt admonishment" (112). The boy "bowed low / To God who thus corrected my desires" (*1799*, I.359–60); the speaker calls on God to be his "help and stay secure" (139).

What these parallels suggest, along with the others I have discussed (in the Matthew poems, "Michael," and the "Matron's Tale"), is that during the three years prior to the composition of "Resolution and Independence" Wordsworth was repeatedly concerned about, if not preoccupied with, a son's anxiety over separation from, or loss of, his father or a father figure. This is not to take the speaker in the poem as Wordsworth but to suggest that such an anxiety figured significantly in Wordsworth's representation of himself as the speaker. It underlies his "dejection," "fears and fancies," and "blind thoughts." His early characterization of himself as a "boy" (18) and a "child" (31), and of the Leech-gatherer as an "old Man" (85, 128), underscores the particular oedipal character of the self-representation in his imaginative re-creation of the encounter. Moreover, the two brother poets that the speaker mentions, and feels a fateful identification with, were both fatherless, Chatterton having lost his father before his own birth, Burns having lost his when the poet was twenty-four, aspects of their lives that would have been known to Wordsworth.¹⁵

---

14. Although this line was not added until 1820, and for that reason may not seem to fit into the context of my discussion of several poems dealing with father-son relationships composed prior to "Resolution and Independence," it gives expression to a longing that is implicit in the original conception of the poem as an account of a saving encounter between a young poet and an old man.

15. Several critics have argued that Wordsworth had Coleridge in mind when thinking of the fates of improvident poets. "It was Coleridge, not Wordsworth,"

Yet it is precisely here, in its handling of the anxiety of loss, that "Resolution and Independence" differs so strikingly from the second spot of time. The poem dramatizes a sudden appearance rather than an unexpected loss, and the discovery of a father figure rather than the loss of one. The speaker's use of "Now" at the beginning of stanza 8, not only as an adverb referring to a particular time but as a conjunctive adverb like "therefore," hinting at a certain logic of inevitability in the Leech-gatherer's unexpected appearance, is designed to represent the encounter as a turning point, one that marks a transformation from an old to a new self. In retelling the story of the encounter the speaker imagines the Leech-gatherer as a ceaseless wanderer on the lonely moors, as if he were the Wandering Jew (as Dorothy reports John imagined when he saw him) or the ghost of Hamlet's father. Given the repeated loss of fathers in the poems composed prior to the composition of "Resolution and Independence" that I have discussed, it is not surprising that an anxiety of loss would figure centrally in the poem. What is surprising is that the speaker represents the encounter with the old man as a reversal of loss—in effect, as a rescue—and that the agent of rescue is the speaker's own idealizing imagination. He structures the encounter so that it comes in a moment of profound distress, while he is thinking of Chatterton, Burns, madness, and the fates of poets, and he employs his idealizing imagination in his vision of the Leech-gatherer to make the encounter

---

Meyer insists, "who took the necessities of life for granted, made repeated claims on others for support and love, and did little or nothing but talk to improve his situation" ("*Resolution and Independence:* Wordsworth's Answer," 69). Heath includes Coleridge but adds Robert Ferguson: "Even though Wordsworth mentions only Chatterton and Burns directly, and surely has Coleridge in mind, a recollection of Ferguson's fate also lies behind these stanzas on the fate of the poet" (*Wordsworth and Coleridge,* 131). More recently, Ruoff has made a strong case for the idea that when Wordsworth heard or read Coleridge's verse letter to Sara Hutchinson in April 1802, which chronicles "his emotional and spiritual misfortunes," Wordsworth "must have been led inevitably to think of Burns" and to include him instead of Coleridge in the poem he would begin to compose in May (*Wordsworth and Coleridge,* 125). For Douglas B. Wilson, "the main subtext is the unnamed Coleridge . . . the primary target among the generic class of endangered poets" (*The Romantic Dream: Wordsworth and the Poetics of the Unconscious,* 76). Another association in Wordsworth's mind, aside from the concern about improvidence and the general fate of poets, may have been the fact that Chatterton, Burns, Coleridge, and, of course, Wordsworth himself lost their fathers early.

seem, Wordsworth wrote to Sara Hutchinson, as if "I was rescued from my dejection and despair almost as an interposition of Providence."[16] The speaker's longing to be comforted (or rescued) is ultimately gratified by his own imagination through a reinstatement of the reassuring image of a father-figure. "In my mind's eye I seemed to see him" (129) and "I'll think of the Leech-gatherer" (140) indicate that such an image has been reinstated in the mind's "I."

Wordsworth's staging of the encounter as sudden and unexpected, coupled with his haunting description of the Leech-gatherer, is designed to suggest an effect of the uncanny. To a certain extent, the effect is created by the speaker's blurring of the boundaries between imagination and reality in the characterization of the Leech-gatherer as the "oldest man . . . that ever wore grey hairs" and as neither "all alive nor dead . . . in his extreme old age" (56, 64–65), in the suggestion that he had "A more than human weight upon his frame" (70), and in the invoking of "Wonder" in the stone and sea-beast similes. But the extraordinary power that the speaker attributes to the Leech-gatherer derives less from the blurring of boundaries and the indeterminate features of character in the description of him, which together belong more to a simultaneous and equally important representation of the sublime in the encounter, than from the speaker's uncanny sense that what appears strange in the old man is also somehow familiar—"And the whole body of the Man did seem / Like one whom I had met with in a dream" [109–10]). Wordsworth seems to anticipate Freud's definition of the uncanny as "in reality nothing new or alien, but something which is familiar and old-established in the mind and which has become alienated from it only through the process of repression."[17] What has been repressed is the anxiety of loss, and what causes the speaker to experience a return of the repressed is the compulsion to repeat, which Freud sees as an important dynamic in the activation of a sense of the uncanny.[18] Only

---

16. *Letters: The Early Years*, 366.

17. Freud, "The Uncanny," in *Standard Edition*, 17:241. In this part of my discussion I am indebted to Manning's essay " 'My Former Thoughts Returned,' " which includes a quotation of the same passage from Freud and provides a reading of the poem rich with psychological insight.

18. Freud traces the uncanny back to a compulsion to repeat that he claims is "probably inherent in the very nature of the instincts," and he goes on to say that "whatever reminds us of this inner 'compulsion to repeat' is perceived as uncanny"

such a combination of the repressed anxiety of loss and the compulsion to repeat could explain the effect of the uncanny in the sudden appearance of the Leech-gatherer. When the speaker says that the old man seemed "Like one whom I had met with in a dream" (110), a reader may recall the Old Man Travelling, Matthew, and Michael and imagine that for Wordsworth, while composing the poem, these and other similar figures were not very far from consciousness.

It is the self-dramatizing design of the speaker's utterance, artfully disguised in the narrative of the encounter, that produces the effect of the uncanny. The effect was not a part of the original encounter, as we know from Dorothy's matter-of-fact report. The speaker's dramatization of it as a climactic moment in his life, like the initial effort to split the self into an earlier and later self, is one of the strategies of the act of self-representation that is the poem. M. H. Abrams has linked such climactic moments in Romantic literature to revelatory moments in Western religious tradition, arguing that they represent a secular appropriation of that tradition. Although he does not discuss "Resolution and Independence," it provides another example of a crisis poem in which the speaker experiences a revelatory moment that becomes a turning point in his life. In stanza 8 the speaker uses religious language to invoke the tradition of the revelatory moment in the notion of "peculiar grace," in the use of the biblical "befel" ("Yet it befel that, in this lonely place"), and in the imaginative restaging of the encounter "Beside a pool bare to the eye of heaven." One of the striking features of the tradition, going back to Augustine and earlier, is that it repeatedly portrays father-son relationships displaced upwards to a spiritual realm. The echo of Matthew 6 at the end of stanza 6 ("But how can He expect that others should / Build for him, sow for him . . . who for himself will take no heed at all"), as Manning has pointed out, subtly invokes a spiritual father-son relationship: the speaker's "allusion to the Redemptive Son and the Heavenly Father who renders worry unnecessary mitigates the anxieties which provoked the poem."[19] In his appropriation of the

---

("Uncanny," 17:238). He refers his reader to "another work, already completed" (but not yet published), *Beyond the Pleasure Principle*, which discusses the compulsion to repeat in a larger context, and in greater detail, but which would not appear until the following year, 1920.

19. Abrams, *Natural Supernaturalism*, 385–90; Manning, " 'My Former Thoughts Returned,' " 401.

revelatory moment in "Resolution and Independence," Wordsworth exploits as much as he perpetuates the religious tradition. The speaker's idealization of the Leech-gatherer, his dramatization of the encounter as a climactic moment, and his representation of it as providentially ordained are all part of an attempt to resolve a crisis through an act of self-representation. The speaker uses the drama of the moment, defining it in both natural and visionary, human and spiritual, terms, to validate the enabling fiction that the encounter resulted in a self-transformation, one that left behind the old self given to fears and fancies. Certainly the speaker's use of the notion of divine intervention in stanzas 8 and 16 (where the Leech-gatherer seems to be "a man from some far region sent, / To give me human strength, by apt admonishment" [111–12]) is designed to counter the image of the earlier self as subject to chance, and largely passive.

Nor is the phrasing as neutral as it appears. Although "whether . . . or" constructions, as Hartman has suggested, reflect Wordsworth's general preference for surmise, and for "alternatives rather than exclusions . . . [or] blunt determinateness," Wordsworth's use of one in this instance appears to be an exception.[20] The speaker's rhetorical gesture in the direction of open-minded inquiry ("Now, whether it were by peculiar grace . . . [or] a something given") gives no alternative to the explanation of divine intervention he proposes: "peculiar grace," "A leading from above," and "a something given" all come to the same thing. This is true even if one reads these phrases as appositional and the construction as "whether or not," for the phrasing would still favor the notion that the old man's appearance was providential. The suddenness of the encounter and the role of the uncanny in Wordsworth's speaker's perception of the Leech-gatherer indicate the extent to which the speaker is committed to a representation of the encounter as providential, and to a view of himself as one of the chosen.

3

If the function of the revelatory moment of encounter with the Leech-gatherer in the speaker's act of self-representation is to reconstitute the self as free from "fears and fancies . . . Dim sadness—and blind

---

20. Hartman, *Wordsworth's Poetry*, 8–9.

thoughts" (27–28), from the perplexity over the fate of "mighty Poets in their misery dead" (116), and from the anxiety of loss, how is the reconstitution or self-transformation represented as achieved? The speaker employs four important strategies of self-dramatization: question-and-answer dialogue, the making of interior images of the Leech-gatherer while listening (and not listening) to him, self-quotation, and narrative repetition and variation. These outward strategies of self-dramatization facilitate and correspond to the inward strategies of internalization and identification on which the possibility of self-transformation rests.

In the other three major lyrics, direct address and apostrophe serve as substitutes for dialogue to represent the presence of an auditor or illusion of an Other and to dramatize the speaker's utterance, but in "Resolution and Independence" Wordsworth employs a dialogue with the Leech-gatherer as one means of dramatizing his speaker's presence. Yet his speaker's use of it is limited to an initial comment to engage the Leech-gatherer's attention ("This morning gives us promise of a glorious day" [84]), a question followed by an observation ("What occupation do you there pursue? / This is a lonesome place for one like you" [88–89]), a follow-up question ("How is it that you live, and what is it you do?" [119]), and a single response from the Leech-gatherer about the scarcity of leeches ("Once I could meet with them on every side; / But they have dwindled long by slow decay; / Yet still I persevere, and find them where I may" [124–26]). The speaker tells us that the Leech-gatherer said much more than is revealed in this single response, using "Choice word and measured phrase" to tell of his coming to this spot to gather leeches, of the hazards of his employment, of his many hardships, and of other matters (stanzas 13–15), but he does not quote him except, as already noted, in lines 124–26. In fact, when one includes the final two lines of the poem, the number of lines the speaker gives to quoting himself is double the number he gives to quoting the Leech-gather. The manuscript of the first version of the poem, "The Leech-Gatherer," reveals that the old man was given at least one full stanza in which to speak of his life.[21] Why is he finally given so little to say? Wordsworth revised the first version and deleted the Leech-gatherer's stanza in part because Sara Hutchinson objected to the "tedious" speech of the old man, but also, I would argue, because the deletion further privileges the

---

21. See *Poems, in Two Volumes, and Other Poems, 1800–1807*, 323.

speaker's presence in the poem, and in doing so enhances the lyrical character of the poem and the speaker's act of self-representation.[22]

The dialogue does more to characterize the speaker and dramatize his presence than to represent the Leech-gatherer. He quotes himself three times, the Leech-gatherer only once. His observation after the first question—"This is a lonesome place for one like you"—characterizes him as presumptuous and naive, as the old man's "flash of mild surprise" indicates (89–90). But it is important to note that the speaker is purposely representing the naïveté of his early self and subtly attributing tolerance and wisdom to the old man as part of the larger dramatic action of his utterance, which moves steadily toward a moment of recognition and reversal. Wordsworth often uses a simple or artless comment, as he does in "The Fountain" ("for thy children dead / I'll be a son to thee!" [61–62]), "A Narrow Girdle of Rough Stones" ("Improvident and reckless . . . The Man must be" [50–51]), and other poems, both to represent a speaker's naive, early self and to set up the dramatic impact of the new awareness and implicit self-transformation he achieves at the end of the poem. The second question is a more pointed version of the first, it is strategically placed closer to the end of the poem, and it concludes a stanza in which the speaker represents himself not only as "Perplexed, and longing to be comforted" (117) but as suddenly afflicted with an intensified version of his melancholy and "former thoughts" ("the fear that kills," "hope that is unwilling to be fed," "all fleshly ills," "And mighty Poets in their misery dead" [113–16]). It is actually two questions in one, combined in the stanza's Alexandrine: "How is it that you live, and what is it you do?" The function of these questions in the speaker's act of self-representation is to dramatize his disturbed state of mind, his continuing astonishment at the strange/familiar figure of the Leech-gatherer, and his need to be comforted. In doing so he makes the old man's smile, his indulgent willingness to repeat what he has already said, and his perseverance in the next stanza seem all the more astonishing.

At the same time that the speaker is representing himself in a dialogue with the Leech-gatherer, however, he is also representing himself as engaged in a process of creating interior images of the Leech-gatherer.

---

22. See *Letters: The Early Years*, 366–67. Although the tone of Wordsworth's letter to Sara Hutchinson is defensive, his deletion of the Leech-gatherer's stanza indicates that he took some of her criticism to heart.

The voice of the old man fades away ("now his voice to me was like a stream / Scarce heard; nor word from word could I divide" [107–8]), and with it much if not all of the speaker's perception of him. What the speaker sees now is wholly different:

> And the whole body of the Man did seem
> Like one whom I had met with in a dream;
> Or like a man from some far region sent,
> To give me human strength, by apt admonishment. (109–112)

An image like this "the excited spirit mainly / Builds for herself," another Wordsworthian speaker says immediately after narrating the encounter with the Blind Beggar and similarly recalling that he felt "As if admonished from another world" (*Prelude*, 7.651–52, 649). In another passage, this one just prior to the encounter with the Discharged Soldier in the 1805 version of the poem, Wordsworth notes the "beauteous pictures" that rise in the mind at the very moment he is looking at a landscape lit by the Moon: "they rose / As from some distant region of my soul / And came along like dreams." Yet the pictures do not simply rise in the mind; they leave "Obscurely mingled with their passing forms . . . A self-possession felt in every pause / And every gentle movement of my frame" (*1805*, 4.392–99). What Wordsworth calls the building of images or the rising of pictures in the mind is a version of internalization that, in "Resolution and Independence," results in an idealized image of the old man. The process is repeated in stanza 19: "In my mind's eye I seemed to see him pace / About the weary moors continually, / Wandering about alone and silently" (129–31). The afterimage of the old man is more than a recollection; it is an internalized ideal that substitutes for the lost father we have traced in the speaker's language and thought, as well as in various of Wordsworth's other poems, and that reconstitutes the "I."

The speaker's repetition/variation of his questions and of his building interior images of the old man is a dramatic strategy designed to intensify his representation of his self-doubts and need to be comforted, and thereby to enhance the force of the new awareness announced in the final lines of the poem. He asks a question in stanza 13 ("What occupation do you there pursue?"), gets an answer in stanzas 14–15 (in "Choice word and measured phrase"), and builds an image of the old man as someone sent to him in stanza 16. Then in stanza 17 he experiences a return of his "former thoughts" and presents a more explicit statement of his anxiety than he has offered before ("the fear that kills . . . And mighty Poets in their misery dead") and again asks his question ("How is it that you live, and what is it you do?"); in stanza 18 he again gets an answer but now presents it more explicitly in the Leech-gatherer's own words ("Once I could meet with them on every side . . . they have dwindled . . . Yet still I persevere. . . ."); and in stanza 19 he again builds an image of the old man, but now a darker one that is "troubled" by his sense of "the lonely place, / The old Man's shape, and speech" ("In my mind's eye I seemed to see him pace / About the weary moors continually, Wandering about alone and silently"). We observed a similar strategy of delaying and intensifying in the speaker's recounting of the two sublime moments in "Tintern Abbey." In both poems the speakers use the strategy to enhance the climactic moments of new awareness and in both the strategy is central to the speakers' efforts at self-dramatization.

In the final stanza the speaker uses self-quotation—"'God,' said I, 'be my help and stay secure; / I'll think of the Leech-gatherer on the lonely moor!'"—to dramatize both the moment of new awareness and the resolution that he represents himself as having achieved. By representing himself as addressing the providence directly that he earlier had only obliquely suggested had intervened in his life, he tries to reinforce a newfound sense of resolution. Self-quotation is a familiar strategy in Wordsworth's poetry. In some poems a speaker uses it not as a dramatization of the moment of new awareness but as a setup for it, as in "The Fountain" and "A Narrow Girdle," where, as we have already noted, the speakers' quoted thoughts represent a naive or mistaken view that gets corrected, the correction becoming the basis of the new awareness. The strategy is used most memorably, perhaps, in the Imagination passage of the Crossing of the Alps episode in *The Prelude* ("But to my conscious soul I now can say—'I recognise thy glory'" [6.598–99]), where he has discovered an internal "Power" (592, 594) that had previously been thought to exist outside himself in Nature. In "Resolution and Independence" the speaker employs self-quotation in a similarly self-dramatizing way: to perform (in the double sense of acting out and achieving) a recognition of an internal strength or sense of resolution that he has prior to this moment seen only in the Leech-gatherer.

What is the specific content of the recognition or new awareness? That it contains a moral dimension is implicit in the idealized image of the old man as a stoic figure pacing the moors continually and supported by Wordsworth's reference to "the moral dignity of the old man's character" in his letter to Sara Hutchinson. Yet the specific moral or other content in the image or character of the old man is never made explicit. Wordsworth seems to have preferred placing the emphasis on the internalized image of the old man, with the implication that it has the emotional power to bring the speaker to a new sense of himself. Making the content explicit in moral or other terms would have risked reducing the speaker's complex emotional and psychological response to the encounter with the Leech-gatherer, as well as Wordsworth's own "feeling of spirituality or supernaturalness" in the experience, to a convenient but distorting phrase or two.[23] Clearness or explicitness, as Burke wrote in his *Enquiry*, and as Wordsworth may have recalled, would have been in conflict with that degree of obscurity necessary for the speaker to preserve a sense of the power of the sublime that he experienced in his encounter of the old man. This is not to say, however, that the content of the new awareness is only a mere gain of intensity of feeling. The speaker's resolution to "think of the Leech-gatherer on the lonely moor" involves an attempt at identification with an idealized if not mythopoeic image of the old man.[24] That image includes moral, psychological, and philosophical contents which, though never articulated, are implicit in various aspects of the idealized image

23. *Letters: The Early Years*, 366.

24. Jared Curtis has persuasively argued that the revisions of "The Leech-Gatherer" that Wordsworth made in transforming the poem into "Resolution and Independence" "function to pull the old man out of his literalness into the realm of myth" (*Wordsworth's Experiments with Tradition: The Lyric Poems of 1802*, 108). If the speaker's use of "decrepit" to describe the Leech-gatherer in the last stanza seems to signal a changed view of him that no longer emphasizes vision and myth, making him now appear to be ordinary, it should also be noted that the speaker continues to think of the old man's speech as "stately in the main" (136), recalling the earlier characterization of it as "a lofty utterance ... Choice word and measured phrase, above the reach / Of ordinary men ... stately" (94–96).

of the Leech-gatherer—his economic independence, his solitariness, his perseverance.[25] The speaker's earlier insistence that the old man used "Choice word and measured phrase, above the reach / Of ordinary men: a stately speech" (95–96) provides still another basis for an identification with him as a poet in spirit, if not in fact, recalling Wordsworth's identification of his brother John as "A *silent* Poet" in "When, to the Attractions of the Busy World" (80).

By the end of the poem when the speaker quotes himself for dramatic emphasis, the Leech-gatherer has become an internalized ideal on which the speaker bases his sense of having achieved a new awareness and a newfound resolution. To the extent that he has achieved a transformation or reconstitution of self, it is dependent, as I have tried to show, on a mode of self-representation that employs a variety of dramatic, rhetorical, and psychological strategies. I have emphasized these strategies (splitting, the staging of the encounter, dialogue, internalization, identification, the staging of the recognition, self-quotation) because they make clear both the self-dramatizing character of the speaker and the process by which his sense of a self-transformation is represented as achieved. Rather than the historical or empirical Wordsworth, he is a self-dramatizing figure who represents a transitional self of the poet. The poem, with its memories of lonely moors and an uncanny encounter with the Leech-gatherer, becomes the cultural space, to use D. W. Winnicott's term, in which this transitional self attempts to perform (again, in the double sense of acting out and achieving) a self-transformation through a lyrical utterance. If the achievement of resolution and independence is to be (or can be) maintained, the act of self-representation will have to be repeated, as the last line of the poem indicates. At some point in the future the speaker will again have to "think of the Leech-gatherer on the lonely moor" and reconstitute himself in the light of that internalized ideal, just as Wordsworth will have to write another lyric and employ another speaker to act out still another self-representation and reconstitution of self.

---

25. For an illuminating consideration of the ethical implications of the speaker's relationship with the Leech-gatherer in its social and economic contexts, see R. Clifton Spargo, "Begging the Question of Responsibility: The Vagrant Poor in Wordsworth's 'Beggars' and 'Resolution and Independence.'"

4 ❖ The "I" of the Ode

Public Performance,
Subjective Transformation

Although the "I" of the Intimations Ode is the most complex and elusive self-representation of any of the major lyrics, in his comments about the poem Wordsworth often suggests a deceptively straightforward identification of himself with the speaker, particularly in his emphasis on the autobiographical experience on which the poem is supposed to be based. In a letter to Catherine Clarkson in January 1815, for example, he commented that "This poem rests entirely upon two recollections of childhood, one that of a splendour in the objects of sense which is passed away, and the other an indisposition to bend to the law of death as applying to our own particular case." He made the most substantial of his comments to Isabella Fenwick in 1843: "To the attentive & competent reader the whole sufficiently explains itself," he says, "but there may be no harm in adverting here to particular feelings or *experiences* of my own mind on which the structure of the poem partly rests." He then goes on to cite the difficulty he had had in childhood of admitting the notion of death "as a state applicable to my own being," the way he "used to brood over the stories of Enoch & Elijah & almost to persuade myself that whatever might become of others I s[houl]d be translated in something of the same way to heaven," and the way his own inner world was more real to him than the external world, remembering that "Many times while going to school have I grasped at a wall or tree to recall myself from this abyss of idealism to the reality."[1] Wordsworth again emphasizes his sense of the greater reality of his inner world in his reply to Bonamy Price's request for an explanation of those "Fallings from us, vanishings": "There was a time in my life when I had to push against something that resisted, to be sure that there was anything outside me. I was sure of my own mind; everything else fell away, and vanished into thought."[2] With each of these comments Wordsworth makes clear that

---

1. *Letters: The Middle Years*, 2:189; *Fenwick Notes*, 61.
2. Quoted from William Knight's edition, *The Poetical Works of William Wordsworth* (1883), 4:58. Another of Wordsworth's comments about the experience of the

he thinks of the Intimations Ode, as he did of "Tintern Abbey" and "Resolution and Independence," as an autobiographical lyric.

Yet the comments do not support the quite different notion that the speaker is the poet in his own person. Indeed, in the Fenwick note Wordsworth calls attention to a distinction between the speaker and himself, remarking that, though "in the poem" he regarded "the dream-like vividness & splendour which invests objects of sight in childhood . . . as presumptive evidence of a prior state of existence," outside the poem he did not mean "to inculcate such a belief." "It is far too shadowy a notion," he went on to say, "to be recommended to faith." Rather than a firmly held conviction, the notion was an Archimedean point from which to advance the validity of his intimations of immortality. "I took hold of the notion of preexistence," he says, "as having sufficient foundation in humanity for authorizing me to make for my purpose the best use of it I could as a Poet." Because these comments were made to Isabella Fenwick nearly forty years after completing the poem, they may appear to be only a retrospective invention of a distinction between the speaker and the poet. But in a letter to Lady Beaumont on May 21, 1807, shortly after the appearance of the Ode in *Poems, in Two Volumes*, Wordsworth maintains a similar distinction with regard to the speaker in the sonnet "With ships the sea was sprinkled far and nigh." Speaking of himself as he appears in the sonnet, he writes, "I am *represented* in the Sonnet . . . my mind *may be supposed* to float up and down. . . . this continued till that feeling *may be supposed* to have passed away" (emphasis added).³ As we saw in Chapter I, Wordsworth frequently emphasizes in his prefaces and essays the autobiographical experience on which his poetry is based, and often claims that in his verse he is speaking in his own person, yet at

---

"abyss of idealism," this one, to R. P. Graves, is also quoted by Knight and has often been linked to the Ode in the critical literature: "I remember Mr Wordsworth saying, that at a particular stage of his mental progress, he used to be frequently so rapt into an unreal transcendental world of ideas that the external world seemed no longer to exist in relation to him, and he had to reconvince himself of its existence by *clasping a tree*, or something that happened to be near him" (4:58). But in this instance the connection to the Ode was made by Graves, not Wordsworth.

3. *Fenwick Notes*, 61–62; *Letters: The Middle Years*, 1:148.

the same time retains the license to conjure and dramatize in ways that fictionalize his self-representation in the poetry.

The fact is that Wordsworth changes his self-representation from poem to poem to suit the lyrical, dramatic, thematic, and other purposes of each work, and this is nowhere clearer than in the contrast between the speaker of the Ode and the speakers of "Tintern Abbey" and "Resolution and Independence." In stanza 5 of the Ode the speaker begins with the bold and unequivocal claim that "Our birth is but a sleep and a forgetting: / The Soul that rises with us, our life's Star, / Hath had elsewhere its setting, / And cometh from afar." He treats preexistence as a reality, not as the "notion" that Wordsworth would say in the Fenwick note "is far too shadowy . . . to be recommended to faith," and he continues to develop and rely upon the myth of preexistence throughout the poem. His confident and assertive tone stands in marked contrast to that of the speaker of "Tintern Abbey." He does not use the conditional mood, either here or elsewhere, the way the speaker of "Tintern Abbey" repeatedly does ("*If this / Be* but a vain belief," "I *would* believe," and "Nor, perchance, / *If I should be*" [49–50, 87, 146–47, emphasis added]), nor does he equivocate in the way the speaker of "Resolution and Independence" does, preserving a distinction between appearance and reality ("The oldest man he *seemed*," "Such *seemed* this Man," "the Man did *seem* / Like one whom I had met with in a dream" [56, 64, 109–10, emphasis added]).

To these contrasts in grammatical mood, qualified statement, and tone should be added the different conceptions of psychological and intellectual development in the poems. In "Tintern Abbey" and "Resolution and Independence," the individual develops from a limited to a greater understanding, and in "Tintern Abbey" he proceeds in almost linear fashion from early youth to mature adulthood, whereas in the Ode the pattern is reversed, the individual beginning a long decline at the moment of birth. Although in the last two stanzas the speaker makes gestures in the direction of development in his mention of the "years that bring the philosophic mind" (187) and in his claim that he loves "the Brooks . . . Even more than when I tripped lightly as they" (193–94), they remain consolatory gestures, never becoming an abundant recompense that could alter the dominant pattern of thought in the poem. These and the other contrasts I have mentioned between the two earlier lyrics and the Ode indicate differences in modes of self-representation difficult if not impossible to reconcile with a univocal notion of the poet always speaking in his own person.

Similarly, the Ode and *The Prelude*, though occasionally paralleling each other in thought, appear at other times to contradict each other to an extent that raises questions about the autobiographical authenticity of their respective speakers. In the Ode the speaker says "But yet I know, where'er I go, / That there hath past away a glory from the earth" (17–18), that "The things which I have seen I now can see no more" (9), and that "the radiance which was once so bright" is "now for ever taken from my sight" (176–77). Yet in *The Prelude* Wordsworth says that "for me / Life's morning radiance hath not left the hills, / Her dew is on the flowers" (6.50–52), and that the "Earth, [is] nowhere unembellished by some trace / Of that first Paradise whence man was driven" (3.110–11). Again, while in the Ode the speaker says that the adult sees "the vision splendid . . . die away, / And fade into the light of common day" (74–77), Wordsworth in *The Prelude* emphasizes his "Unfading recollections! at this hour / The heart is almost mine with which I felt, / From some hill-top on sunny afternoons, / The paper kite high among fleecy clouds / Pull at her rein like an impetuous courser" (1.491–95).

The major difference between the speaker of the Ode and the speakers of "Tintern Abbey," "Resolution and Independence," and *The Prelude* is that the "I" of the Ode is a more public and dramatic self-representation that fits with the Pindaric tradition in which the Ode is written. Although the poem does not achieve what Stuart Curran calls the level of "impetuous rhapsody" to which the Pindaric tradition aspired, it is nonetheless, by comparison with Wordsworth's other major lyrics, distinctly more dramatic, particularly in its use of questions, apostrophes, exclamations, and other features of voice and self-representation, and in this way the speaker seems to belong to the more performative and public tradition of the eighteenth-century Pindaric ode.[4] Reinforcing the more public character of the speaker is the sudden shift from the "I" of

---

4. Curran, *Poetic Form and British Romanticism*, 78. On the public tradition of the eighteenth-century ode, see Norman Maclean, "From Action to Image: Theories of the Lyric in the Eighteenth Century," and Anne Williams, *Prophetic Strain: The Greater Lyric in the Eighteenth Century*.

stanzas 1–4 to the "we" of stanza 5 and the rest of the poem. Although in "Tintern Abbey" Wordsworth employs a similar shift from "I" to "we" in certain passages ("we are laid asleep / In body, and become a living soul . . . We see into the life of things," "Our cheerful faith, that all which we behold / Is full of blessings" [45–49, 133–34]), the "I" remains profoundly personalized by memories of the earlier visit to the Wye valley, by particulars of past and present experience, and by his relationship with his sister. In contrast, the emphasis in the Ode is on representative rather than personal experience. The questions in stanzas 1–4, as Wolfson has pointed out, "issue from the self, [but] are not directed to the self."[5] There is no reference to the time of a particular experience or encounter, no "Five years have past . . . and again I hear / These waters" ("Tintern Abbey," 1–3) or "To me that morning did it happen so" ("Resolution and Independence," 26). Although there is the puzzling reference to a "timely utterance" that gave relief to the speaker's disturbing or mournful thought, it hardly compares to the specific references in the two earlier poems.[6] While several of the verbal similarities between the Ode and the Sonnets of Liberty that Wordsworth wrote in 1802–1803 appear to be references to the French Revolution and Wordsworth's experience and disappointment in the 1790s, as Levinson has argued, they are more public than personal.[7] The only specific references to the poet's life are extratextual, contained in Wordsworth's remarks about the poem to Catherine Clarkson, Isabella Fenwick, and others. Even the melancholy is of a public kind, derived more from a general nostalgia for the visionary splendor of childhood (to which "every one . . . if he would look back," Wordsworth says in the Fenwick note, "could bear testimony")[8] than from any personal experience of depression in the loneliness of the city, and under "the heavy and the weary weight / Of all this unintelligible world," as in "Tintern Abbey" (39–40), or from the fear of "Solitude, pain of heart, distress, and poverty" and the self-accusatory feelings of one "who for himself will take no heed at all," as in "Resolution and Independence" (35, 42).

5. Susan J. Wolfson, *The Questioning Presence: Wordsworth, Keats, and the Interrogative Mode in Romantic Poetry*, 170–71.
6. For two of the best-known speculations on the "timely utterance," see Lionel Trilling, "The Immortality Ode," and Hartman, "'Timely Utterance' Once More."
7. Levinson, *Wordsworth's Great Period Poems*, 88–89.
8. *Fenwick Notes*, 61.

As public as the "I" of the Ode is, however, it reflects a preoccupation with self or subjectivity greater than that found in the two earlier major lyrics, for the speaker of the Ode takes himself as an object. He situates himself in relation to earlier selves rather than, as is common in the greater Romantic lyric, to an Other such as Nature, a personified Dejection, a spirit of Intellectual Beauty, a Nightingale, or a Grecian Urn. In addition, there is no silent auditor such as the sister in "Tintern Abbey," no respondent such as the Leech-gatherer in "Resolution and Independence," and no addressee such as Beaumont in "Elegiac Stanzas." His primary concern throughout the poem is to relate himself to versions of the self: the earlier self that sees the world "Apparelled in celestial light" (4), the pre-existent "Soul that rises with us" (59), the "growing Boy" who "beholds the light" (68–70), the "Youth, who daily farther from the east / Must travel" (72–73), the man who perceives the light fade into common day (76–77), the idealized Child-Philosopher of stanza 8, and the present self that is preoccupied with its persistent memories of obstinate questionings, vanishings, and shadowy recollections. In other words, it is in the presence of these self-representations rather than in the presence of a single, idealized object that the "I" poses and seeks answers to questions, experiences moments of profound sadness and extreme elation, and tries to act out a self-transformation.

Even Wordsworth's change of epigraphs reflects the poem's preoccupation with the self rather than intersubjective relationships.[9] The first epigraph, *Paulo maiora canamus*, "Let us sing a nobler song," taken from Virgil's fourth eclogue, preserved the tradition of invoking the authority or ironic perspective of another poet or voice as a foundation for or commentary on the views represented in the work the epigraph heads. When he changed the epigraph, however, to three lines from his own "My Heart Leaps Up"—

> The Child is father of the Man;
> And I could wish my days to be
> Bound each to each by natural piety

---

9. See Peter J. Manning, "Wordsworth's Intimations Ode and Its Epigraphs," for an important examination of the implications in the change of epigraphs and a persuasive reading of the poem (*Reading Romantics: Texts and Contexts*, 68–84).

—the speaker's implied relationship with the poet and authority represented by the Virgilian epigraph disappeared. In its place was substituted in the new epigraph a relationship between an earlier self (the child that fathers the man) and a later (the "I" that wishes for natural continuity). That relationship is charged with unresolved tension between the two selves, as the still unfulfilled "wish" that the days could be "Bound each to each by natural piety" indicates. The change in epigraphs reflects not only a significant shift in relations from those between a younger poet and an older (or a modern and an ancient) to those between a present self and an earlier self, but also an internalization of all relations, signaling the poem's preoccupation with internal or intrapsychic presences rather than intersubjective relations. It also suggests that, despite the more public and representative character of the "I" of the poem, the traditionally performative and dramatic features of the Pindaric form will in this ode be self-dramatizing, focusing on the subjectivity of the speaker.

The act of taking himself as an object and relating himself throughout the poem to different versions of the self is an obvious form of splitting, familiar from its earlier use in "Tintern Abbey" and "Resolution and Independence." The splitting now, however, serves a quite different function. In the two earlier poems it functions in the speaker's narrative account of his development and in his reflections on it as a defense against fears and anxieties associated with an earlier depressed and vulnerable self. In effect, it is a strategy used to reassure the speaker of the growth and self-transformation that he claims and takes some pains to represent as achieved. But in the Ode, where the speaker idealizes the earlier self and conceives of growth and maturation as a falling away from an ideal state, splitting cannot function in the speaker's act of self-representation in the same way. It functions rather as a defense against an anxiety associated with his present self, a sense of loss experienced as emptiness ("there hath past away a glory from the earth" [18]), diminished power ("The things which I have seen I now can see no more" [9]), and a consciousness of "man's mortality" (199). "The Transientness is Poison in the Wine," Coleridge would write in his verse letter to Sara Hutchinson shortly after hearing the first four—and at that time only—stanzas of Wordsworth's ode, in his response calling attention to its preoccupation with human mutability and death. As the poem looked in 1802, with only the first four stanzas written, it was, as Kenneth Johnston has remarked, "Wordsworth's ode to mortality, not immortality." Yet even in the completed version as it appeared in *Poems, in Two Volumes* in 1807 and in other editions through 1815, the burden of mortality continues to weigh on the speaker's consciousness, as we know from four lines Wordsworth later deleted from the address to the Child-Philosopher in stanza 8 in which he imagines the possession of consciousness in the grave: "To whom the grave / Is but a lonely bed without the sense or sight / Of day or the warm light, / A place of thought where we in waiting lie." Although in her *Grasmere Journals* Dorothy says that Wordsworth thought "it would be sweet . . . to lie . . . in the grave, to hear the *peaceful* sounds of the earth & just to know that ones dear friends were near," the line he substituted for the three deleted lines does not seem to lessen but increase the speaker's consciousness of mortality—"In darkness lost, the darkness of the grave" (118). If the deletion looks like an act of suppression (in response to Coleridge's view in *Biographia Literaria* that the original lines represented "the frightful notion of lying awake in [the] grave"), the substitution looks like a return of the repressed.[10] It is this consciousness of mortality that drives Wordsworth to imagine an earlier self blissfully free of a sense of loss.

I

The speaker's preoccupation with his own subjectivity is reflected in the three-part structure of the ode.[11] Stanzas 1–4 identify a profound split in the speaker's self and represent it as a crisis brought on by the loss of the celestial vision. Stanzas 5–8 attempt to resolve the crisis by

---

10. "*A Letter to* _____" in *Coleridge's "Dejection,"* 28 (line 160); Johnston, *Hidden Wordsworth*, 777; *Poems, in Two Volumes, and Other Poems, 1800–1807*, 274–75; Dorothy Wordsworth, *Grasmere Journals*, 92; Coleridge, *Biographia Literaria*, 2:139.

11. Lionel Trilling divides the poem into two parts, with part one (stanzas 1–4) posing questions that part two (stanzas 5–11) answers ("Immortality Ode," 137). Helen Vendler, in general disagreement with Trilling's reading of the poem, including his view of its structure, sees the poem divided into three parts, stanzas 1–4, 5–8, and 9–11 ("Lionel Trilling and the *Immortality Ode*," 77), which is the view I adopt here. Curran also finds a tripartite structure, but sees "the recognizable triad of stanzas" as 1–4, 5–9, and 10–11 (*Poetic Form and British Romanticism*, 78).

means of a myth of origins that provides a naturalistic explanation of the loss but at the same time actually deepens the crisis to the point where, as the speaker predicts will be the case for the blessed Child of stanza 8, "Full soon thy Soul shall have her earthly freight, / And custom lie upon thee with a weight / Heavy as frost, and deep almost as life!" (127–29). Stanzas 9–11 then present a second and more successful attempt to resolve the crisis by representing a discovery of gain in loss and by finding consolation "In years that bring the philosophic mind" (187). What is not represented in this brief summary of the structure of the Ode, and what I shall be concerned to show in the remainder of this chapter, is the dramatic design of the structure and the self-dramatizing nature of the speaker's utterance.

A lyric, of course, may have a dramatic plot that directs the unfolding of the speaker's thoughts toward a moment of recognition and reversal. Wordsworth unfolds the speaker's thoughts in the Intimations Ode in a structure designed to highlight the climactic moment reached in stanza 9. The first four stanzas show him not only representing but dramatizing a sense of loss (for many readers, the most genuine expression of feeling and poignant moment in the poem) to set the stage for the mythical explanation in 5–8 and the recognition and fortunate reversal in 9. The first stanza provides an elegiac expression and definition of the sense of loss, the second a dramatization of it.

> There was a time when meadow, grove, and stream,
> The earth, and every common sight,
>   To me did seem
>   Apparelled in celestial light,
> The glory and the freshness of a dream.
> It is not now as it hath been of yore;—
>   Turn wheresoe'er I may,
>   By night or day,
> The things which I have seen I now can see no more.
>
>   The Rainbow comes and goes,
>   And lovely is the Rose,
>   The Moon doth with delight
> Look round her when the heavens are bare,
>   Waters on a starry night
>   Are beautiful and fair;

> The sunshine is a glorious birth;
> But yet I know, where'er I go,
> That there hath past away a glory from the earth.

The first five lines of stanza 1 adopt the past tense of a traditional narrative beginning ("There was a time . . .") and the next four, though in the present tense, also emphasize the past ("not now," "yore," and "no more").[12] Stanza 2, on the other hand, begins in the present tense, enumerating some of the beauties of nature visible to the speaker, yet ends with a "But" and a statement that undercuts any sense that "the glory and freshness of a dream" are still visible, even in the sunshine's "glorious birth." Stanza 1 is elegiac in its poetics of lament, stanza 2 dramatic in its performance of the loss that stanza 1 described, first listing the beauties that can be seen, then undercutting the sight of them with "But yet I know, where'er I go, / That there hath past away a glory from the earth."

Stanzas 3 and 4 have a similar structural relationship to each other. Although the speaker reverts briefly to his sense of loss in the mysterious lines "To me alone there came a thought of grief: / A timely utterance gave that thought relief" (22–23), in the remainder of stanza 3 he describes a happy scene of nature ("The cataracts blow their trumpets from the steep . . . I hear the Echoes through the mountains throng, / The Winds come to me from the fields of sleep, / And all the earth is gay" [25–28]). Whatever else may be said about stanza 3 and some of the puzzling references and images in it that have attracted so much critical attention, particularly the "timely utterance" and "the fields of

---

12. A number of lines in the first stanza appear to echo a poem of uncertain authorship that appeared in the London *Morning Post* on October 13, 1800, entitled "The Voice from the Side of Etna; or, The Mad Monk: An Ode, in Mrs. Ratcliff's Manner," particularly the second stanza ("There was a time when earth, and sea, and skies, / The bright green vale and forest's dark recess, / When all things lay before mine eyes / In steady loveliness. / But now I feel on earth's uneasy scene / Such motions as will never cease! / I only ask for peace / Then wherefore must I know, that such a time has been?" [*Lyrical Ballads, and Other Poems, 1797–1800*, 804–5]). For a review of the controversy concerning whether Coleridge or Wordsworth wrote the poem, see idem, 802–4. No matter who wrote "The Mad Monk," it is worth noting that the echoed lines are spoken by a character in a dramatic situation.

sleep,"[13] it is clear that the last lines ("And all the earth is gay . . . Thou Child of Joy, / Shout round me, let me hear thy shouts, thou happy Shepherd-boy!" [29–35]) anticipate and lead into a radical shift in the speaker's tone in stanza 4, where he strains at a joy he does not feel.

> Ye blessèd Creatures, I have heard the call
>   Ye to each other make; I see
> The heavens laugh with you in your jubilee;
>   My heart is at your festival,
>   My head hath its coronal
> The fulness of your bliss, I feel—I feel it all.
>   Oh evil day! if I were sullen
>   While Earth herself is adorning,
>   This sweet May-morning,
>   And the Children are culling
>   On every side,
>   In a thousand valleys far and wide,
>   Fresh flowers; while the sun shines warm,
> And the Babe leaps up on his Mother's arm:—
>   I hear, I hear, with joy I hear! (36–50)

As many readers have felt, there is something forced in the celebratory tone of these lines. We sense it especially in the speaker's claim about the "fulness of [his] bliss" ("I feel—I feel it all" [41]) and in his protests-too-much exclamation ("I hear, I hear, with joy I hear!" [50]). Yet the lines are dramatically appropriate because, as Cleanth Brooks pointed out, "The poet under the influence of the morning scene, feeling the

---

13. These phrases have tested the critical ingenuity of several generations of commentators. For speculations on "timely utterance," see note 6. For an informative discussion of "fields of sleep," see Gene W. Ruoff, "Fields of Sheep: The Obscurities of the Ode, I–IV." Whatever it may refer to in Wordsworth's life, the "timely utterance" and the claim "I again am strong" appear in dramatic context to be another of those staged false recoveries designed to set off by contrast the dejection that comes with a return of the sense of loss at the end of stanza 4, just as the speaker of "Resolution and Independence" says after the storm "My old remembrances went from me wholly; / And all the ways of men, so vain and melancholy" (20–21), only to fall (as it more than "sometimes chanceth") into a profound dejection.

winds that blow 'from the fields of sleep,' tries to relive the dream . . . and fails."[14] In other words, the speaker's effort to relive the dream, from the perspective of the dramatic design of the poem, is a reenactment of the sense of loss acknowledged in stanzas 1 and 2 ("The things which I have seen I now can see no more") and in that way it dramatizes rather than merely expresses the sense of loss. Stanza 4 thus deepens the melancholy tone of the first part of the poem by staging a failed effort to reexperience the lost bliss and provides an excellent example of how the art of self-representation in the poem involves self-dramatization, not simply self-expression.

2

The speaker's shift from "I" to "we" at the beginning of stanza 5 is a sudden and radical change in self-representation. In the first four stanzas, written in 1802, Wordsworth presents the speaker in an elegiac mode. But when he returned to the poem in 1804 he moved beyond the elegiac "I" to a more public and bardic "we," reflecting a new and authoritative tone of a poet-prophet:

> Our birth is but a sleep and a forgetting:
> The Soul that rises with us, our life's Star,
>   Hath had elsewhere its setting,
>   And cometh from afar:
>   Not in entire forgetfulness,
>   And not in utter nakedness,
> But trailing clouds of glory do we come
>   From God, who is our home. (58–65)

The shift from a personal to a public voice, along with the shift from private to representative experience, is accompanied by a change in subject matter that is, if anything, even more abrupt and dramatic, for it involves a change from a preoccupation with individual loss to a radically new and wholly unexpected subject, one that remains surprising even after many readings: a concern with a universal myth of celestial origins and naturalistic decline. As suddenly and boldly as the speaker shifts from "I"

---

14. Cleanth Brooks, *The Well Wrought Urn: Studies in the Structure of Poetry*, 135–36.

to "we," he reconceives the experience of loss as only a failing of memory inherent in the process of growing up and he introduces a naturalistic myth that accounts for the visionary loss and spiritual decline, as well as the psychological and social maturation. The imaginative and narrative force of the myth is so great that it seems to recast the poem, transforming elegy into narrative. While the Ode employs narrative in significant ways, however, it is not a poem in which Wordsworth subordinates lyric to a narrative plot but one in which he briefly appropriates narrative for a larger lyrical and dramatic framework.[15] It is important to understand how the narrative in these stanzas functions in the structure of the poem as an aspect of the speaker's conception and representation of himself.

The introduction of the sun-soul metaphor is one of the breathtaking moments in Wordsworth's poetry, comparable in its combination of images of temporal and spatial immensity invoking a sense of the sublime to some of the most powerful moments in *The Prelude*. It enables the speaker for the first time in the poem to reconstitute himself in ways that defend against the sense of loss dramatized in stanzas 1–4 and his consciousness of mortality recurrent throughout. Although images of the sun or of a star crossing the heavens are common enough in poetry, and Wordsworth may have recalled the one from *Lycidas* in the lines "the star that rose, at evening, bright, / Toward heaven's descent had sloped his westering wheel" (30–31), his introduction of the sun-soul metaphor in stanza 5 functions in a uniquely appropriate way for his speaker's act of self-representation. The speaker uses the metaphor to redefine the soul in ways that give it life and immediacy and that, more importantly, bring it into historical time without surrendering its celestial vision and aspect more sublime. For, although the metaphor initiates the myth of human development and naturalistic decline that ends in stanza 8 with the Soul under the "inevitable yoke" of its years and burdened with "her earthly freight" (125–27), it also establishes in the lyrical plot of the speaker's thoughts a link with the lost world of celestial light that will prove to be both conceptually and dramatically crucial in stanza 9, since the notion that "Though inland far we be, / Our Souls have sight of that immortal sea" (163–64) is part of the extended sun-soul metaphor. Between "The Youth, who daily farther

---

15. For a different view, see Joseph C. Sitterson, "The Genre and Place of the Intimations Ode."

from the east / Must travel" (72–73) and the "Souls" far inland but still able to "see the Children sport upon the shore, / And hear the mighty waters rolling evermore" (167–68) emerges a conception of the speaker's self that insists on continuity of self in the several stages of human existence. Despite the self-diminishing sense of loss in stanzas 1–4, the ironic view of human nature in stanzas 6–7, and the many tensions inherent in a soul blindly at strife with its own blessedness in stanzas 7–8, the speaker uses the sun-soul metaphor to project a sense of unity in his efforts to redefine the soul and reconstitute himself. However defensive and fragile this sense of unity may be, it nonetheless enables him to reconstitute himself in ways that appear, even if only temporarily, to resolve the crisis of irrevocable loss in stanzas 1–4.

More important than the unifying effect of the sun-soul metaphor for the speaker's self-representations in stanzas 5–9, however, is his depiction of himself as the prophet-hero of a family romance in which human nature's mortal parents are replaced by a divine parent.[16] In accord with Wordsworth's persistent concern in this poem to present the speaker as a representative rather than personal or autobiographical "I," the speaker overlooks his mortal parents in his account of his origins, characterizes himself as the "Foster-child" of Earth as a "homely Nurse," and traces his lineage to a divine parent: "Trailing clouds of glory do we come / From God, who is our home" (64–65). Wordsworth introduces a similarly spiritual element of family romance into one of several passages in book 8 of *The Prelude* concerned with defining human nature. "Man" is said to be, "though born / Of dust, and kindred to the worm," nonetheless "a Being . . . instinct / With godhead" (485–93). The speaker of the Ode, by laying claim to descent from godhead for the human soul, establishes the basis for solving the crisis of loss by making it into a developmental phenomenon not in conflict with the assumption of divine origin and immortality. In this way his use of

---

16. See Freud, "Family Romances," in *Standard Edition*, 9:237–41. Jerome Christensen has pointed out that since the "God" of line 66 is the paternity who is the subject of stanzas 5–9, "the eternal deep is *in* the child but *of* the father—an extension in the child of the eternity of the godhead" ("'Thoughts That Do Often Lie Too Deep for Tears': Toward a Romantic Concept of Lyrical Drama," 53). See also Manning, who sees a configuration of a family romance in the "satiric dismissal of the parents" in stanzas 6 and 7 ("Wordsworth's Intimations Ode," 71).

splitting in his self-representation appears to be a natural outcome of human development rather than the defense against mortality that it is.

Two changes in the speaker's representation of himself in stanzas 6 and 7 significantly alter the character of his efforts at self-dramatization. First, with the completion of the shift from "our" and "we" to "he," the speaker moves away from the bardic voice adopted in stanza 5 (and still further from the elegiac tone of stanzas 1–4) to a lyrical-narrative and at times ironic voice. Second, accompanying this change in voice is a change of characters in the family romance from divine to earthly parents and from the universal "Soul" (with which the speaker's "I" becomes merged at the beginning of stanza 5) to the serial and almost allegorical representations of self in the figures of the "growing Boy," "Foster-child," and "six years' Darling of a pygmy size" (68, 83, 87) used to depict the various stages of human development. As a result of these changes, the perspective, tone, and self-representation of the speaker change. Throughout stanza 5 the light imagery brought forward from stanzas 1–4 and now forming a part of the sun-soul metaphor remains prominent in the myth of human origins that the speaker creates and it enables him to maintain for the growing Boy (and implicitly himself) a connection with the divine paternal figure in the family romance (the Boy "Beholds the light," "He sees it in his joy," "The Youth . . . by the vision splendid / Is on his way attended" [70–75]). But by stanza 6 the light imagery has completely disappeared, except for the nostalgic glance back in line 84 to the "glories" of the celestial light, and with its disappearance, as well as with the change in the characters of the family romance and its relocation from a divine to an earthly setting (the "light upon him" in stanza 7 is "from his father's eyes" [90]), the speaker's role changes from participant in to observer of the human history he narrates.

Although the shifts from "I" in stanzas 1–4 and "we" in stanza 5 to "he" in stanzas 6–7 establish an observer-narrator role for the speaker that appears to reduce his self-dramatizing to a minimum, the shifts are in fact part of the speaker's act of self-representation, enabling him to adopt a superior and ironic perspective on the little drama of human development he narrates. Stanza 7 presents a staged scene as much as it tells a story, and the voice of the speaker is as much self-dramatizing as it is narrative. In his use of direct address in "Behold" and "See" ("Behold the Child among his new-born blisses," "See, where 'mid work of his own hand he lies," "See, at his feet, some little plan or chart" [86, 88, 91]), the speaker subordinates the narrative mode to the dramatic. He calls the attention of an unspecified silent auditor to a scene of human life in which the child is shown to be playacting in "A wedding or a festival / A mourning or a funeral," or fitting "his tongue / To dialogues of business, love, or strife" (94–95, 98–99). The vocative of direct address, calling upon a silent auditor to look at the imaginary scene, in effect transforms a narrative description of human development into a dramatic scene, as if immediately before the eye of the speaker and the auditor. Near the end of the stanza the speaker emphasizes the staged character of the scene by employing a theatrical metaphor:

> The little Actor cons another part;
> Filling from time to time his "humourous stage"
> With all the Persons, down to palsied Age,
> That Life brings with her in her equipage;
>   As if his whole vocation
>   Were endless imitation. (103–8)

The little actor is also father of the man, ironically mirroring the way in which the speaker now attempts to assist in the process of maturation by acting out and displaying a narrator's omniscient and gently satirical perspective on that process. The real drama in stanza 7 is not that of the little actor but that of the speaker who, in a performative/transformative act, attempts to reassure himself of a significant advance beyond his sense of loss in stanzas 1–4 and his consciousness of human mortality throughout the poem.

From his relatively limited use of addressing a silent, unidentified auditor in the imperatives of "Behold" and "See" at the beginning of the three sentences of stanza 7, the speaker turns abruptly in stanza 8 to address the Child in an apostrophe that he then elaborates throughout the stanza ("Thou, whose exterior semblance doth belie / Thy Soul's immensity," "Thou best Philosopher," "thou Eye among the blind," "Mighty Prophet! Seer Blest," "Thou, over whom thy Immortality / Broods like the day"). This is the most extended use of apostrophe in the Ode, as well as in the other major lyrics, and it presents an example of Jonathan Culler's observation that apostrophes are embarrassing.[17]

---

17. Jonathan Culler, "Apostrophe." In his "Apostrophe Reconsidered: Wordsworth's 'There Was a Boy,' " J. Douglas Kneale points out that Culler does not

Wordsworth's use of apostrophe in stanza 8 aroused in Coleridge a famous outburst in which he remarked that it is an example of the fifth and last defect to be found in Wordsworth's poetry—namely, "thoughts and images too great for the subject . . . an approximation to what might be called *mental* bombast." Much of the potential for embarrassment at the apostrophe in stanza 8 lies in a reader's sense of its extreme implausibility, as Coleridge's questions about it make clear ("In what sense is a child of that age a *philosopher?* In what sense does he *read* 'the eternal deep'? In what sense is he declared to be *'for ever haunted'* by the Supreme Being? or so inspired as to deserve the splendid titles of a *mighty prophet*, a *blessed seer*? By reflection? by knowledge? by conscious intuition? or by *any* form or modification of consciousness?'"). We know that the lyric, as Northrop Frye has said, "turns away, not merely from ordinary space and time, but from the kind of language we use in coping with ordinary experience."[18] But does Wordsworth's use of apostrophe in stanza 8 (not only to insist on the fiction of addressing the Child but of taking it as a philosopher) go so far, as it seemed to Coleridge to do, that it strains to the breaking point one's willing suspension of disbelief in the imaginative power of the lyric?

In having his speaker suddenly turn to the Child and address him as he does, and in implicitly insisting that the Child is a potentially responsive subject on such lofty matters, Wordsworth certainly risks embarrassment as a response from his readers. But the dramatic context of this apostrophe makes its use understandable, if not fully justifiable. It dramatizes the passionately felt consternation of the speaker over the haunting paradox lying at the heart of human development as he has

---

distinguish between *apostrophe* and *address*, and he is persuasive in showing that there is a long tradition of defining *apostrophe* as a movement of voice, "a turning from an original (implicit or explicit) addressee to a different addressee, from the proper or intended hearer to another" (17). In my discussion of the apostrophe in stanza 8 I continue to draw on Culler's essay, however, for two points that seem especially relevant and valuable: (1) that apostrophe (and address) can be embarrassing in those instances, very common in Romantic poetry, when a speaker addresses an object or a person incapable of understanding what is being said, and (2) that apostrophe (and address) can be a device for constituting the speaker's own subjectivity.

18. Coleridge, *Biographia Literaria*, 2:136–38; Northrop Frye, "Approaching the Lyric," 34.

sketched it: that we will (or at least eagerly accept) the loss we later lament. The exaggerated praise of the Child in lines 109–23 preceding the question ("Why with such earnest pains dost thou provoke / The years to bring the inevitable yoke, / Thus blindly with thy blessedness at strife?" [124–26]) is part of the dramatic context, designed to heighten or intensify the emotional effect of the question. Many of the rhetorical and dramatic features of the speaker's utterance that we have seen before are again employed here in the service of an emotional intensification of the apostrophic moment: exaggeration, the elongated sentence, the series of appositional phrases ("Thou, whose exterior . . . Thou best Philosopher . . . thou Eye among the blind"), and other forms of repetition ("eternal deep . . . eternal mind," "darkness lost . . . darkness of the grave").

Wordsworth's use of apostrophe to dramatize the speaker's passion and incredulity is part of a larger function the apostrophe serves—that of reconstituting the self of the speaker.[19] In stanza 8 the speaker, who addresses the Child with a mixture of exaggerated praise and disturbed questioning, is in the process of reconstituting himself as someone in whom the earlier sense of loss is now far more deeply interfused with a profound understanding of the paradox by which the loss that one must undergo is both inevitable and provoked. Much of the change in the speaker's representation of himself may be seen in his different uses of apostrophe—in stanzas 1–4 to dramatize his sense of loss, in stanza 8 to dramatize his understanding of the dark consequences of the loss. Although the elegiac tone of stanzas 1–4 returns to the speaker's voice in the question he poses and in the prophetic gloom of the last three lines ("Full soon thy Soul shall have her earthly freight, / And custom lie upon thee with a weight, / Heavy as frost, and deep almost as life!" [127–29]), the difference now is that the earlier sense of loss has been transformed into a profound despair. Human loss is shown to be, in the words of Gene Ruoff, "divinely, systematically, and irreversibly determined."[20] The earlier sense of loss now seems almost naive and the speaker represents himself at the end of the stanza as utterly changed by

---

19. See Culler on apostrophe as a poetic device for self-constitution ("Apostrophe," 142).
20. Ruoff, *Wordsworth and Coleridge*, 251.

his dark vision of human fate. The extended apostrophe in this stanza has played no small part in this self-representation.

4

Among the strategies used to dramatize the great climactic moment in stanza 9 when the speaker achieves a new awareness, the plotting of his thoughts in the first eight stanzas is perhaps the easiest to overlook. It is no accident that in the development of his thoughts the sense of loss in stanzas 1–4 has deepened into a despair in 5–8 that now cries out for resolution. The myth of naturalistic decline provided an explanation of the sense of loss but not a means of dispelling it. The heavy weight of custom in the Soul at the end of stanza 8 creates a moment of extreme suspense. Although there are no obvious dramatic props in the representation of the moment of new awareness in stanza 9 (no sudden encounter, as in "Resolution and Independence," or external event in Nature inspiring and paralleling the moment of internal illumination, as in the Mount Snowdon episode), the speaker does employ other strategies to dramatize the passion of the moment, as well as the conceptual power of the recognition that makes it a turning point.

For example, the abrupt transition from the despair at the end of stanza 8 to the joy at the beginning of stanza 9—"O Joy! that in our embers / Is something that doth live"—signals an unmistakable shift in tone. More important, the long sentence that begins at line 134 ("The thought of our past years . . .") and runs to lines 160–61 ("Nor all that is at enmity with joy, / Can utterly abolish or destroy!"), at twenty-seven lines the longest in the poem, and itself longer than any of the other stanzas, is a remarkable vehicle for dramatizing the speaker's passionately felt new understanding. After the initial assertion ("The thought of our past years in me doth breed / Perpetual benediction"), the sentence delays progress toward resolution with the qualifications of the two "not for that" constructions that tell us what he is not praising ("not indeed / For that which is most worthy to be blest . . . Not for these I raise / The song of thanks and praise" [135–41]). These two constructions and their qualifications intensify the suspense and serve as an introductory ascent to the main thought:

> those obstinate questionings
> Of sense and outward things,
> Fallings from us, vanishings;
> Blank misgivings of a Creature
> Moving about in worlds not realised,
> High instincts before which our mortal Nature
> Did tremble like a guilty Thing surprised:
> But for those first affections,
> Those shadowy recollections,
> Which, be they what they may,
> Are yet the fountain light of all our day;
> Are yet a master light of all our seeing . . . (142–53)

Far more than a mere rhetorical flourish, the appositional phrases that are never quite synonymous ("obstinate questionings," "Fallings from us," "vanishings," "Blank misgivings," "High instincts," "first affections," "shadowy recollections") dramatize the speaker's passionate effort to articulate a thought that remains elusive. Wordsworth explains this pattern of repetition and tautology in his "Note to 'The Thorn' ":

> Words, a Poet's words more particularly, ought to be weighed in the balance of feeling, and not measured by the space which they occupy upon paper. For the Reader cannot be too often reminded that Poetry is passion: it is the history or science of feelings: now every man must know that an attempt is rarely made to communicate impassioned feelings without something of an accompanying consciousness of the inadequateness of our own powers, or the deficiencies of language. During such efforts there will be a craving in the mind, and as long as it is unsatisfied the speaker will cling to the same words, or words of the same character. (*Poetical Works*, 2:513)

The speaker's use of gerunds ("questionings," "fallings," "vanishings," "misgivings"), anaphora ("Are yet the fountain light . . . Are yet the master light"), and other forms of repetition ("But for those . . . But for those," "those first affections . . . those shadowy recollections," "of all our day . . . of all our seeing") dramatizes his "consciousness of the inadequateness of [his] powers" to fully communicate his impassioned feelings. The entire passage provides support for Wordsworth's claim that "repetition and apparent tautology are frequently beauties of the highest kind" (*Poetical Works*, 2:513).

The most revealing of the speaker's efforts to dramatize his new awareness, however, is his investing the moment with a sense of the sublime. Like the Wordsworth of the boat-stealing episode, the encounter with the Blind Beggar, the ascent of Mount Snowdon, and other episodes in *The Prelude*, the speaker of the Ode relies on a number of conventional features of the experience of the sublime that were described by Burke in his *Philosophical Enquiry into the Origin of Our Ideas of the Sublime and Beautiful* (1757) and were long familiar to Wordsworth either directly from Burke or indirectly from Gilpin's *Observations on the Lakes* (1786).[21] Aside from the abrupt transition at the beginning of stanza 9, the three main elements of the sublime that the speaker invokes are vastness, obscurity, and power. Vastness, along with infinity, is invoked in the spatial image of the adult "Moving about in worlds not realised," suggesting that the mind contains within itself an infinite potential that is conceptualized in spatial terms ("Moving," "worlds"). The image of "High instincts before which our mortal Nature / Did tremble like a guilty Thing surprised" further suggests a spiritual elevation of great magnitude within the mind, as if the newly discovered "High instincts" tower over lowly mortal nature and cause it to tremble. In certain details the image bears a striking resemblance to the scene in the boat-stealing episode in *The Prelude*, composed only a few years before: The "huge cliff" is now the "High instincts," the boy's "trembling" in his use of the oars is now the speaker's "trembl[ing] like a guilty Thing surprised" before those high instincts, and the mix of fear and astonishment in the two passages is due to a new awareness "Of unknown modes of being" and "worlds not realised" (*1799*, I.108, 114, 122).[22] Infinity is also invoked in the temporal image of "noisy years" as "moments in

---

21. Duncan Wu says that at Hawkshead Wordsworth "would have learnt of the sublime through Gilpin's *Observations on the Lakes*, where Burke is frequently cited. And he may have consulted the fourth edition of the *Enquiry* (1764), donated to the Hawkshead School Library in 1789" (*Wordsworth's Reading, 1770–1799*, 21–22). He also mentions a borrowing from the *Enquiry* in Wordsworth's letter to Dorothy of September 6, 1790. See also Nicola Trott, "Wordsworth and the Picturesque: A Strong Infection of the Age."

22. The most striking difference between the two passages—the fact that the new awareness in the boat-stealing episode is provoked by an encounter with an external object, whereas in the Ode the provoking agency is internal—is really a similarity, for in both passages the experience of the sublime derives from a sense

the being / Of the eternal Silence" (155–56). Obscurity as a quality contributing to the sense of the sublime at work in the passage may be seen in the indeterminate nature of the "questionings," "vanishings," and "shadowy recollections." It calls to mind the passage in book 2 of *The Prelude* in which the soul

> Remembering how she felt, but what she felt
> Remembering not, retains an obscure sense
> Of possible sublimity, whereto
> With growing faculties she doth aspire,
> With faculties still growing, feeling still
> That whatsoever point they gain, they yet
> Have something to pursue. (2.316–22)

Yet the result of this almost formulaic use of infinity and obscurity to create a sense of the sublime is finally more Kantian than Burkean to the extent that the speaker's astonishment (which Burke says is "the effect of the sublime in its highest degree") is not caused by any external object but by unexpected internal sources of power.[23] We

---

of power. "Power awakens the sublime," Wordsworth wrote in his essay-fragment "The Sublime and the Beautiful," "either when it rouses us to a sympathetic energy & calls upon the mind to grasp at something towards which it can make approaches but which it is incapable of attaining . . . or, 2dly, by producing a humiliation or prostration of the mind before some external . . . Power at once awful & immeasurable" (*Prose*, 2:354). Both effects are at work in the Ode. The appositional phrases represent the speaker's attempt to grasp at something that he is "incapable of attaining," and the image of fear and trembling implies the presence of a "Power at once awful & immeasurable."

23. Edmund Burke, *A Philosophical Enquiry into the Origin of Our Ideas of the Sublime and Beautiful*, 57. Scholars are divided on the question of whether Wordsworth read Kant. Weiskel, *Romantic Sublime*, and Theresa M. Kelley, *Wordsworth's Revisionary Aesthetics*, assume that Wordsworth read some of the *Critique of Judgement*, while Duncan Wu states that there is no evidence that he read Kant (see *Wordsworth's Reading, 1800–1850*, 261–62). No one is in doubt, however, that, as Raimonda Modiano has said, Wordsworth "discussed the subject of the sublime with Coleridge, who was, of course well versed in Kantian philosophy" (*Coleridge and the Concept of Nature*, 129), or that Wordsworth at times displays ideas that are similar to Kant's, though, as Kelley has cautioned, the differences are more important (see *Wordsworth's Revisionary Aesthetics*, especially 23–42).

see this particularly in the image of fear, guilt, and power in the lines "High instincts before which our mortal Nature / Did tremble like a guilty Thing surprised" (147–48). Anne Williams finds a Miltonic echo in these lines, recalling the way Adam and Eve after the fall "trembled before God as guilty things surprised."[24] Other readers see in the lines an allusion to *Hamlet,* particularly to Horatio's remark that at the crowing of the cock the ghost of Hamlet's father "started like a guilty thing / Upon a fearful summons" (I.I.148–49), and interpret the allusion as revelatory of oedipal tensions in both the poem and Wordsworth's life.[25] Douglas Wilson, reading the lines as referring to Hamlet's father's ghost, sees an uncanny analogy in them: "Because this ghost has crossed the boundary between the living and the dead, it trembles at a summons back to the underworld. By uncanny analogy, the boy's mortality trembles at an encounter with a world beyond death."[26] Whichever echo we choose to emphasize, it is clear that the speaker uses an image of fear to suggest the way the boy at one time trembled before "High instincts" and the way his own consciousness still trembles at the powerful implications of remembering the "obstinate questionings," "Fallings from us, vanishings," "Blank misgivings," and "shadowy recollections." As Adam and Eve tremble before God, or as the ghost trembles at the summons back to the underworld, so the speaker trembles not only before his present memory of the fallings and vanishings but before a new understanding of their significance, one that is as much new interpretation as new understanding, transforming loss into gain.

Experiences of the sublime in Wordsworth's poetry are generally followed by a representation of some form of self-transformation. In

---

24. Williams, *Prophetic Strain,* 141. See also Vendler, "Lionel Trilling and the Immortality Ode," 82.

25. See, for example, Jonathan Wordsworth, who says that "the poet associated the 'blank misgivings' and 'high instincts' of childhood with his father's death, and with the guilt that has been taken over from the Ghost" (*William Wordsworth: The Borders of Vision,* 64), and Peter Manning, who sees in the lines a hint "at the oedipal contest of Shakespeare's play, the son's obligation to his absent father, his duty to punish his 'foster' father/uncle and his derelict mother, his allegiance to a home in comparison to which the present one is a prison, even as Wordsworth's allegiances make the world a prison-house" ("Wordsworth's Intimations Ode," 72).

26. Wilson, *Romantic Dream,* 37.

the Intimations Ode the sublime is followed by a consolation for loss that invokes the beautiful. As Theresa Kelley has observed, the end of the poem "complexly enacts the aesthetic work required when the beautiful brings (or imposes) its sense of order and relation on . . . thoughts 'too deep for tears.' "[27] In stanza 9 an experience of the sublime was used to dramatize the speaker's discovery of a reason for consolation. Although the celestial vision is gone and the speaker could recall only the experience of losing it, he was consoled by the fact that his memory of the process of forgetting remains vivid and by his claim that one continues to "have sight of that immortal sea" and the ability to "hear the mighty waters rolling evermore" (164, 168). He reinterprets loss as gain and memories of loss as intimations of immortality.[28] In stanzas 10 and 11 the transforming effect of the discovery must be dramatized. What the speaker must do now in stanzas 10 and 11 in order to bring his entire dramatic utterance to a persuasive conclusion is to perform an acceptance of the consolation as a means of showing—or attempting to prove—that a transformation of self has indeed taken place.

Just as stanza 9 ends with "Hence" ("Hence in a season of calm weather, / Though inland far we be"), representing both an argumentative and emotional sense of a conclusion having been reached, so stanza 10 continues with "Then":

> Then sing, ye Birds, sing, sing a joyous song!
>   And let the young Lambs bound
>   As to the tabor's sound!
> We in thought will join your throng,
>   Ye that pipe and ye that play,
>   Ye that through your hearts to-day
> Feel the gladness of the May! (169–75)

27. Kelley, *Wordsworth's Revisionary Aesthetics*, 157.

28. In the words of Kenneth Johnston, "He knows he knows it, and the fact that he has forgotten it—was in fact always in the process of forgetting it—becomes a solid consolation for the loss of it" ("Recollecting Forgetting: Forcing Paradox to the Limit in the 'Intimations Ode,'" 63). See also the fine essay by Stuart Sperry (to whom Johnston is responding) on the premonitory function of memory in the Ode, in contrast to its constitutive function in "Tintern Abbey" ("From 'Tintern Abbey' to the 'Intimations Ode': Wordsworth and the Function of Memory").

The use of apostrophe here is considerably diminished from its earlier use in the poem. The speaker is no longer so concerned with invoking the presence of the birds, young lambs, and others ("that pipe and . . . play") who represent the time and spirit of his earlier self. Rather than address the Child in idealized terms, as he does in stanzas 4 and especially 8, the speaker now uses apostrophe to support the argument and spirit of consolation with which he wants to conclude his utterance. The argumentative grounds for consolation are further developed with the two qualifying "though" clauses ("What though the radiance which was once so bright," "Though nothing can bring back the hour / Of splendour in the grass" [176, 178–79]), which lead into the subdued but more sustainable mood of consolation. The argumentative turn in the speaker's thoughts continues with the "not this/rather that" construction ("We will grieve not, rather find / Strength in what remains behind"), but the consolatory nature of the thought is given emotional support with a series of appositional phrases that are, again, never quite synonymous ("in what remains behind," "In the primal sympathy," "In the soothing thoughts," "In the faith," "In years that bring the philosophic mind" [180–87]).

The function of the rhetoric and mood of consolation in stanzas 10 and 11 is to dramatize the self-transformation that the speaker is claiming he has experienced as a result of the discovery made in stanza 9. If after the celestial vision is gone he can remember the process of loss as one of forgetting, and if the "vanishings" and "shadowy recollections" are perceived as intimations of immortality, then he can seem to himself to have achieved a new awareness and to have undergone a self-transformation. Now with an increased use of the first-person singular in stanza 11, after six stanzas in which it made only three appearances (twice in stanza 9 at lines 134 and 140 and once in 10 at line 177), and with a shift in focus to the consequences of his reflections, he seeks to emphasize the rewards of the new awareness: "Yet in my heart of hearts I feel your might," "I only have relinquished one delight," "I love the Brooks . . . Even more than when I tripped lightly as they," "To me the meanest flower that blows can give / Thoughts that do often lie too deep for tears." But the rewards remain consolatory, attempting to allay the grief for the loss expressed in stanzas 1–4. The fact that the speaker now returns to the first-person singular, uses apostrophe less, supports the consolation with argument, and relies much less on splitting

suggests that Wordsworth was determined to have his speaker act out a performance of the consolation to demonstrate the achievement of a change in self that is supposed to result from the new awareness.

Despite the efforts of the speaker (and the apparent determination of Wordsworth), however, the speaker appears at the end of the poem to be somewhat subdued, especially when compared with the speakers at the end of "Tintern Abbey" and "Resolution and Independence." He stands alone, without the support of the mirroring and self-enhancing presence of the sister in the earlier poem or the reassuring presence of the Leech-gatherer in the later. Like the speakers of those two poems, he looks to the future, but with less confidence. The "cheerful faith, that all which we behold / Is full of blessings" in "Tintern Abbey," even though it was not unqualified, and was to some extent defensive, now appears to be only a shadow of its former self, a "faith that looks through death" (186), a lingering into adulthood of Wordsworth's childhood "indisposition to bend to the law of death, as applying to our own particular case."[29] The faith that allowed the speaker in "Resolution and Independence" to call on God and to expect to be strengthened in a moment of crisis by thinking of the Leech-gatherer has been reduced to sober reflections on "The Clouds that gather round the setting sun," on "man's mortality" (197–99), and on the way the passing years "bring the philosophic mind" (187). In the differences between the endings of "Tintern Abbey" and "Resolution and Independence," on one hand, and the ending of the Intimations Ode, on the other, and especially in the differences between their respective speakers, one senses a gradual movement in Wordsworth's psychological and intellectual development, in the years from 1798 to 1804, toward a broader sense and acceptance of human limitations.

Although the art and psychology of self-representation, not Wordsworth's development, is the primary concern of this study, one is never far away from, and is always returning to, an awareness that Wordsworth is the poet responsible for all these self-representations. The movement that can be discerned here seems to anticipate, even before the crisis brought on by John Wordsworth's death, the darker strains of "Elegiac Stanzas." The speaker of the Ode is closer to the speaker of "Elegiac Stanzas" than he is to the speakers of the earlier poems. Both have been

29. *Letters: The Middle Years,* 2:189.

changed by submission to an awareness that "A power is gone, which nothing can restore" ("Elegiac Stanzas," 35). Both seek consolation and resolve to "grieve not, rather find / Strength in what remains behind" (180–81) and to "welcome fortitude, and patient cheer" ("Elegiac Stanzas," 57–58). Both represent themselves in the end as having achieved an understanding that takes them beyond the experience of loss to thoughts that "lie too deep for tears" (204) and to a sense of "what is to be borne!" ("Elegiac Stanzas," 58).

5 ❖ "Elegiac Stanzas"

The Poet in His Letters and the "I" of the Poem

Although "Elegiac Stanzas" resembles "Tintern Abbey," "Resolution and Independence," and other poems in being based on a specific experience in the poet's life, it differs from them in two significant ways. First, the event on which it is based is not taken from "ordinary life" or "things of every day" (to use Coleridge's language in characterizing Wordsworth's subject matter in *Lyrical Ballads*) such as a return to a favorite landscape or an encounter with an old man. It is based instead on a tragic event that had an immediate and profound effect on Wordsworth, the death of his brother John in the wreck of the *Earl of Abergavenny* on February 5, 1805. On receiving his brother Richard's letter six days later informing him of John's death, he penned a brief reply in which, after expressing shock over "this catastrophe" and the "great affliction" it had brought, he concluded that "the set is now broken" and wrote out his prayer, "God keep the rest of us together!"[1] John's death not only intensified Wordsworth's sense of his own mortality but also reawakened traumatic memories of the early loss of their parents and the experience of becoming an orphan. It had not been that long since Wordsworth, in the spring of 1804 while composing what would become the 1805 *Prelude*, recalled his mother's death—"she who was the heart / And hinge of all our learnings and our loves"—and characterized the still unbroken set of four brothers and a sister as "left . . . destitute, and as we might / Trooping together" (*1805*, 5.257–60). The lines reflect Wordsworth's strong sense of the children as that part of the family unit still intact, held together by their common fate of having become orphans after their parents' death.

At the time of his death, John was the brother that Wordsworth felt closest to. In the 1805 *Prelude* he is said to be one of the two brothers—the other was Richard—with whom Wordsworth dwelt in their father's house when he died Christmas of 1783 ("I and my two brothers, orphans then, / Followed his body to the grave" [11.366–67]). Now, after his death, he seemed to Wordsworth to have been "meek,

---

1. *Letters: The Early Years*, 540.

affectionate, silently enthusiastic, loving all quiet things, and a Poet in every thing but words." Dorothy seems to speak for her brother William as well as herself when she says that "the Image of our departed Brother haunts me with many a pang in the midst of happy recollections of him," one of them being his eight-month visit to Dove Cottage in 1800 and the pride he took in the cottage and the fact that their "Father's Children had once again a home together."[2] In "Tintern Abbey" and "Resolution and Independence" Wordsworth uses incidents from his past that could be imaginatively transformed and integrated into a version of his personal history, but the incidents themselves (the return to the Wye valley and the encounter with an old man who gathered leeches) had no immediate and disruptive impact on his life. Like most of the incidents drawn from his personal history and incorporated into *The Prelude*, these two were chosen less for any intrinsic significance they possessed than for the significance given to them by the aroused poetic spirit and what it brought to memory—what Keats would call the poet's "greeting of the spirit." Unlike the death of John, they were not painful and irreversible interventions in his life.

A second important difference between "Elegiac Stanzas" and the other major lyrics based on a particular autobiographical incident or experience lies in the fact that there is a substantial body of letters dealing with the incident, not only John's death but the controversy surrounding his actions as captain of the ship after it struck the reef and until it sank seven hours later. Wordsworth's repeated reference to the shipwreck as a "catastrophe" is no exaggeration. Over 260 lives and a cargo worth more than two hundred thousand pounds were lost. The accounts in the newspapers and in several pamphlets, two of which claimed in their titles to be *An Authentic Narrative of the Loss of the* Earl of Abergavenny, were—not surprisingly—inconsistent and inaccurate, but they offered reports of John's behavior that, as Wordsworth remarked in a letter to Sir George Beaumont on March 12, "tended to throw discredit on my Brother's conduct and personal firmness."[3] Among the charges against

---

2. Ibid., 541, 649.

3. Ibid., 557. For the best account of the shipwreck and the sensationalizing narratives of it that appeared in the following months, including one that Wordsworth apparently read and underlined some passages of, see Richard E. Matlak, "Captain John Wordsworth's Death at Sea." For an earlier account of the

John in the various accounts that became public, the two most damaging were that he had failed to have the ship's boats hoisted out, thus causing unnecessary loss of life, and that he made no effort to save his own life. Over the next few months Wordsworth wrote many letters to various people seeking information, defending John's behavior, expressing his grief, and trying to make moral and philosophical sense of John's death. These letters, most of which were written between February and July, present Wordsworth in an epistolary voice quite different from that of the poem (though naturally marked with certain striking similarities) and in this way they provide a unique opportunity to compare and contrast two treatments of the same general subject, one by the poet in his letters, the other by the "I" of the poem.

I

The most introspective and revealing of the surviving letters are to Sir George Beaumont, but there are other relevant letters to his brothers Christopher and Richard, to Southey and Scott, and to Thomas Clarkson, James Losh, Richard Sharp, and Thomas Evans. The whereabouts of some of the most valuable letters, those written to Charles Lamb, are unfortunately not known. Wordsworth wrote to Lamb because, as a clerk in the East India Company, which had owned the ship of which John was captain, Lamb would be able to question survivors and give a more detailed account than the rather scant one Richard Wordsworth had sent, and a more accurate one than the sensationalizing newspapers and pamphlets were providing. Nevertheless, the available letters reveal in considerable detail Wordsworth's state of mind. In them he often reverts to the use of conventional—at times even formulaic—phrasing in expressing his grief. John's death, for example, is repeatedly referred to as a "calamity" and an "affliction" ("great affliction," "miserable affliction," "grievous affliction," "burden of our affliction," and "depths of our affliction"). Indeed, five of the major themes running through the letters find expression in such phrasings: (1) the idea that the event is "a calamity [or affliction] with which it has pleased God to visit us"; (2) the

---

shipwreck, the narratives, and Wordsworth's efforts to gather information, see E. L. McAdam, "Wordsworth's Shipwreck." See also Frank Prentice Rand, *Wordsworth's Mariner Brother*, 94–109.

conviction that Wordsworth "will never forget" John and that his death is an "irreparable loss"; (3) the idea that "the set is now broken"; (4) the awareness that "grief will . . . have its course" and that "Time only can give us regular tranquillity"; and (5) the notion that the death was the will of God. I mention Wordsworth's reliance on conventional language for the expression of grief not to bring the sincerity of his feelings into question, but to begin to distinguish the voice of the letters from the voice of the poem.[4]

Five other themes, though conventional enough in the experience and literature of grief, particularly the pastoral elegy, receive more elaborate treatment: (6) description and discussion of the death and its cause (the shipwreck); (7) idealization of the mourned object's character; (8) recollection of the poet's indebtedness to John; (9) recognition of the need for fortitude; and (10) philosophical reflection on life, on "the great Cause and ruler of things,"[5] and on immortality.

It is a matter of some surprise that, of these ten themes running through the letters, only two appear in the poem. The first, perhaps the most persistent in the letters, is the sense of John's death as an irreparable loss that will never be forgotten. Memorable variations on this theme may be seen in the lines "A power is gone, which nothing can restore" (35) and "The feeling of my loss will ne'er be old" (39), echoing a sentiment Wordsworth expressed to Thomas Clarkson on February 16, "Our loss is one which never can be made up," as well as to James Losh a month later, "there is something cut out of my life which cannot be restored."[6]

The second theme is the recognition of the need for fortitude, which appears in the last stanza of the poem ("But welcome fortitude, and patient cheer, / And frequent sights of what is to be borne!" [57–58]). Wordsworth mentions the family's need of fortitude several times in the letters, but on the one occasion when he discusses fortitude at some length (in his March 12 letter to Beaumont) he attributes it to John. He begins by quoting a passage he ran across in a review offering a

---

4. *Letters: The Early Years*, 540, 541, 544, 552, 566, 540–70 passim, 543, 540 and 571, 540, 542 and 565, and 544. McFarland has compiled in a single paragraph a list of expressions of grief by Wordsworth that make clear how profoundly he was affected by the death of John; see *Romanticism and the Forms of Ruin*, 169n.
5. *Letters: The Early Years*, 556.
6. Ibid., 544–45, 565.

synopsis of virtues and vices defined by Aristotle: "It is . . . the property of fortitude not to be easily terrified by the dread of things pertaining to death: to possess good confidence in things terrible, and presence of mind in dangers; rather to prefer to be put to death worthily than to be preserved basely." He concludes by saying that John "might have sate for this picture," except for the fact that "he was of a meek and retired nature, loving all quiet things."[7] Yet when the theme of fortitude is mentioned in the last stanza of the poem ("But welcome fortitude, and patient cheer"), it refers to the speaker, not to John.

Of the themes in the letters that do not appear in the poem, philosophical reflection is the most conspicuous by its absence. In this regard the poem stands in striking contrast to three of the most famous elegies in English tradition, "Lycidas," "Adonais," and *In Memoriam*, in each of which the speaker is moved by the death of a lost friend and poet to raise questions about life and the powers that control it, often in an accusatory tone. The speaker in "Elegiac Stanzas" does not raise or speculate on ultimate questions. The closest he comes is in the ambiguous understatement of the final line, "Not without hope we suffer and we mourn," which may or may not reflect a sense of consolation that makes a gesture toward religious thought.[8]

But the letters reveal that Wordsworth not only felt the weight of such questions on several occasions ("Alas! what is human life!") but on two went far beyond the kind of conventional submission to divine will ("it was the will of God that he should be taken away") that recurs in his and Dorothy's thoughts during this time of grief.[9] On the first occasion, in a letter written February 12, one day after he learned of the shipwreck, Wordsworth responded to Southey's letter of condolence by remarking,

---

7. Ibid., 557–58. The editors note that "The review has not been identified. The second edition of John Gillies's translation of Aristotle's *Ethics and Politics* appeared in 1804" (558).

8. For differing views, see Hartman, who says that Wordsworth's "letters after John's death do show him turning toward the idea of another world, but in 'Peele Castle' the consolation is purely human. If he has religious thoughts . . . he does not tap them; he is yet strong enough in himself" (*Wordsworth's Poetry*, 287), and J. D. O'Hara, who raises the question of how we are to understand the hope in the last line "if not as tapped religion" ("Ambiguity and Assertion in Wordsworth's 'Elegiac Stanzas,'" 81).

9. *Letters: The Early Years*, 541, 548; see also 544, 550, 579.

> Oh! it makes the heart groan, that, with such a beautiful world as this to live in, and such a soul as that of man's is by nature and gift of God, we should go about on such errands as we do, destroying and laying waste; and ninety-nine of us in a hundred never easy in any road that travels towards peace and quietness! And yet, what virtue and what goodness, what heroism and courage, what triumphs of disinterested love everywhere; and human life, after all, what is it! Surely, this is not to be forever, even on this perishable planet.[10]

Although much remains unclear in these remarks (does he have John in mind when he speaks of men going on errands that end in destruction and waste? or when he speaks of "virtue . . . and . . . goodness . . . heroism and courage"? what is the antecedent of "this" when he says "Surely, this is not to be forever"?), Wordsworth's willingness to acknowledge his despair and to ask fundamental questions is very clear ("and human life, after all, what is it!").

On the second occasion, however, in a much longer letter written to Beaumont a month later, on March 12, Wordsworth is far more direct in his use of questions to express profound religious doubt:

> a thousand times have I asked myself, as your tender sympathy led me to do, "why was he taken away?["] and I have answered the question as you have done. In fact, there is no other answer which can satisfy and lay the mind at rest. Why have we a choice and a will, and a notion of justice and injustice, enabling us to be moral agents? Why have we sympathies that make the best of us so afraid of inflicting pain and sorrow, which yet we see dealt about so lavishly by the supreme governor? Why should our notions of right towards each other, and to all sentient beings within our influence differ so widely from what appears to be his notion and rule, if every thing were to end here? Would it be blasphemy to say that upon the supposition of the thinking principle being destroyed by death, however inferior we may be to the great Cause and ruler of things, we have *more of love* in our Nature than he has? The thought is monstrous; and yet how to get rid of it except upon the supposition of *another* and a *better world* I do not see.[11]

While the series of questions in this brief section of the letter that I have quoted is designed to lead to the consoling thought of an afterlife

---

10. Ibid., 543.
11. Ibid., 556.

("the supposition of *another* and a *better world*") and to make reaching that conclusion seem to be a logical imperative, Wordsworth phrases his questions in ways that allow him, as he moves toward the consoling thought, to register several strong charges against the "ruler of things." First, the questions suggest that the ruler may be not only less sensitive to inflicting pain and sorrow than humans, but also "lavish" in his willingness to deal them out, suggesting indifference or cruelty. The phrase "supreme governor" does not suggest the "God" in whom, on other occasions, Wordsworth or one of his speakers expresses trust ("'God,' said I, 'be my help and stay secure, / I'll think of the Leech-gatherer on the lonely moor!'") but rather a distant ruler of "things," not unlike the god of the deists, and in certain ways similar to Hardy's unfeeling and maleficent divine forces, Crass Casualty and the Spinner of the Years, in "Hap" and "The Convergence of the Twain." Finally, with an awareness of (and some self-consciousness concerning) the accusatory nature of his questions ("Would it be blasphemy to say that . . . we have *more of love* in our Nature than he has?"), Wordsworth makes a charge against the "supreme governor" that implies humans are the moral superior of "the Great Cause and ruler of things," a possibility that, had he been willing to explore it, might have radically altered everything he would think, write, and revise for the next forty-five years.

Since, however, Wordsworth has already answered the question "Why was he taken away?" with the reassurance of an immortal life ("I have answered the question as you have done. . . . [T]here is no other answer which can satisfy and lay the mind at rest"), the accusatory force of the questions is limited. In the rhetorical design of this section of the letter, they appear to be asked in a hypothetical way only to prove the necessity of concluding that there must be an afterlife. But in posing them, even in the protective rhetorical framework he employs, Wordsworth is genuinely engaged, however briefly, in questioning the purpose of life and speculating in an accusatory vein about the nature of the supreme being, and in doing so he displays forms of behavior common to the mourning process, as well as to the pastoral elegy, but not present in "Elegiac Stanzas" or elsewhere in his letters.

There are several ways to account for the absence of this and other important themes (for example, Wordsworth's sense of indebtedness to John, his idealization of his brother's character, and his awareness that the "set" is "broken"). For one thing, there is a gap of more than a year between the shipwreck in February 1805 and the composition of the poem in 1806 (probably between May 20 and June 27).[12] The immediate shock of the loss, the memories and anxieties it reawakened, and the pressing force of the questions that death always poses would have gradually diminished, succumbing over a period of time to the routine and renewal of daily life. The controversy in the newspapers and pamphlets over the shipwreck and John's behavior had largely exhausted itself, and when that happened Wordsworth's feeling that he had to continue to defend his brother's reputation must have decreased, and with it, perhaps, some of the preoccupation with the loss and the related anxieties often repeated in the letters through July 1805.

Another way to explain the absence of themes in the letters is to recall that during this period Wordsworth wrote several poems, particularly "Elegiac Verses in Memory of My Brother, John Wordsworth" and his third poem with the title "To the Daisy," that enabled him, as he said, "to give vent to [his] feelings."[13] At first he had difficulty writing ("I had a strong impulse to write a poem that should record my Brother's virtues and be worthy of his memory. . . . [B]ut I was overpowered by my subject and could not proceed"), perhaps because he was too close to the event. But he eventually succeeded and, although neither "Elegiac Verses" nor "To the Daisy" possesses the conceptual sophistication and emotional intensity of "Elegiac Stanzas," each allows him some expression of grief. Moreover, each develops two of the themes from the letters, idealization and indebtedness. In "Elegiac Verses" Wordsworth characterizes John as "The meek, the brave, the good" (38) and in "To the Daisy" as "a gentle Soul and sweet" and "A meek Man and a brave!" (47, 52). Another opportunity to express his feelings came with the death of Lord Nelson on October 21, 1805, and the composition of "The Character of the Happy Warrior" in the winter of 1805–1806. In a remark to Isabella Fenwick made many years later, Wordsworth said that "many elements

---

12. See Mark Reed, *Wordsworth: The Chronology of the Middle Years, 1800–1815*, 324.

13. Reed says that both poems were probably composed between May and July 1805 (see *Wordsworth: The Chronology*, 290). For the phrase "give vent to my feelings" in reference to Wordsworth's efforts to compose a poem about John, see the May 1 letter to Beaumont, in *Letters: The Early Years*, 586. For the other two poems with the same title, as well as still another poem, "To the Same Flower," all composed in 1802, see *Poems, in Two Volumes, and Other Poems, 1800–1807*, 65–69 and 238–41.

of the character here pourtrayed were found in my brother John. . . . His messmates used to call him the Philosopher, from which it must be inferred that the qualities & dispositions I allude to had not escaped their notice."[14]

In "Elegiac Verses" he joins the theme of idealization to that of indebtedness in an effort to memorialize John: "—Brother and friend, if verse of mine / Have power to make thy virtues known, / Here let a monumental Stone / Stand—sacred as a Shrine" (61–64). His sense of indebtedness was a continuing concern throughout this period. In a letter to Losh on March 16 in which he recalls how John had said "I will work for you . . . and you shall attempt to do something for the world," he concludes that "I have much yet to do and pray God to give me strength and power—his part of the agreement between us is brought to an end, mine continues." And in May he wrote to Beaumont, "I shall . . . never be at peace till, as far as in me lies, I have done justice to my departed Brother's memory."[15] The poems cannot have laid these concerns to rest, but they enabled Wordsworth to express his feelings and they may account, at least in part, for the absence of these themes in "Elegiac Stanzas."

Still another way to account for the absence in the poem of some of the concerns revealed in the letters is to acknowledge the strong tendency toward consolation in much of Wordsworth's poetry, representing one of the most persistent patterns in his thought, and by its very presence undoubtedly repressing certain parts of his experience of the loss. In his first letter to Beaumont after learning of John's death, written on February 11, the day he received Richard's letter informing him of it, Wordsworth remarked, "My poor Sister, and Wife who loved him almost as much as we did (for he was one of the most amiable of men) are in miserable affliction, which I do all in my power to alleviate; but heaven knows I want consolation myself."[16] Even in the more reflective March 12 letter to Beaumont, in which he raised serious doubts about the moral nature of the ruler of the universe, he was determined, as we have seen, to find consolation in the supposition of an afterlife. New Historicist readers have argued that Wordsworth sought consolation in his poetry as an escape from history, particularly the social, economic,

---

14. *Letters: The Early Years*, 586; *Fenwick Notes*, 40–41.
15. *Letters: The Early Years*, 563, 565, 586.
16. Ibid., 541.

and political conditions of the day. Certainly the absence of any mention in the poem of the great loss of life, the commercial nature of the ship's voyage, and Wordsworth's investment in it could be interpreted as a repression or denial of important social and economic aspects of the tragedy. Yet the letters Wordsworth wrote throughout the spring and summer of 1805 indicate that personal history was the more immediate and important object of concern and repression. His remark to Richard that "the set is now broken," an allusion to the five orphaned children after his parents' death, reveals one of the concerns expressed in the letters but repressed in the poem. The allusion disguises as much as it reveals, however, for it was the death of Wordsworth's mother when he was eight that initiated him into the experience of death as traumatic loss and that remained a shaping force in his creative life. The death of John involved him in an unconscious repetition of that first experience of traumatic loss and, despite the effects of the work of repression and displacement in the poem, the unconscious priorities of that first experience are clear enough in the contrast between the one relatively insignificant reference to John in the brief address to Beaumont ("Then, Beaumont, Friend! who would have been the Friend, / If he had lived, of Him whom I deplore" [41–42]) and the prominence of a Nature that, as Richard Onorato has shown, Wordsworth had much earlier conceived as maternal and providential as a defense against "his irrational and distressing feelings of betrayal by the mother herself." "With the death of John, Wordsworth felt in another way the 'betrayal' by Nature of the gentle heart that loved her."[17] It should also be mentioned that the desire for consolation becomes stronger in the normal course of mourning, especially as one moves further in time from the event, resulting eventually in the repression of many of the most painful and disturbing aspects of the experience of loss.

Yet these and other ways of accounting for certain absences in the poem, while they have both plausibility and explanatory value, can neither minimize nor explain away the striking differences in self-representation between the Wordsworth of the letters and the Wordsworth of the poem.[18] On the contrary, they call attention to them.

17. Onorato, *Character of the Poet*, 391.
18. Prominent among the other ways of accounting for absences in the poem is Levinson's New Historicist argument that Wordsworth repressed his hopes in

The biographical and psychological context provided by the letters highlights important contrasts between his epistolary and poetic voices and ultimately between the two modes of being represented by epistolary and poetic forms. The contrasts, however, are not only a matter of absence but also of presence, of something characteristic of Wordsworth present in the poem but not in the letters, particularly the dramatic self-representation of the speaker. More than any other feature, it defines the difference between the Wordsworth of the letters and the "I" of the poem.

2

Turning now to the poem, we note several concerns and emphases not present in the letters. The full title—"Elegiac Stanzas Suggested by a Picture of Peele Castle, in a Storm, Painted by Sir George Beaumont"—points to a major concern with representation. There is a representation of Peele Castle in the picture, another in Wordsworth's memory, and still another in his imagination as he would have represented it in 1794, when he spent the month of August in Rampside, was its "neighbour" (1), and saw it every day. The remembered picture, the one described in the first three stanzas, is "doubly pictorial," as James Heffernan has observed, for it includes both the "rugged Pile" and the mirror representation of its "Form . . . sleeping on a glassy sea" (4). The double representation in the speaker's memory is not unlike the two images of Lancelot that Tennyson's Lady of Shalott sees in her mirror, "From the bank and from the river."[19] Of the two representations, Wordsworth appears to be more interested in his memory of the mirror image of the castle, for he emphasizes it in the second stanza when he has the speaker say, "Whene'er I looked, thy Image was still there," trembling on the calm waters (7–8). The primary effect of the emphasis on representation is conceptual. Wordsworth reconceives the experience of loss in a way that

---

the French Revolution and mourned the lost promise of Napoleon and the power of the autonomous imagination that he represented (see *Wordsworth's Great Period Poems*, 101–34).

19. James A. W. Heffernan, *Museum of Words: The Poetics of Ekphrasis from Homer to Ashbery*, 98; for a discussion of the double representation in "The Lady of Shalott," see Christopher Ricks, *Tennyson*, 80–81.

distances it from the actual world of shipwrecks, a drowned brother (who, as I have already noted, is referred to only once, and then obliquely), and a collective, family grief, and relocates it entirely in the realm of the mind, appropriating it for his own purposes in a maneuver characteristic of the Wordsworthian or egotistical sublime. In thus reconceiving loss in terms of representation, representation becomes a concern with self-representation.

There is also a concern with time, a predictable definition of it in internal, psychological terms, and a division of it into a "before" and an "after." In an illuminating discussion, E. D. Hirsch argued that the "before" of the poem, when "the mighty Deep" and implicitly all of Nature seemed "the gentlest of all gentle Things" (11–12), involved a "temporal-eternal perspective" in which nothing appears to be lost and that the "after," when the speaker rejects the former notion as "the fond illusion of my heart" and "a dream" (29, 54), resulted in a change characteristic of the poet's later viewpoint.[20] I am less concerned with the notion of any permanent change in Wordsworth such a rejection may have caused than with the way the before-and-after theme is employed to structure the speaker's experience of loss in ways that are designed to persuade him such a change has taken place and facilitate his act of self-representation.

Wordsworth also now introduces into the poem, as he did not into the letters, a consideration of Nature and his speaker's relationship to it, though this new theme is more substitution (or screen) than addition. In his philosophical reflections in his March 12 letter to Beaumont, in which he raised the question of "why was [John] taken away?" he defined his sense of injustice in the universe by rhetorically situating himself in an accusatory opposition to "the great Cause and ruler of things." But now he situates his speaker in relation to Nature and the substitution enables him to evade the larger questions raised in the letter, as well as the risk of blasphemy that he expressed concern about. Alan Liu has argued forcefully that Nature in Wordsworth is never the primary object of concern, but "stands in the *middle* ground," with history occupying the background and the "I" the foreground.[21] Nature is a mediating rather than primary figure. From the perspective of Wordsworth's letters,

---

20. E. D. Hirsch, *Wordsworth and Schelling.*
21. Liu, *Wordsworth: The Sense of History,* 11.

Nature in "Elegiac Stanzas" does indeed seem to stand in the middle ground and the "I" of the poem in the foreground. But I would argue that it is not social, economic, or political history that is in the background so much as that part of Wordsworth's personal history immediately following the death of John when Wordsworth felt compelled to raise fundamental questions about existence in relation to "the great Cause and ruler of things." In the poem Wordsworth does not situate himself in relation to this Cause, nor does he raise questions about causation. Nature is introduced instead as a substitute that is first represented as having been embraced and is then redefined, but never questioned or challenged.

Yet these concerns with representation, time, and Nature, though they appear to be the immediate objects of the speaker's attention, and give a strong degree of thematic and structural unity to his thoughts, are subordinate in importance to his larger concern with self-representation. In contrast to the Wordsworth of the letters, the speaker of the poem stages a drama in the theater of his mind in which memory and illusion are represented as suffering a defeat at the hands of experience but in the service of increasing awareness and achieving a sense of resolution. The purpose of the drama is to enact a self-transformation that will resolve anxieties reawakened by the death of John and dealt with inconclusively in the letters. While the letters reveal Wordsworth undergoing a process beginning in profound shock and despair, extending to religious doubt, and ending inconclusively in a sense of resignation, the poem dramatizes the speaker's transformation from innocence to sudden new awareness and resolution.

There is of course nothing in the letters comparable to the dramatization of the turning point in the poem. More than anything else, it is this act of self-representation that deserves critical attention, for in it one can discern the ways in which the speaker is and is not the poet in his own person.

The structure of "Elegiac Stanzas" that divides the speaker's life into a "before" and an "after" is familiar to us from numerous other poems. The speaker's self was once sealed in slumber, he had no human fears; then he awakes to death or an end of innocence or some new awareness. Or he experienced dejection and fears of despondency and madness, and then discovers resolution and hope by a peculiar grace. But here, too, as in other poems, the before-and-after structure is a form of splitting that the speaker employs as a means of self-representation. Its purpose is not only to represent that change has taken place but to stage it in a dramatic way so that the accompanying levels of intensity and resolution will suggest or seem to ensure that the change is both crucial and permanent, one that achieves a significant self-transformation.

Of the various self-dramatizing techniques that Wordsworth employs in representing the speaker's pursuit of self-transformation in this poem, apostrophe is particularly notable because of its uncharacteristically ironic use. The speaker begins by addressing the castle of his memory (recalled while viewing the castle of the painting):

> I was thy neighbour once, thou rugged Pile!
> Four summer weeks I dwelt in sight of thee:
> I saw thee every day; and all the while
> Thy Form was sleeping on a glassy sea.
>
> So pure the sky, so quiet was the air!
> So like, so very like, was day to day!
> Whene'er I looked, thy Image still was there;
> It trembled, but it never passed away. (1–8)

Apostrophe, as Jonathan Culler has said, attempts to establish presence and relationship: "to apostrophize is to will a state of affairs, to attempt to call it into being by asking inanimate objects to bend themselves to your desire." Apostrophe "takes the crucial step of constituting the object as another subject with whom the poetic subject might hope to strike up a harmonious relationship."[22] In its attempt to establish presence and relationship, apostrophe is typically a defense against anxiety over absence and death.

That is not its use, however, in "Elegiac Stanzas." It is true that Wordsworth uses apostrophe to invoke presence in the first two stanzas, even representing his speaker as slipping into a reverie in the third stanza, as if to reexperience his old, idealized relationship with Nature.

> How perfect was the calm! it seemed no sleep;
> No mood, which season takes away, or brings:

---

22. Culler, "Apostrophe," 139, 143.

> I could have fancied that the mighty Deep
> Was even the gentlest of all gentle Things. (9–12)

But at the same time he resists full enchantment by his use of the past conditional "I could have" and the word "fancied" in line 11, both calling attention to the uncertain status of this remembered and apostrophized presence. In the fourth stanza Wordsworth again emphasizes a certain degree of self-consciousness about the immediate situation of viewing Beaumont's painting and meditating on it ("Ah! THEN, if mine had been the Painter's hand, / To express what then I saw"), but returns to a conditional use of apostrophe in stanzas 5 and 6:

> I would have planted thee, thou hoary Pile
> Amid a world how different from this!
> Beside a sea that could not cease to smile;
> On tranquil land, beneath a sky of bliss.
>
> Thou shouldst have seemed a treasure-house divine
> Of peaceful years; a chronicle of heaven;—
> Of all the sunbeams that did ever shine
> The very sweetest had to thee been given. (17–24)

The qualified, self-conscious use of apostrophe and the abandonment of it after stanza 6 make the speaker's use of it both ironic and dramatic. Instead of being used to evoke a presence that could, for the brief moment of the poem, be imagined to continue to exist in the speaker's consciousness and life, as the evoked "presence" in "Tintern Abbey" is represented as having become a permanent part of the speaker's consciousness, apostrophe in "Elegiac Stanzas" is used to evoke presence solely for the purpose of pointing up and dramatizing its disappearance and absence. The abandonment of apostrophe after stanza 6 is part of the speaker's attempt to dramatize his sense of having reached a turning point in his thoughts. It is, in its own way, an attempt to say farewell both to the old dream of a beneficent Nature and an earlier self that believed in the dream. It is true that there are two other uses of apostrophe, one in stanza 11 when the speaker addresses Beaumont ("Then, Beaumont, Friend! who would have been the Friend / If he had lived, of Him whom I deplore" [41–42]), and a second in stanza 14 when he addresses his previous self ("Farewell, farewell the heart that lives alone, / Housed in a dream" [53–54]). But in these two instances the use of apostrophe is not central to the drama of the speaker's utterance. In the first, he invokes the name of Beaumont as a way of reinforcing an immediate present that emphasizes his distance from the "before" of the first seven stanzas, thereby reinforcing a sense of change, and in the second he invokes the idea of a past self in order to say farewell to it primarily as a way of attempting to guarantee or establish the presence of the new self.

The predominantly ironic use of apostrophe in "Elegiac Stanzas," therefore, has the general purpose of serving the act of self-dramatization. Not only does the use of it in the first half of the poem briefly restore and dramatize the early self that saw a sea always calm, a "tranquil land," and a "sky of bliss" (20), and thereby support the contrast between an earlier and later self, an innocent and more mature self, but the abandonment of it after stanza 6 suddenly withdraws the principal emotional and dramatic prop for the illusion of presence and relationship. The absence of apostrophe haunts the second part of the poem, representing the loss the speaker feels and deepening the tone of disenchantment in his elegiac strains.

The turning point derives much of its sobering power from that absence:

> So once it would have been—'tis so no more;
> I have submitted to a new control:
> A power is gone, which nothing can restore;
> A deep distress hath humanised my Soul.
>
> Not for a moment could I now behold
> A smiling sea, and be what I have been:
> The feeling of my loss will ne'er be old:
> This, which I know, I speak with mind serene. (33–40)

Complementing the abandonment of apostrophe is the speaker's use of a grammatical shift that further marks the turning point as an irrevocable loss of "the fond illusion of my heart" (29). The change from the past conditional "would have been" to the present indicative " 'tis" in line 33 ("So once it would have been—'tis so no more") is a grammatical shift reflecting the speaker's climactic move from the illusory potential of the past to the new reality of absence. The speaker's change from the past conditional to the present indicative is part of a larger dramatic strategy designed to dramatize the turning point, as well as the recognition and reversal central to the effort at self-transformation. The strategy includes a strong representation of radical change or reversal traditionally accompanying moments of recognition. The moment here is supported by the verb phrases that the speaker uses ("would have been," "have submitted," "is gone," "what I have been,") and by the repetition of phrases of negation ("no more," "gone," "nothing," "Not for a moment," "ne'er be old"). Even the modulation of "o" sounds in the last words of each line ("so no more," "control," "restore," "Soul"), as if a moan has been only half-suppressed, contributes to the emotional power of stanza 9.

The speaker's grammatical shift is thus used both to dramatize the turning point and to enhance his sense of self-transformation. The all-important line "So once it would have been—'tis so no more" not only asserts change but identifies it as a reversal of a prior state of mind that "nothing can restore," one of the two themes from the letters, we recall, that makes its way into the poem. The opening lines of the next stanza, "Not for a moment could I now behold / A smiling sea," repeat the notion that the change is a reversal, in effect insisting that the reversal is irreversible because the loss is irrecoverable. "The feeling of my loss will ne'er be old" is a way of saying that the change will never change. The speaker's confident assertions ("I have submitted to a new control," "Not for a moment could I now behold," "This, which I know, I speak with mind serene") are to some extent defensive, attempting to ensure that the experience of loss is in the past and that the future is not vulnerable to it. As Marjorie Levinson has observed, the speaker is attempting "to validate his present vision by reference to his brave exposure of his illusionary past."[23] It is true that when he says "The feeling of my loss will ne'er be old" he appears to be preserving the sense of loss rather than putting it in the past. But preserving the memory of loss can be a way of defending against the possibility of again becoming susceptible to "A smiling sea" or vulnerable to its loss, and therefore preserving the memory of loss can be a way of imprisoning the old self in the past.

The turning point, the dramatic emphasis given to it, and the sense of irreversible change all emanate, of course, from a profound recognition. The recognition, however, does not come to us as a complete surprise.

23. Levinson, *Wordsworth's Great Period Poems*, 110.

For one thing, the lyric speaker, like a storyteller or dramatist, plots his thoughts in a sequential order that leads to a recognition. At first we are given the supposed actual past when he was the neighbor of Peele Castle, then a hypothetical past in which he would have painted a different picture of the castle from the one Beaumont painted, and finally the present in which he recognizes the justness of Beaumont's representation and looks to the future. For another, his use of the conditional mood early in the poem ("I could have fancied that the mighty Deep / Was even the gentlest of all gentle Things," "if mine had been the Painter's hand," "I would have planted thee" [11–12, 13, 17]) depends upon his knowledge of the content of the recognition before he reveals it. The conditional mood repeatedly alerts us to the fact that the view of Nature he wishes to restore is hypothetical. It creates both grammatical and dramatic suspense that can only be resolved by a recognition that replaces the conditional mood with the indicative and that suggests a move from a false understanding to a true.

Critical readers of the poem have tended to equate the content of the recognition with a profound sense of loss, though they differ in their definitions of the loss. For many years the accepted view was that what has been lost is Wordsworth's faith in Nature. Geoffrey Hartman, however, argued that the loss was "definitely not his faith in nature": "It is quite true that nature led him on, to a conception that proved false; but it is clearly his own soul which betrayed him through the 'fond delusion' that nature is more than it can be." What has been lost, Hartman says, is a "potentiality . . . [a] capacity for generous error and noble illusion, which made life correspond to the heart's desire." In a psychoanalytic reading, Peter Sacks argues that Wordsworth's rejection of "the fantasy, like that of the mirror stage, of a quasimaternal natural continuity in which the erotically powerful 'rugged Pile' seemed to be forever 'sleeping on a glassy sea' of contentment 'beneath a sky of bliss'" represents his submission "not just to the presence of death, but more crucially to the irrevocable loss of his own power . . . to a previously unrecognized control." In Marjorie Levinson's view, "the subject of Wordsworth's lament is neither John Wordsworth nor a Nature experienced as constant and nurturing . . . [nor] *pace* Hartman . . . his former 'capacity for generous error and noble illusion, which made life correspond to the heart's desire.' The subject of this elegy—the loss deplored—is that binary apparatus whereby Mind redeems itself (i.e., subjectivity escapes itself) by recurrent, dialectical engagements with an alien and impenetrable objectivity."[24] The real loss mourned in the poem, Levinson argues, is Napoleon and the hope and promise he had inspired.

While strong arguments have been made for each of these views, as well as for others, it can also be argued that the actual sense of loss that Wordsworth experienced at the time of John's death was traumatically overdetermined, something the letters strongly suggest, and cannot be reduced to a single content. As Peter Sacks has observed about the experience of loss in his study of the English elegy, "each loss recapitulates a prior loss."[25] The loss represented in "Elegiac Stanzas" is similarly overdetermined, representing not only the death of John and the deaths of Wordsworth's parents but also, one could argue, the experience of being orphaned, the separation from Dorothy, the loss of Nature as a maternal substitute, and the loss of Nature, in Hartman's phrase, as a noble illusion corresponding to the heart's desire.

A more important dimension of the content of the recognition than the loss, however, is the sense of something gained that Wordsworth devotes the last six stanzas of the poem to developing. Not surprisingly, his representation of the speaker's new awareness invokes the sublime in the description of the scene in Beaumont's painting:

> O 'tis a passionate Work!—yet wise and well,
> Well chosen is the spirit that is here;

---

24. Hartman, *Wordsworth's Poetry*, 284–85 (Hartman quotes "fond delusion" from line 29 of the 1807 *Poems, in Two Volumes*); Peter M. Sacks, *The English Elegy: Studies in the Genre from Spenser to Yeats*, 144; Levinson, *Wordsworth's Great Period Poems*, 113.

25. Sacks, *English Elegy*, 23. MacFarland suggests something similar in his comments on the relationship between John's death and earlier experiences of loss. John's death "was shattering not only in its own right but as a confirmation and reawakening of the losses of his father, and especially of his mother, in his childhood" (*Romanticism and the Forms of Ruin*, 161). Wordsworth's remark to his brother Richard that "the set is now broken" may have been an unconscious reference to his earlier characterization (in the spring of 1804, while composing the 1805 *Prelude*) of the five children as a still unbroken set left "Trooping together" after her death (*1805*, 5.256–60), suggesting how intertwined and inescapable the thoughts of loss were in his mind, and how naturally the thought of one loss would have recalled others.

That Hulk which labours in the deadly swell,
This rueful sky, this pageantry of fear!

And this huge Castle, standing here sublime,
I love to see the look with which it braves,
Cased in the unfeeling armour of old time,
The lightning, the fierce wind, and trampling waves. (45–52)

The ship's labouring "in the deadly swell" under the "rueful sky" and the entire scene, with its "sea in anger, and that dismal shore" (44) and its "pageantry of fear," evoke a Burkean sense of the fear and power that repeatedly appear in Wordsworth's representations of an experience of the sublime. Especially evocative of a possible sublimity in the presence of Nature are the images of "The lightning, the fierce wind, and trampling waves," which of course stand in marked contrast to the quiet of the sea and the image of the castle reflected in the trembling waters in the remembered earlier scene of the first three stanzas.[26] Wordsworth's contrast of the picturesque word-picture of the sea and the castle that the speaker had painted in his mind with the sublime he sees in Beaumont's painting is designed to dramatize the speaker's recognition and the transformation of self it is supposed to represent. The representation of change in the speaker's consciousness is in part a change from the quiet of the picturesque or beautiful to the drama of the sublime, from "So pure the sky, so quiet was the air!" (5) and "the mighty Deep . . . the gentlest of all gentle Things" (11–12) to an image of "the sea in anger" (44), the shore as "dismal," the sky as "rueful," and the entire scene as a "pageantry of fear!" (46–49). What is most striking about the contrast is that Wordsworth employs the imagery of the picturesque to define that

---

26. For a discussion of the differences between Wordsworth's representation of the sea and the castle in the poem and their representation in the smaller oil painting that is believed to have been the inspiration for the poem, and that has been reproduced in Jonathan Wordsworth et al., eds., *William Wordsworth and the Age of English Romanticism*, see Heffernan, *Museum of Words*, 106–7. I am indebted to Richard Matlak for calling to my attention that the larger oil Beaumont painted, which is held in the Leicester Museum and Art Gallery and has been reproduced in *Sir George Beaumont, 1753–1827: A Painter's Eye, a Poet's Heart*, corresponds more closely in a number of details to Wordsworth's description and may have been the inspiration for the poem.

part of the content of the speaker's recognition associated with loss, but relies upon the imagery of the sublime to define that part of the content associated with gain. Only the imagery of the sublime could support the sense of fortitude that Wordsworth shows the speaker attempting to adopt in the face of loss. Wordsworth dramatizes the reversal in the speaker's consciousness not only by showing him approve of the passion he finds in Beaumont's picture ("O 'tis a passionate Work!—yet wise and well, / Well chosen is the spirit that is here" [45–46]) but also by having him identify with—or, to use Wordsworth's term from his essay "The Beautiful and the Sublime," "participate" in—the spirit of fortitude displayed by "That Hulk which labours in the deadly swell" and by the castle braving the elements in the lines "I love to see the look with which it braves, / Cased in the unfeeling armour of old time / The lightning, the fierce wind, and trampling waves" (50–52).

Yet the speaker identifies not with the forces in Nature that evoke a sense of the sublime but rather with the human power of resistance, the castle "standing here sublime" against the wind and waves. In this poem, as in the other major lyrics, Wordsworth has adapted the aesthetics of the sublime to the poetics of dramatizing a recognition and reversal in the speaker's consciousness and a transformation of self. But in viewing Beaumont's picture the speaker sees the sublime not in Nature but in the human spirit that defies the elements. The "spirit that is here" (46), represented by the huge castle with its "unfeeling armour of old time" (49, 51), is the model of fortitude that he chooses.

In the last two stanzas, the speaker attempts to dramatize the transformation of self that his identification with the spirit of the castle is designed to confirm he has achieved. He again employs the strategies of splitting and apostrophe, addressing that part of the self that is supposed to have been left behind: "Farewell, farewell the heart that lives alone, / Housed in a dream, at distance from the Kind!" (53–54). The word *housed* is ironic, standing in obvious contrast to the stronger castle, as well as suggesting the vulnerability of the "Poet's dream" (16) and "fond illusion of my heart" (29) that "shouldst have seemed a treasure-house divine" (21). The ironic implications reinforce the notion here at the end of the poem that the speaker has indeed undergone a radical change. The phrasing "distance from the Kind!" is problematic, however, since the use of "the Kind" for "humankind" has the strange effect of seeming to "distance" or estrange the speaker from the very ideal of community that he now claims to support. Be that as it may, the speaker is determined to represent himself as resolved to turn away from the fond illusion of the past ("Such happiness, wherever it be known, / Is to be pitied; for 'tis surely blind" [55–56]) and, in the last stanza, to turn toward the future:

> But welcome fortitude, and patient cheer,
> And frequent sights of what is to be borne!
> Such sights, or worse, as are before me here.—
> Not without hope we suffer and we mourn. (57–60)

As in the conclusions to the other major lyrics, it proves to be impossible to domesticate the sublime, and as a result the resolution in the last two stanzas is supported not by the dramatic effect of the speaker's use of the imagery of power but by a spirit of resignation and hope. If such a spirit ("Not without hope we suffer and we mourn") seems dangerously close to a return to the old illusion, or a version of it, the speaker's emphasis of "sights of what is to be borne" and "worse" should be noted, for they indicate an attempt to assume an attitude of stoicism that is nowhere to be found in the earlier version of the self in the poem.

6 ❖❖ *Conclusion*

The Prelude as a Major Lyric

To conclude, I want to address briefly a question that, though not having appeared in any explicit form so far, may seem to have haunted the argument throughout: Can the critical understanding of the subjectivity of the speakers of the major lyrics that I have presented in the foregoing chapters be applied to the speaker-narrator of Wordsworth's longest autobiographical poem? Although I have referred to *The Prelude* throughout, at times pointing to differences in self-representation between it and the major lyrics, at other times to similarities, I have yet to deal with this question or to sketch the implications of the argument for constructions of the speaker-narrator's subjectivity. The psychoanalytic model I have proposed for understanding the art and psychology of self-representation in the major lyrics, it could be argued, must be capable of being extended to *The Prelude* if it is to have critical value. Let me now, therefore, turn to *The Prelude* and, in doing so, begin with the problem of the obvious differences in form between it and the major lyrics.

In relying on traditional poetic forms to represent the feelings and thoughts of his speakers in the major lyrics, Wordsworth submits his representations of the subjectivity of the "I" in each poem to the shaping influence of literary tradition. As Susan Wolfson has observed, "The poetic 'I' comes into being in form cast as a system that precedes it, takes possession of it, and defines it."[1] In "Tintern Abbey," for example, Wordsworth's choice of the meditative and locodescriptive tradition of topographical poetry of the late eighteenth century seems to determine that the speaker will be stationed as an observer of a landscape, depicted in a reflective and self-reflexive mood, and represented as a man speaking in the supposedly natural but uplifted tone and language of someone thinking aloud on a serious subject. The choice of the ode form for his exploration of his intimations of immortality, on the other hand, seems to determine that the speaker's utterance will be in a more public and performing mode, with a highly complex versification scheme and stanzaic structure to modulate a greater range of voice and mood, from

---

1. Wolfson, *Formal Charges*, 28.

celebration to despair. In these and other ways, the "I" of each major lyric is shaped by the poetic form that Wordsworth chooses for a particular act of self-representation.

Yet it is also true that none of the major lyrics is pure in form and that in each of them Wordsworth draws on more than one poetic tradition. Although he did not call "Tintern Abbey" an ode, we remember, he said that "it was written with a hope that in the transitions, and the impassioned music of the versification, would be found the principal requisites of that species of composition" (*Poetical Works*, 2:517). The Intimations Ode appears in the first four stanzas to be more of an elegy than an ode, but by the end it is clear that it represents a composite form of the two principal ode traditions, the Pindaric and the Horatian, and that, along the way, it incorporates elements of satire, romance, and the pastoral. "Resolution and Independence," like most of the poems in the 1798 *Lyrical Ballads*, is a mixed form, a lyrical and autobiographical narrative, and "Elegiac Stanzas" incorporates elements of elegy, autobiography, and narrative. The form of *The Prelude* is perhaps the most mixed of all Wordsworth's poems, being at once autobiography, epic, elegy, verse epistle, romance, pastoral, and, of course, lyric, that most protean and versatile of forms.[2] His reliance on more than one form—or, to be more accurate, more than one tradition of poetic forms—in each of the major lyrics and *The Prelude* suggests that it takes more than one poetic tradition to represent the subjectivity of the speaker in each work. Wordsworth adopts a form such as the ode or the elegy or the epic, but he appropriates from various poetic traditions whatever is necessary, within certain generic and formal limits, to enable the "I" in its act of self-representation in each work to achieve its expressivist, constitutive, and self-transformative aims.

Of the various traditions that Wordsworth employs or draws upon in representations of the subjectivity of his speakers, it is the lyrical, not

---

2. For a discussion of form in *The Prelude*, see Curran, *Poetic Form and British Romanticism*, 182–90. Curran identifies epic as the poem's "subsuming genre" and verse epistle as its "most important secondary form" (183, 184), but he also notes various genres and modes incorporated into the poem, including, in addition to those I mention above, mock-heroic, dream vision, and satire. For an excellent discussion of the poem's reliance on epic tradition, see Brian Wilkie, *Romantic Poets and Epic Tradition*, chapter 2.

surprisingly, that is most central to their aims. In the category of "The Lyrical" he includes only "the Hymn, the Ode, the Elegy, the Song, and the Ballad" (*Prose*, 3:27), but several generations of critics have included a meditative-descriptive poem such as "Tintern Abbey," and one is justified in also including both a narrative such as "Resolution and Independence" in which the speaker's presence and reflections figure so prominently and an extended narrative such as *The Prelude*. Although *The Prelude* relies on several narrative traditions—epic, romance, and pastoral—in structuring the poet's episodic account of his personal history, it is also a poem that draws extensively on lyrical tradition to represent the most important moments in that history. Indeed, the poet-speaker repeatedly privileges the lyrical over the narrative in his representations of these moments. It is true that the more narrative parts of *The Prelude*, particularly the accounts of the speaker-hero's life at Cambridge in book 3, his residence in London in book 7, and his stay in France in books 9–11, situate the speaker in social and political contexts that tend to define his consciousness in historical and social and therefore intersubjective terms. Nevertheless, the direction of his thoughts and thus of the poem itself is always toward impassioned moments of supposed individual transcendence that the lyrical tradition is best suited to explore and celebrate.[3] To the extent that the speaker of *The Prelude* is preoccupied with these moments, he represents a subjectivity more concerned with internal crises than external events, more concerned with the dramatic potential of his utterance to perform a self-transformation than with the potential of the narration of his relations with the external world to lead to a desirable conclusion. This is not to say that these relations and the intersubjective construction of the character of the speaker implicit in the narrative are less important as keys to and determinants of his subjectivity than the self-representations revealed in the more lyrical moments of the poem, or that we should accept on the speaker's own terms his privileging of the lyrical over the narrative in his self-representations. But it is to say that his privileging of the lyrical and more dramatic moments of the poem points to the performative intentions behind his utterance and

---

3. For two discussions of the ways in which history and ideology shape the subjectivity of the speaker of *The Prelude*, see Richard Gravil, "'Some Other Being': Wordsworth in *The Prelude*," and Brooke Hopkins, "Wordsworth's Voices: Ideology and Self-Critique in *The Prelude*."

to his effort to act out the self-transformation or growth of the poet's mind that the poem narrates and describes. These intentions, I have been arguing in the previous chapters, are central to an understanding of the transitional self represented by the "I" of the major lyrics, and they are equally important for an understanding of the subjectivity of the speaker of *The Prelude*.

Wordsworth incorporates into *The Prelude* several features of the major lyrics that allow the speaker-hero's lyrical and self-dramatizing voice to assume predominance over his recollective, narrative, and other voices. The speaker's expressivist and performative impulses repeatedly interrupt the progress of the narrative, transforming it into a dramatic utterance with hymns, philosophical reflections, apostrophes, and impassioned descriptions and narrations in which the speaker, by slipping into the mood of the experience recollected, in effect reenacts it. A poet has the disposition and ability, we recall Wordsworth saying in the Preface to the second edition of *Lyrical Ballads*, "to be affected more than other men by absent things as if they were present," to "[conjure] up in himself passions," and "to let himself slip into an entire delusion, and even confound and identify his own feelings" with those of the persons whose feelings he describes (*Prose*, I:138). In the case of the major lyrics and *The Prelude*, the person whose feelings Wordsworth describes, identifies with, and conjures up the feelings of is less the empirical Wordsworth that he wanted his readers to think of when he used the phrase "the poet in his own person" than the imaginatively reconstituted self he prefers to remember or tries to become.

In most of these lyrical effusions, Wordsworth uses the present tense to enhance the dramatic illusion of the immediacy and authenticity of the speaker's experience and the presence of his voice. In book 1, for example, he introduces what is essentially a hymn to Nature—"Dust as we are, the immortal spirit grows / Like harmony in music" (1.340–56)—as a prelude to the boat-stealing episode. The "Blest the infant Babe" passage in book 2 is another example of a hymn, this time to the feelings emanating from the maternal presence that, once internalized by the infant, become "the first / Poetic spirit of our human life" (2.260–61), and it interrupts—really, usurps—the narrative form in this section of the poem. At the beginning of book 5, on the other hand, he provides a lyricized philosophical reflection in the present tense, supported initially by an apostrophe ("Even then I sometimes grieve for thee, O Man, / Earth's paramount Creature" [5.4–5]), as an introduction to the dream vision of the Arab. A stunning example of the use of the present tense to dramatize the speaker's voice and presence appears at the beginning of the poem in the "glad preamble" (1.1–45), which, as I noted in Chapter 3, is similar to the first two stanzas of "Resolution and Independence." It represents the speaker as experiencing the blessing of the gentle breeze, the escape from the city, and the Adamic prospect of the earth all before him at the moment of his utterance. As in "Tintern Abbey," the dramatic illusion of the utterance coinciding with the moment of the experience supports the immediacy of the voice and presence of the speaker, as well as the drama of the moment. Although we learn from his address to Coleridge in the third verse paragraph that the moment was only staged in the present tense ("Thus far, O Friend! did I, not used to make / A present joy the matter of my song, / Pour out *that day* my soul in measured strains, / Even in the very words which I have here / Recorded" [*1805*, 1.55–59, emphasis added]), and that the dramatic illusion will not be sustained (as it is throughout "Tintern Abbey"), we are alerted in the first fifty lines of the poem to the fact that the speaker will often dramatize rather than simply narrate his thoughts and experiences. The 1805 version's more specific "in the very words which I have here / Recorded" calls attention to the staging of the glad preamble in a way that the 1850 version's somewhat muted "strains / That would not be forgotten, and are here / Recorded" (1.48–50) does not.

The speaker's use of apostrophe in his frequent turns away from the history he is relating in order to address Coleridge or, more commonly, a spirit or supernatural power ("Wisdom and Spirit of the universe! Thou Soul that art the eternity of thought" [1.401–2]), is the most obviously dramatic of the strategies that he employs in his act of self-representation. Through his use of apostrophe he not only invokes the presence of the person or object or supernatural power addressed but also reconstitutes himself in a clearly self-dramatizing fashion. Indeed, when the speaker invokes the Wisdom and Spirit of the universe, just as when the speaker of "Tintern Abbey" addresses the Wye ("How oft, in spirit, have I turned to thee, / O sylvan Wye!" [55–56]) or the speaker of the Ode addresses the child philosopher in stanza 8 ("Thou best Philosopher . . . Mighty Prophet! Seer blest!" [111–15]), it is less the invoked spirit than the voice and presence of the speaker himself that is brought to life. His voice seems to reach across the two centuries since Wordsworth began to compose the poem and insist, against time and common sense, on the dramatic illusion of the continuing now of his utterance and the immediacy of his presence. Even an ironic use of apostrophe of the kind found in "Elegiac Stanzas" is, as we have seen, finally dramatic in aesthetic function and effect. *The Prelude* is replete with apostrophes not only to supernatural powers ("Wisdom and Spirit of the universe! / Thou Soul that art the eternity of thought" [1.401–2]) but also to poets and other writers ("Ye dreamers, then, / Forgers of daring tales!" [5.523–24]), to his "conscious soul" ("I recognise thy glory" [6.598–99]), to the Maid of Buttermere ("and this bright innocent [the prostitute's son], Mary, may now have lived till he could look / With envy on thy nameless babe that sleeps . . . undisturbed" [7.378–81]), to all those who "pore / On the dead letter, [and] miss the spirit of things" (8.296–97), to human nature ("Here must thou be, O Man! / Power to thyself" [14.209–10]), and to Dorothy ("Child of my parents! Sister of my soul!" [14.232–33]). Their recurrence throughout the narrative, along with the addresses to Coleridge, is a repeated appeal to, an insistence upon, the dramatic illusion of the speaker's immediacy of voice and presence. Wordsworth's use of apostrophes goes a long way toward transforming the epic form of the poem into what Mary Jacobus has aptly called "an extended personal lyric."[4]

The most important feature of the major lyric that Wordsworth incorporates into *The Prelude*, however, is its primary focus on episodes or moments of crisis in his life as a structural and dramatic principle for the representation of the speaker's subjectivity. It is in these selected moments, these lyricized spots of time, rather than in the numerous other events recounted in the narrative, that the speaker seeks to dramatize his presence and experience and to perform through his dramatic utterance the achievement of a self-transformation that he would make permanent by linking it with some form of timeless being. The moments are drawn from out of the past, and from deep within the speaker's memory ("The days gone by / Return upon me almost from the dawn / Of life" [12.277–79]), and are then privileged in the overall structure of the poem by their representations of turning points in the speaker's life, by

---

4. Jacobus, *Romanticism, Writing and Sexual Difference*, 176.

the strategic place they are given in the narrative, and by the speaker's efforts to dramatize them. They are designed to support the dramatic illusion that the speaker is experiencing or reexperiencing a recognition or new awareness at the moment he gives voice to his memories, thoughts, and reflections.

In some of the episodes the epiphanic moment is represented as taking place in the now of the speaker's utterance and reflections. In the "Crossing of the Alps" episode, for example, the speaker's structuring of his narration of the events leading to the climactic moment of new awareness in the famous "Imagination" passage (6.592–616) in effect reenacts the experience of remembering the events and making a discovery about them. He introduces the episode as an example of how his "under-thirst" for great things, his "hopes that pointed to the clouds" (6.587), was sometimes disappointed, and, in the 1850 version, he begins with an almost formulaic narrative phrasing, "let one incident make known" (6.561). What he does not reveal at this point, however, is that a discovery will follow this recollection of the disappointment, and that the disappointment is recounted now only to set the stage for it. The discovery will appear in the next verse paragraph as a sudden and dramatic intervention in the act of remembering and narrating the events, one that employs apostrophe ("I recognise thy glory") to lift the speaker's self out of the narrative time-past into the lyric's more dramatic time-present. His withholding of any mention of the discovery is deliberate, part of his self-dramatizing intention that will enable him to reenact the suddenness with which the discovery was made. At this point in the narration he is primarily concerned with setting the stage for the moment of discovery by narrating the climb "Along the Simplon's steep" (6.563), his and his companion's separation from their guide, their eager choice of the ascending road, their encounter with the peasant who informed them they had taken the wrong path, and their disappointment in learning *"that we had crossed the Alps."*

The abruptness of transitions characteristic of the ode is nowhere more evident in *The Prelude* than in the beginning of the 1805 "Imagination" passage:

> Imagination—lifting up itself
> Before the eye and progress of my song
> Like an unfathered vapour, here that power,

> In all the might of its endowments, came
> Athwart me. I was lost as in a cloud,
> Halted without a struggle to break through,
> And, now, recovering, to my soul I say
> "I recognise thy glory." (6.592–99)

Although Wordsworth uses the theme of traveling and becoming lost to connect the two passages, his emphasis is on dramatic juxtaposition rather than narrative or thematic transition. In the original draft (March 1804) the two passages were separated by an extended simile of a cave that allowed him to develop further his sense of disappointed expectations at having crossed the Alps. At some point prior to the completion of the 1805 version, however, he removed the simile and made it a part of his description of London in book 8 (*1805*, 8.711–27). One reason for removing it would have been, as Jonathan Wordsworth has explained, that the simile, with its description of the roof of the cave becoming clearly visible and its conclusion of "The scene before him . . . in perfect view / Exposed, and lifeless as a written book" (*1805*, 8.726–27), was in conflict with the central thought in the "Imagination" passage of "something evermore about to be" (*1805*, 6.542). Even though it allowed Wordsworth to represent the sense of anticlimax he felt, it went against the "border quality of imminence" that had become for Wordsworth "a guarantee of human potential."[5] Another reason may have been that the removal enhances the dramatic effect of the juxtaposition of the two passages and enables the speaker to dramatize not only the radical shift in mood and thought from disappointment to celebration, but the moment of self-discovery in the "Imagination" passage.

The speaker's use of apostrophe and the shift to the present tense further reinforce his break out of the constraints on self-representation imposed by the narrative mode and his move toward the more expressivist mode of the lyric. His address to his "soul" at the moment of discovery is predicated on the kind of splitting we have seen in each of the major lyrics, and his use of apostrophe at this crucial moment, like the

---

5. For Jonathan Wordsworth's discussion of the simile and the "impressive juxtaposition" of the two passages, see his *William Wordsworth: The Borders of Vision*, 189–91, and his note to *1805*, 6.530 in *The Prelude: 1799, 1805, 1850*.

speaker's address to his sister in the final verse paragraph of "Tintern Abbey," is an attempt to represent himself as having already achieved the self-transformation that is being described. When the "I" addresses "soul" and says that now he recognizes its glory, he is claiming to have experienced that idealized state of being toward which the "I" has all along been striving, a state of being represented by the word *soul,* and when he says that "In such strength / Of usurpation, in such visitings / Of awful promise, when the light of sense / Goes out in flashes that have shewn to us / The invisible world, doth greatness make abode" (*1805*, 6.532–36), he is again claiming to have become "a living soul" ("Tintern Abbey," 46). Taken together, the abrupt transition, the shift to the present tense, the use of apostrophe, the invocation of a sense of the sublime, and the impassioned music of the remainder of the passage all contribute to our sense of this as one of the great lyrical and dramatic moments in the poem, one in which the speaker's efforts at self-dramatization give him a presence that stands out from and above the self-depiction in the narrative elsewhere.

In other episodes the epiphanic moment is represented as having taken place in the past, but the speaker becomes so involved in the experience he is describing or narrating in the past tense, and the verse so impassioned, that he does not merely describe the experience; he in effect reenacts it and re-creates the drama of the earlier moment. For example, after his description of the idealized life of the shepherd in book 8, he begins his recollection of having seen the shepherd and "felt his presence in his own domain" (8.257). He then offers a composite description (rather than one based on a single, actual experience) of seeing him "distant a few steps" and in the description uses a number of standard features of the rhetoric of the sublime:

> When up the lonely brooks on rainy days
> Angling I went, or trod the trackless hills
> By mists bewildered, suddenly mine eyes
> Have glanced upon him distant a few steps,
> In size a giant, stalking through thick fog,
> His sheep like Greenland bears; or, as he stepped
> Beyond the boundary line of some hill-shadow,
> His form hath flashed upon me, glorified
> By the deep radiance of the setting sun:

> Or him have I descried in distant sky,
> A solitary object and sublime,
> Above all height! like an aerial cross
> Stationed alone upon a spiry rock
> Of the Chartreuse, for worship. (8.262–75)

In each of the three recollections of the shepherd (first "distant a few steps," then "Beyond the boundary line of some hill-shadow," and finally stationed as "A solitary object and sublime") there is an attempt to recapture the suddenness of the encounter, a sense of magnitude attributed to or associated with the shepherd, and a sense of obscurity or mystery that would, together, reenact an experience of the sublime.

The best example of such a descriptive and narrative reenactment is the Mount Snowdon episode. Although it is based on a trip to Wales that Wordsworth made in the summer of 1791, prior to his second trip to France in November of the same year, it is placed after books 9–11 dealing with his stay in France. In altering the chronology in this way Wordsworth gave to the episode the crucial role of bringing the poem to conclusion. Wordsworth has the speaker narrate the ascent of Snowdon and its visionary experience in the past tense, but he structures the narrative to re-create the drama of discovery and recognition as he supposedly had experienced it at the time. Yet Wordsworth's first account of the scene on Snowdon, composed in 1792 and published the following year in *Descriptive Sketches*, differs substantially from the one in *The Prelude* and indicates, as Jonathan Wordsworth has suggested, that "whatever else he was thinking about, it is not likely to have been the creative imagination. It was only by a gradual process that the scene came to have its later implications. Wordsworth himself had to learn to see in Wordsworthian terms."[6] Among the differences between the two accounts, the most important for the self-dramatization that I have been concerned with throughout this study is the prominence of the speaker's presence in the scene and the effort to represent his feelings and thoughts. In the account in *Descriptive Sketches*, the observer of the scene is not, as in *The Prelude*, the speaker. The observer is referred to by the narrator only in the last two lines: "Think not, suspended from the cliff on high / He looks below with undelighted eye" (1793,

---

6. Jonathan Wordsworth, *William Wordsworth: The Borders of Vision*, 310.

510–11). In contrast, the speaker in *The Prelude* assumes the central role in his narrative of the ascent of Snowdon and his is the active consciousness that experiences the climactic moment of recognition when the scene is suddenly illuminated by the moon. His concern is not with describing the scene but with reenacting the moment and representing himself as having achieved a new awareness and a sense of self-transformation.

Several elements of sublime experience as it is typically represented in Wordsworth's poetry underscore his effort to dramatize the moment and his experience: the darkness and quietness preceding surprise ("the dead of night," "silence," "forehead bent / Earthward" [14.26–29]), the suddenness of the appearance of the object that initiates the experience of the sublime ("For instantly a light upon the turf / Fell like a flash" [14.38–39]), and the objects of geographical and spatial immensity that suggest something infinite and incomprehensible ("The Moon hung naked in a firmament / Of azure without cloud," "this still ocean; and beyond, / Far, far beyond," "the ethereal vault," the "sovereign elevation" of "the full-orbed Moon" [14.40–62]). The speaker's reenactment of the climactic moment is punctuated with the exclamation "and lo! as I looked up, / The Moon hung naked" (14.39–40).

In the meditation that follows the speaker employs several devices to continue the drama of the moment.

> When into air had partially dissolved
> That vision, given to spirits of the night
> And three chance human wanderers, in calm thought
> Reflected, it appeared to me the type
> Of a majestic intellect, its acts
> And its possessions, what it has and craves,
> What in itself it is, and would become.
> There I beheld the emblem of a mind
> That feeds upon infinity, that broods
> Over the dark abyss, intent to hear
> Its voices issuing forth to silent light
> In one continuous stream; a mind sustained
> By recognitions of transcendent power,
> In sense conducting to ideal form,
> In soul of more than mortal privilege. (14.63–77)

In shifting his narration from a past event to past reflection, there is a subtle shift from the narrated past to the dramatic present. Although the speaker makes clear that he is describing his past reflections as they occurred to him immediately after the experience, his use of the analogy between the workings of Nature in the vision and the workings of a higher mind ("the type / Of a majestic intellect, its acts / And its possessions") shifts his attention to the analogous object, the "mind / That feeds upon infinity" and "broods / Over the dark abyss" (echoing Milton's description of the Almighty "brooding on the vast abyss" in *Paradise Lost*, 1.21), and since this object is timeless his reflections turn from the past to the present. The analogy itself eventually leads his thoughts away from the vision that Nature had shadowed forth on Mount Snowdon and toward the comparable power of the human mind. What Nature revealed is thought to be "the express / Resemblance of that glorious faculty / That higher minds bear with them as their own" (14.88–90), the imagination, and the description that follows becomes an impassioned hymn celebrating its workings and the higher minds who possess such powers of imagination. These higher minds use their imaginations to "send abroad / Kindred mutations," "create / A like existence," "build up greatest things," "live, / By sensible impressions not enthralled," and "hold fit converse with the spiritual world" (14.93–109).

In addition to the shift from past to present tense in his move from the narration of the ascent of Snowdon to the reflections following it, the speaker also shifts from a personal to a public voice. Although there is no explicit shift from "I" to "we" of the type found in crucial moments of "Tintern Abbey," the Intimations Ode, and other poems, the shift is implied in the speaker's identification with those higher minds whose powers of imagination he describes, and whose voice he assumes at the end of the poem when, addressing Coleridge, he says "we will teach" men and nations, "Instruct them how the mind of man becomes / A thousand times more beautiful than the earth / On which he dwells" (14.449–52). And since the speaker identifies not only with these higher minds but with the deity (in the echo of Milton noted above, as well as in the claim that "Such minds are truly from the Deity" [14.112]), what appears to be a hymn celebrating the powers of the human mind becomes in effect a hymn to the self. The speaker's claim that those higher minds achieve "the highest bliss / That flesh can know . . . the consciousness / Of Whom they are" (14.113–15) is in effect, by means of identification, his attempt to act out a moment of supreme self-awareness and self-transformation.

In this brief look at *The Prelude,* my purpose has been to show that the speaker, by employing strategies of self-dramatization identical or similar to those employed by the speakers of the major lyrics, reveals himself to be equally preoccupied with the aim of self-transformation. What is at stake here, as it has been throughout this study, is the way we conceptualize the "I" and the subjectivity it represents. To think of the speaker of "Tintern Abbey" or another of the major lyrics as Wordsworth is both natural and critically appropriate, especially in biographical, historical, and intertextual contexts. Yet it is also true that the substitution of the proper noun *Wordsworth* for the "I" of a poem (or the use of the very different term *persona*) begs the question of how the self or subjectivity of the "I" is constituted. My argument has been for a conception of subjectivity that gives greater recognition to its personal, psychological dimension than recent explanations of the speaker's subjectivity have tended to do. It is true that the "self" that is the object of the supposed transformation in each poem remains more of a signifier than a signified, more of an idealized process of becoming than an achieved state of being, and that it contains political, intertextual, gendered, and other contents that reveal its social and cultural (and therefore intersubjective) constructedness. Yet the speaker's repeated efforts at self-dramatization and his preoccupation with experiences of loss, dejection, "the fear that kills," and hopes sublime suggest an emotional intensity and psychological complexity that cannot be fully explained in ideological, literary-historical, or cultural terms. No single approach, of course, can fully account for the subjectivity of the "I" of Wordsworth's major lyrics. In an ideal, comprehensive explanation, one would no doubt want to assimilate the views of all relevant critical approaches. That ideal lies beyond the limited scope of this study. What I have tried to do, more simply, is make the case, at this particular point in the history of Wordsworth criticism, for the importance of taking into account, in our conceptions of the speaker's subjectivity, the art and psychology involved in the acts of self-representation in the major lyrics.

Works Cited

Abrams, M. H. *Natural Supernaturalism: Tradition and Revolution in Romantic Literature.* New York: Norton, 1971.

———. "On Political Readings of *Lyrical Ballads.*" In *Doing Things with Texts: Essays in Criticism and Critical Theory*, 364–91. New York: Norton, 1989.

———. "Structure and Style in the Greater Romantic Lyric." In *The Correspondent Breeze: Essays on English Romanticism*, 76–108. New York: Norton, 1984.

Armstrong, Isobel. "'Tintern Abbey': From Augustan to Romantic." In *Augustan Worlds*, ed. J. C. Hilson, M. M. B. Jones, and J. R. Watson, 261–79. New York: Harper and Row, 1978.

Beaumont, George. *Sir George Beaumont, 1753–1827: A Painter's Eye, a Poet's Heart.* Leicester: Leicester Museum and Art Gallery, 1973.

Berger, Harry. "Reconstructing the Old New Criticism." *Journal of Comparative Literature and Aesthetics* 9 (1986): 1–36.

Bialostosky, Don H. *Making Tales: The Poetics of Wordsworth's Narrative Experiments.* Chicago: University of Chicago Press, 1984.

———. *Wordsworth, Dialogics, and the Practice of Criticism.* Cambridge: Cambridge University Press, 1992.

Blank, G. Kim. *Wordsworth and Feeling: The Poetry of an Adult Child.* Cranbury, N.J.: Associated University Presses, 1995.

Bloom, Harold. *The Anxiety of Influence: A Theory of Poetry.* New York: Oxford University Press, 1973.

Brisman, Susan Hawk, and Leslie Brisman. "Lies against Solitude: Symbolic, Imaginary, Real." In *The Literary Freud: Mechanisms of Defense and the Poetic Will*, ed. Joseph H. Smith, 29–65. Vol. 4 of *Psychiatry and the Humanities.* New Haven: Yale University Press, 1980.

Brooks, Cleanth. *The Well Wrought Urn: Studies in the Structure of Poetry.* New York: Harcourt, Brace, and World, 1975.

Brooks, Peter. "The Idea of a Psychoanalytic Literary Criticism." *Critical Inquiry* 13 (1987): 334–48.

———. *Reading for the Plot: Design and Intention in Narrative.* Oxford: Clarendon Press, 1984.

Burke, Edmund. *A Philosophical Enquiry into the Origin of Our Ideas of the*

Sublime and Beautiful. 1757. Ed. J. T. Boulton. South Bend: University of Notre Dame Press, 1968.

Caruth, Cathy. *Unclaimed Experience: Trauma, Narrative, and History.* Baltimore: Johns Hopkins University Press, 1996.

Cave, Terence. *Recognitions: A Study in Poetics.* Oxford: Clarendon Press, 1988.

Chase, Cynthia. "Oedipal Textuality: Reading Freud's Reading of *Oedipus.*" In *Decomposing Figures: Rhetorical Readings in the Romantic Tradition,* 175–95. Baltimore: Johns Hopkins University Press, 1986.

Chayes, Irene. "Rhetoric as Drama: An Approach to the Romantic Ode." *PMLA* 79 (1964): 67–79.

Christensen, Jerome. " 'Thoughts That Do Often Lie Too Deep for Tears': Toward a Romantic Concept of Lyrical Drama." *The Wordsworth Circle* 12 (1981): 52–64.

Coleridge, Samuel Taylor. *Biographia Literaria.* Ed. James Engell and W. Jackson Bate. 2 vols. Princeton: Princeton University Press, 1983.

———. *Coleridge's "Dejection": The Earliest Manuscripts and the Earliest Printings.* Ed. Stephen Maxfield Parrish. Ithaca: Cornell University Press, 1988.

———. *The Complete Poetical Works of Samuel Taylor Coleridge.* 2 vols. Ed. E. H. Coleridge. London: Oxford University Press, 1912.

———. *Lectures, 1808–1819: On Literature.* Ed. R. A. Foakes. 2 vols. Princeton: Princeton University Press, 1987.

———. *The Statesman's Manual.* In *Lay Sermons,* ed. R. J. White. Princeton: Princeton University Press, 1972.

Culler, Jonathan. "Apostrophe." In *The Pursuit of Signs: Semiotics, Literature, and Deconstruction,* 135–54. Ithaca: Cornell University Press, 1981.

Curran, Stuart. *Poetic Form and British Romanticism.* Oxford: Oxford University Press, 1986.

Curtis, Jared. *Wordsworth's Experiments with Tradition: The Lyric Poems of 1802.* Ithaca: Cornell University Press, 1971.

Davie, Donald. "On Sincerity: From Wordsworth to Ginsberg." *Encounter* 31 (October 1968): 61–66.

Derrida, Jacques. *Of Grammatology.* Trans. Gayatri Chakravorty Spivak. Baltimore: Johns Hopkins University Press, 1976.

———. "Structure, Sign, and Play in the Discourse of the Human Sciences." In *The Structuralist Controversy: The Languages of Criticism and the*

Sciences of Man, ed. Richard Macksey and Eugenio Donato, 247–65. Baltimore: Johns Hopkins University Press, 1972.

Douglas, Wallace W. *Wordsworth: The Construction of a Personality.* Kent, Ohio: Kent State University Press, 1968.

Fay, Elizabeth. *Becoming Wordsworthian: A Performative Aesthetics.* Amherst: University of Massachusetts Press, 1995.

Ferguson, Frances. *Wordsworth: Language as Counter-Spirit.* New Haven: Yale University Press, 1977.

Foucault, Michel. "What Is an Author?" In *Language, Counter-Memory, Practice: Selected Essays and Interviews,* trans. Donald F. Bouchard and Sherry Simon, 113–38. Ithaca: Cornell University Press, 1977.

Freud, Sigmund. *The Standard Edition of the Complete Psychological Works of Sigmund Freud.* 24 vols. Trans. James Strachey, Anna Freud, Alix Strachey, and Alan Tyson; ed. James Strachey. London: Hogarth Press, 1953–1974.

Frye, Northrop. "Approaching the Lyric." In *Lyric Poetry: Beyond New Criticism,* ed. Chaviva Hošek and Patricia Parker, 31–37. Ithaca: Cornell University Press, 1985.

Gerard, Albert. *English Romantic Poetry: Ethos, Structure, and Symbol in Coleridge, Wordsworth, Shelley, and Keats.* Berkeley and Los Angeles: University of California Press, 1968.

Gittings, Robert. *John Keats.* London: Heinemann, 1968.

Gravil, Richard. "'Some Other Being': Wordsworth in *The Prelude.*" *Yearbook of English Studies* 19 (1989): 127–43.

Hartman, Geoffrey. "Romanticism and 'Anti-Self-Consciousness.'" In *Romanticism and Consciousness: Essays in Criticism,* ed. Harold Bloom, 46–56. New York: Norton, 1970.

———. "'Timely Utterance' Once More." In *The Unremarkable Wordsworth,* 152–62. Minneapolis: University of Minnesota Press, 1987.

———. *Wordsworth's Poetry, 1787–1814.* New Haven: Yale University Press, 1964.

Heath, William. *Wordsworth and Coleridge: A Study of Their Literary Relations in 1801–1802.* Oxford: Clarendon Press, 1970.

Heffernan, James A. W. *Museum of Words: The Poetics of Ekphrasis from Homer to Ashbery.* Chicago: University of Chicago Press, 1993.

———. "The Presence of the Absent Mother in Wordsworth's *Prelude.*" *Studies in Romanticism* 27 (1988): 253–72.

Hirsch, E. D. *Wordsworth and Schelling.* New Haven: Yale University Press, 1960.

Homans, Margaret. *Bearing the Word: Language and Female Experience in Nineteenth-Century Women's Writing.* Chicago: University of Chicago Press, 1986.

———. *Women Writers and Poetic Identity: Dorothy Wordsworth, Emily Brontë, and Emily Dickinson.* Princeton: Princeton University Press, 1980.

Hopkins, Brooke. "Wordsworth's Voices: Ideology and Self-Critique in *The Prelude.*" *Studies in Romanticism* 33 (1994): 279–99.

Jackson, Geoffrey. "Nominal and Actual Audiences: Some Strategies of Communication in Wordsworth's Poetry." *The Wordsworth Circle* 12 (1981): 226–31.

Jacobus, Mary. *Romanticism, Writing, and Sexual Difference: Essays on "The Prelude."* Oxford: Clarendon Press, 1989.

———. *Tradition and Experiment in Wordsworth's Lyrical Ballads (1798).* Oxford: Clarendon Press, 1976.

Jay, Paul. *Being in the Text: Self-Representation from Wordsworth to Barthes.* Ithaca: Cornell University Press, 1984.

Johnston, Kenneth R. *The Hidden Wordsworth: Poet, Lover, Rebel, Spy.* New York: W. W. Norton, 1998.

———. "Recollecting Forgetting: Forcing Paradox to the Limit in the 'Intimations Ode.'" *The Wordsworth Circle* 2 (1971): 59–64.

Keats, John. *The Letters of John Keats, 1814–1821.* 2 vols. Ed. Hyder E. Rollins. Cambridge: Harvard University Press, 1958.

———. *The Poems of John Keats.* Ed. Jack Stillinger. Cambridge: Harvard University Press, 1978.

———. *The Poetical Works and Other Writings of John Keats.* 8 vols. Ed. H. Buxton Forman, rev. M. Buxton Forman. New York: Scribner's, 1938–1939.

Kelley, Theresa M. *Wordsworth's Revisionary Aesthetics.* Cambridge: Cambridge University Press, 1988.

Klancher, Jon. *The Making of English Reading Audiences, 1790–1832.* Madison: University of Wisconsin Press, 1987.

Klein, Melanie. "Mourning and Its Relation to Manic-Depressive States." In *Love, Guilt, and Reparation and Other Works, 1921–1945,* 344–69. London: Hogarth Press, 1975.

Kneale, J. Douglas. "Apostrophe Reconsidered: Wordsworth's 'There Was a Boy.'" In *Romantic Aversions: Aftermaths of Classicism in Wordsworth and Coleridge,* 11–27. Montreal: McGill-Queen's University Press, 1999.

Kramer, Lawrence. "Victorian Sexuality and 'Tintern Abbey.'" *Victorian Poetry* 24 (1986): 399–410.

Lacan, Jacques. *Écrits: A Selection.* Trans. Alan Sheridan. New York: W. W. Norton, 1977.

Langbaum, Robert. "The Epiphanic Mode in Wordsworth and Modern Literature." In *The Word from Below: Essays in Modern Literature and Culture,* 33–57. Madison: University of Wisconsin Press, 1987.

———. *The Poetry of Experience: The Dramatic Monologue in Modern Literary Tradition.* New York: W. W. Norton, 1957.

———. "Wordsworth: The Self as Process." In *The Mysteries of Identity,* 25–47. Chicago: University of Chicago Press, 1977.

Laplanche, Jean. *Life and Death in Psychoanalysis.* Trans. Jeffrey Mehlman. Baltimore: Johns Hopkins University Press, 1976.

Laplanche, Jean, and J.-B. Pontalis. *The Language of Psycho-Analysis.* Trans. Donald Nicholson-Smith. New York: W. W. Norton, 1974.

Lau, Beth. *Keats's "Paradise Lost."* Gainesville: University of Florida Press, 1998.

Leader, Zachary. "Wordsworth, Revision, and Personal Identity." *ELH* 60 (1993): 651–83.

Lear, Jonathan. *Open Minded: Working Out the Logic of the Soul.* Cambridge: Harvard University Press, 1998.

Levinson, Marjorie. *Wordsworth's Great Period Poems: Four Essays.* Cambridge: Cambridge University Press, 1986.

Liu, Alan. Review of *Wordsworth's Historical Imagination: The Poetry of Displacement,* by David Simpson. *The Wordsworth Circle* 19 (1988): 172–81.

———. *Wordsworth: The Sense of History.* Stanford: Stanford University Press, 1989.

Maclean, Norman. "From Action to Image: Theories of the Lyric in the Eighteenth Century." In *Critics and Criticism,* ed. R. S. Crane, 408–60. Chicago: University of Chicago Press, 1952.

Magnuson, Paul. *Coleridge and Wordsworth: A Lyrical Dialogue.* Princeton: Princeton University Press, 1988.

Mahler, Margaret. *On Human Symbiosis and the Vicissitudes of Individuation.* London: Hogarth Press, 1969.

Maniquis, Robert M. "Comparison, Intensity, and Time in 'Tintern Abbey.'" *Criticism* 11 (1969): 358–82.

Manning, Peter J. "'My Former Thoughts Returned': Wordsworth's *Resolution and Independence.*" *The Wordsworth Circle* 9 (1978): 398–405.

———. *Reading Romantics: Texts and Contexts.* New York: Oxford University Press, 1990.

Matlak, Richard E. "Captain John Wordsworth's Death at Sea." *The Wordsworth Circle* 31 (2000): 127–33.

———. "Classical Argument and Romantic Persuasion in 'Tintern Abbey.'" *Studies in Romanticism* 25 (1986): 97–129.

———. *The Poetry of Relationship: The Wordsworths and Coleridge, 1797–1800.* New York: St. Martin's Press, 1997.

McAdam, E. L. "Wordsworth's Shipwreck." *PMLA* 72 (1962): 240–47.

McFarland, Thomas. *Romanticism and the Forms of Ruin: Wordsworth, Coleridge, and Modalities of Fragmentation.* Princeton: Princeton University Press, 1981.

———. *William Wordsworth: Intensity and Achievement.* Oxford: Clarendon Press, 1992.

McGann, Jerome. *The Romantic Ideology: A Critical Investigation.* Chicago: University of Chicago Press, 1983.

Mellor, Anne. *Romanticism and Gender.* New York: Routledge, 1993.

Mellor, Anne, ed. *Romanticism and Feminism.* Bloomington: Indiana University Press, 1988.

Meyer, George Wilbur. "*Resolution and Independence*: Wordsworth's Answer to Coleridge's *Dejection: An Ode*." *Tulane Studies in English* 2 (1950): 49–74.

Miller, J. Hillis. *Fiction and Repetition: Seven English Novels.* Cambridge: Harvard University Press, 1982.

———. "On the Edge: The Crossways of Contemporary Criticism." *Bulletin of the American Academy of Arts and Sciences* 32 (1979): 13–32.

Milton, John. *The Poems of John Milton.* Ed. John Carey and Alastair Fowler. London: Longmans, Green, 1968.

Modiano, Raimonda. *Coleridge and the Concept of Nature.* Tallahassee: Florida State University Press, 1985.

Moorman, Mary. *William Wordsworth: A Biography.* Vol. I, *The Early Years, 1770–1803.* Oxford: Clarendon Press, 1957.

Nichols, Ashton. *The Poetics of Epiphany: Nineteenth-Century Origins of the Modern Literary Moment.* Tuscaloosa: University of Alabama Press, 1987.

———. *The Revolutionary "I": Wordsworth and the Politics of Self-Representation.* New York: St. Martin's Press, 1998.

The Norton Anthology of English Literature. Vol. 2. 7th ed. General ed. M. H. Abrams. New York: W. W. Norton, 2000.

O'Hara, J. D. "Ambiguity and Assertion in Wordsworth's 'Elegiac Stanzas.'" *Philological Quarterly* 47 (1968): 69–82.

Onorato, Richard J. *The Character of the Poet: Wordsworth in "The Prelude."* Princeton: Princeton University Press, 1971.

Page, Judith W. *Wordsworth and the Cultivation of Women.* Berkeley and Los Angeles: University of California Press, 1994.

Parrish, Stephen M. *The Art of the "Lyrical Ballads."* Cambridge: Harvard University Press, 1973.

Rajan, Tilottoma. *The Supplement of Reading: Figures of Understanding in Romantic Theory and Practice.* Ithaca: Cornell University Press, 1990.

Rand, Frank Prentice. *Wordsworth's Mariner Brother.* Amherst, Mass.: Newell Press, 1966.

Reed, Mark. *Wordsworth: The Chronology of the Middle Years, 1800–1815.* Cambridge: Harvard University Press, 1975.

Ricks, Christopher. *Tennyson.* New York: Macmillan, 1972.

Ross, Marlon. *The Contours of Masculine Desire: Romanticism and the Rise of Women's Poetry.* New York: Oxford University Press, 1989.

———. "Naturalizing Gender: Woman's Place in Wordsworth's Ideological Landscape." *ELH* 53 (1986): 391–410.

Rudnytsky, Peter L. *Freud and Oedipus.* New York: Columbia University Press, 1987.

Ruoff, Gene W. "Fields of Sheep: The Obscurities of the Ode, I–IV." *The Wordsworth Circle* 12 (1981): 45–51.

———. *Wordsworth and Coleridge: The Making of the Major Lyrics, 1802–1804.* New Brunswick: Rutgers University Press, 1989.

Rzepka, Charles J. *The Self as Mind: Vision and Identity in Wordsworth, Coleridge, and Keats.* Cambridge: Harvard University Press, 1986.

Sacks, Peter M. *The English Elegy: Studies in the Genre from Spenser to Yeats.* Baltimore: Johns Hopkins University Press, 1985.

Salvesen, Christopher. *The Landscape of Memory.* Lincoln: University of Nebraska Press, 1968.

Schafer, Roy. *Aspects of Internalization.* New York: International Universities Press, 1968.

Schapiro, Barbara. *The Romantic Mother: Narcissistic Patterns in Romantic Poetry.* Baltimore: Johns Hopkins University Press, 1983.

Schiller, Friedrich. *On the Aesthetic Education of Man.* Trans. and ed. Elizabeth M. Wilkinson and L. A. Willoughby. Oxford: Clarendon Press, 1967.

Schwartz, Murray. "Where Is Literature?" *College English* 36 (1975): 756–65.

Shakespeare, William. *The Riverside Shakespeare.* Ed. G. Blakemore Evans. Boston: Houghton Mifflin, 1974.

———. *Shakespeares Sonnets Never before Imprinted.* 1609. Reprint, in *Twenty of the Plays of Shakespeare*, vol. 4, ed. George Steevens. London, 1766.

Sheats, Paul. *The Making of Wordsworth's Poetry, 1785–1798.* Cambridge: Harvard University Press, 1973.

———. "Wordsworth's Retrogrades and the Shaping of *The Prelude.*" *JEGP* 71 (1972): 473–90.

Shelley, Percy Bysshe. *Shelley's Poetry and Prose.* Ed. Donald H. Reiman and Sharon B. Powers. New York: W. W. Norton, 1977.

Simpson, David. *Wordsworth's Historical Imagination: The Poetry of Displacement.* New York: Methuen, 1987.

Sitterson, Joseph C. "The Genre and Place of the Intimations Ode." *PMLA* 101 (1986): 24–37.

Spargo, R. Clifton. "Begging the Question of Responsibility: The Vagrant Poor in Wordsworth's 'Beggars' and 'Resolution and Independence.'" *Studies in Romanticism* 39 (2000): 51–80.

Sperry, Stuart M. "From 'Tintern Abbey' to the 'Intimations Ode': Wordsworth and the Function of Memory." *The Wordsworth Circle* 1 (1970): 40–49.

Stillinger, Jack. "Multiple Consciousnesses in Wordsworth's *Prelude.*" In *Multiple Authorship and the Myth of Solitary Genius*, 69–95. New York: Oxford University Press, 1991.

Tennyson, Hallam. *Alfred, Lord Tennyson: A Memoir.* 2 vols. New York: Macmillan, 1897.

Thomson, A. W. "Resolution and Independence." In *Wordsworth's Mind and Art*, 181–99. New York: Barnes and Noble, 1970.

Trilling, Lionel. "The Immortality Ode." In *The Liberal Imagination*, 125–54. Garden City, N.Y.: Anchor Press, 1953.

Trott, Nicola. "Wordsworth and the Picturesque: A Strong Infection of the Age." *The Wordsworth Circle* 18 (1987): 114–21.

Tucker, Herbert. "Dramatic Monologue and the Overhearing of Lyric." In *Lyric Poetry: Beyond New Criticism*, ed. Chaviva Hosek and Patricia Parker, 226–43. Ithaca: Cornell University Press, 1985.

Vendler, Helen. "Lionel Trilling and the *Immortality Ode.*" *Salmagundi* 4 (1978): 66–86.
———. " 'Tintern Abbey': Two Assaults." In *Wordsworth in Context,* ed. Pauline Fletcher and John V. Murphy, 173–90. Lewisburg: Bucknell University Press, 1992.
Waldoff, Leon. *Keats and the Silent Work of Imagination.* Urbana: University of Illinois Press, 1985.
Ward, Aileen. *John Keats: The Making of a Poet.* New York: Viking Press, 1963.
Weiskel, Thomas. *The Romantic Sublime: Studies in the Structure and Psychology of Transcendence.* Baltimore: Johns Hopkins University Press, 1976.
Wilkie, Brian. *Romantic Poets and Epic Tradition.* Madison: University of Wisconsin Press, 1965.
Williams, Anne. *Prophetic Strain: The Greater Lyric in the Eighteenth Century.* Chicago: University of Chicago Press, 1984.
Wilson, Douglas B. *The Romantic Dream: Wordsworth and the Poetics of the Unconscious.* Lincoln: University of Nebraska Press, 1993.
Wilson, Edmund. *The Wound and the Bow: Seven Studies in Literature.* Boston: Houghton, Mifflin, 1941.
Winnicott, Donald W. *Playing and Reality.* New York: Basic Books, 1971.
Wolfson, Susan J. *The Questioning Presence: Wordsworth, Keats, and the Interrogative Mode in Romantic Poetry.* Ithaca: Cornell University Press, 1986.
———. "Revision as Form: Wordsworth." In *Formal Charges: The Shaping of Poetry in British Romanticism,* 100–132. Stanford: Stanford University Press, 1997.
Woodring, Carl. "The New Sublimity in 'Tintern Abbey.' " In *The Evidence of the Imagination: Studies of Interactions between Life and Art in English Romantic Literature,* ed. Donald H. Reiman, Michael C. Jaye, and Betty T. Bennett. New York: New York University Press, 1978.
Woolf, Virginia. *A Room of One's Own.* New York: Harcourt Brace, 1929.
Wordsworth, Dorothy. *The Grasmere Journals.* Ed. Pamela Woof. Oxford: Oxford University Press, 1991.
Wordsworth, Jonathan. *William Wordsworth: The Borders of Vision.* Oxford: Clarendon Press, 1982.
Wordsworth, Jonathan, Michael C. Jaye, and Robert Woof, eds. *William Wordsworth and the Age of English Romanticism.* New Brunswick, N.J.: Rutgers University Press, 1987.

Wordsworth, William. *The Fenwick Notes of William Wordsworth.* Ed. Jared Curtis. London: Bristol Classical Press, 1993.

———. *Lyrical Ballads, and Other Poems, 1797–1800.* Ed. James Butler and Karen Green. Ithaca: Cornell University Press, 1992.

———. *Poems, in Two Volumes, and Other Poems, 1800–1807.* Ed. Jared Curtis. Ithaca: Cornell University Press, 1983.

———. *The Poetical Works of William Wordsworth.* Ed. William Knight. 11 vols. Edinburgh: William Paterson, 1882–1889.

———. *The Poetical Works of William Wordsworth.* Ed. Ernest de Selincourt and Helen Darbishire. 5 vols. Oxford: Clarendon Press, 1940–1949.

———. *The Prelude: 1799, 1805, 1850.* Ed. Jonathan Wordsworth, M. H. Abrams, and Stephen Gill. New York: W. W. Norton, 1979.

———. *The Prose Works of William Wordsworth.* Ed. W. J. B. Owen and Jane Worthington Smyser. 3 vols. Oxford: Clarendon Press, 1974.

Wordsworth, William, and Dorothy Wordsworth. *The Early Years, 1787–1805.* 2d ed., rev. Chester L. Shaver. Vol. 1 of *The Letters of William and Dorothy Wordsworth,* ed. Ernest de Selincourt. Oxford: Clarendon Press, 1967.

———. *The Later Years: Parts 1–4, 1821–1853.* 2d ed., rev. Alan G. Hill. Vols. 4–7 of *The Letters of William and Dorothy Wordsworth,* ed. Ernest de Selincourt. Oxford: Oxford University Press, 1978–1993.

———. *The Middle Years: Parts 1–2, 1806–1820.* 2d ed., rev. Mary Moorman and Alan G. Hill. Vols. 2–3 of *The Letters of William and Dorothy Wordsworth,* ed. Ernest de Selincourt. Oxford: Clarendon Press, 1969–1970.

Wu, Duncan. "Wordsworth and Helvellyn's Womb." *Essays in Criticism* 44 (1994): 6–25.

———. *Wordsworth's Reading, 1770–1799.* Cambridge: Cambridge University Press, 1992.

———. *Wordsworth's Reading, 1800–1850.* Cambridge: Cambridge University Press, 1995.

Index

Abrams, M. H., 34n, 35n-36n, 95
Acting out, 32–33, 35, 48, 50, 59, 102, 155, 158, 164. *See also* Reenactment
Addressees, nominal and actual, 55–56
Adler, Alfred, 30n
Agamemnon, The, 39
Apostrophe, 97, 118; as defense against absence and death, 143; as device for self-constitution, 119n, 120, 156; as embarrassing, 118–19; ironic use of in "Elegiac Stanzas," 143–45, 157; in "Intimations Ode," 118–21, 127; in *The Prelude,* 158, 159–60
Aristotle, 11, 39, 134n
Armstrong, Isobel, 61
Augustine, 95

Beaumont, Lady, 104
Beaumont, Sir George, 108, 131–51, *passim;* as addressee in "Elegiac Stanzas," 139, 144
Bialostosky, Don, 6n, 12n, 15, 18, 19, 81–82
Blank, G. Kim, 42n
Bloom, Harold, 6n
Bonaparte, Napoleon, 140n, 148
Brisman, Leslie, 33, 34n
Brisman, Susan Hawk, 33, 34n
Brooks, Cleanth, 113
Brooks, Peter, 31, 38n
Browning, Robert, 27n; "Rabbi Ben Ezra," 20
Burke, Edmund, 101, 123–24
Burns, Robert, 85, 92, 93; "Death and Dr. Hornbook," 20
Byron, Lord: *Childe Harold's Pilgrimage,* 23n, 49

Caruth, Cathy, 43n

Cave, Terence, 37n, 40
Chase, Cynthia, 43n
Chatterton, Thomas, 85, 92, 93
Chayes, Irene, 11
Christensen, Jerome, 116n
Clarkson, Catherine, 50, 103, 107
Clarkson, Thomas, 132, 133
Coleridge, Hartley, 56
Coleridge, Samuel Taylor, 2, 7, 33, 40–41, 48, 92n-93n, 157, 163; addressees in his poems, 56–57; on notion of poet "in his own person," 18–19; on the Shakespearean "I," 17
—Works: *Biographia Literaria,* 110, 119; "Dejection: An Ode," 34, 56, 88, 108; "The Eolian Harp," 56, 74; "Frost at Midnight," 56, 74; "A Letter to ———," 93n, 109; "This Lime-Tree Bower," 37, 56, 74, 75n; "The Mad Monk," 112n; "The Rime of the Ancient Mariner," 37; *The Statesman's Manual,* 26
Coleridge, Sara, 56
Cowper, William, 52
Culler, Jonathan, 118, 143
Curran, Stuart, 6n, 12, 25, 49, 106, 110n, 153n
Curtis, Jared, 101n

Davie, Donald, 19
Deconstruction, 2–4, 27n
Derrida, Jacques, 4
Douglas, Wallace W., 48n, 59n, 71n
Dryden, John, 26

Eliot, T. S., 19, 37
Evans, Thomas, 132

Fay, Elizabeth, 6

Fenwick, Isabella, 1, 17, 47, 49, 51, 77, 103, 104, 107, 137
Ferguson, Frances, 27n
Ferguson, Robert, 93n
Foucault, Michel, 18n
Freud, Sigmund, 9; on repetition and remembering, 38–40; on transference, 12, 29–34, 46; on trauma as deferred action, 42–43
—Works: *Beyond the Pleasure Principle*, 38–39, 40; "The Dynamics of Transference," 29; "Family Romances," 116; "Fragment of an Analysis," 34n; *Interpretation of Dreams*, 89; *Introductory Lectures*, 34n; "Observations on Transference Love," 29; *Project for a Scientific Psychology*, 39; "Remembering, Repeating, and Working-Through," 33n; "Splitting of the Ego in the Process of Defence," 65n; "The Uncanny," 94
Frye, Northrop, 119

Gerard, Albert, 59n
Gillies, John, 134n
Gillies, R. P., 49
Gilpin, William, 48, 123
Gittings, Robert, 42n
Graves, R. P., 104n
Gravil, Richard, 154n
Gray, Thomas: "Elegy Written in a Country Courtyard," 51–52

Hardy, Thomas: "The Convergence of the Twain," 136; "Hap," 136
Hartman, Geoffrey, 10n, 35, 36n, 62n, 80, 96, 107n, 134n, 147, 148
Hazlitt, William, 52n
Heath, William, 78–79, 93n
Heffernan, James A. W., 45, 59n, 140n, 149n
Hirsch, E. D., 141
Homans, Margaret, 6, 59n
Hopkins, Brooke, 154n

Hunt, Leigh, 52n
Hutchinson, Sara, 17, 24, 56, 77, 88, 94, 97, 98n, 101, 109

"I" as lyric speaker: and acting out, 32–33, 48; autobiographical character of, 2, 18, 23, 47–48; autobiographical self vs. historical/cultural self, 28n; conceptions of in recent criticism, 2–7; definition, problems of, 1–2, 7–8, 13–14, 18–21; as historical/biographical Wordsworth in New Historicism, 4–5; identity and role of, 1, 46; intersubjective character of, 32, 154; repetition in life of, 40; as representative or public voice, 17, 64, 106–8, 114, 163; self-dramatizing character of, 12, 25, 28, 36, 48; and self-realization, 35–36, 45; and Shakespearean "I," 17; as transitional self, 29–36, 46, 48
Intertextual analysis, 5, 48, 56n

Jackson, Geoffrey, 56
Jacobson, Edith, 40n
Jacobus, Mary, 35n, 52, 57, 157
Jay, Paul, 35n
Johnston, Kenneth R., 8, 23n, 33n, 48n, 78n, 110, 126n
Jones, Robert, 77

Kant, Immanuel, 124
Keats, John, 2, 38, 131; marginal notes on *Paradise Lost*, 52; on stationing, 52; on Wordsworth, 20
—Works: *Endymion*, 38; "The Eve of St. Agnes," 38; "The Fall of Hyperion," 34; "Hyperion," 52n; "Lamia," 38; "Ode on a Grecian Urn," 37, 38, 108; "Ode to a Nightingale," 38, 108
Kelley, Theresa M., 124n, 126
Klancher, Jon, 7n
Klein, Melanie, 65n
Kneale, J. Douglas, 118n-119n

Kohut, Heinz, 40n
Kramer, Lawrence, 57–58, 73

Lacan, Jacques, 41
Lamb, Charles, 56, 132
Landon, Letetia, 2
Langbaum, Robert, 11, 18, 19, 35n, 36n, 70n
Laplanche, Jean, 43n, 65n
Lau, Beth, 52n-53n
Leader, Zachary, 22n
Lear, Jonathan, 31n
Levinson, Marjorie, 5, 48n, 60n, 107, 146, 147–48
Lichtenstein, Heinz, 40n
Liu, Alan, 5, 141
Lonsdale, Lord. *See* Lowther, James
Losh, James, 132, 133, 138
Lowther, James, 79, 89
Lyttleton, George, 52

Maclean, Norman, 106n
Magnuson, Paul, 5, 48n, 56n, 75n, 88
Mahler, Margaret, 40n
Major lyrics: as autobiographical, 7, 11, 15, 104, 131; defined, 10–11; on defining the "I" in, 15–18; differences in Wordsworth's self-representation in, 105–6; dramatic nature of, 12, 25; repetition in as critical problem, 40; self-dramatizing speaker in, 9, 25, 28, 48, 50; traditions of poetic forms in, 152–53
Maniquis, Robert, 61n
Manning, Peter J., 22n, 89, 94n, 95, 108n, 116n, 125n
Matlak, Richard E., 7n, 55n-56n, 60n, 74, 131n, 149n
McAdam, E. L., 132n
McFarland, Thomas, 41, 68, 133n, 148n
McGann, Jerome, 4, 48n
Mellor, Anne, 6, 35
Meyer, George Wilbur, 88n, 93n

Mill, John Stuart, 27
Miller, J. Hillis, 3
Milton, John: Keats on stationing in, 52; "Lycidas," 115, 134; *Paradise Lost,* 52, 83, 84, 125, 163
Modiana, Raimonda, 124n
Moorman, Mary, 77

Napoleon Bonaparte, 140n, 148
New awareness. *See* Recognition(s)
New Criticism, 15, 19
New Historicism, 4, 34, 47, 138–39
Nichols, Ashton, 7n, 9n, 28n, 37n

Odyssey, The, 39
Oedipus Rex, 39
O'Hara, J. D., 134n
Onorato, Richard J., 22n, 33n, 35n, 42n, 48n, 59n, 71, 139

Page, Judith, 73n
Parrish, Stephen, 12, 28n 56
Persona, 4, 46; in New Criticism, 15, 19; critical problems in use of, 19–20
Poet speaking "in his own person," 4; critical problems in Wordsworth's use of the phrase, 18; and self-dramatizing character of lyric speaker, 25; and self-representation, 27–28; Wordsworth's use of, 1, 15–21, 23–24
Pontalis, J.-B., 43n
Pope, Alexander, 26
Pound, Ezra, 19
Price, Bonamy, 103

Rajan, Tilottama, 7n
Rand, Frank Prentice, 132n
Recognition(s), 37–40, 45, 111; contents of, 29, 70–72, 101–2, 147–50; in "Elegiac Stanzas," 146–51; in the Intimations Ode, 121–23; kinds of described by Aristotle, 39; moments of dramatized, 37–38, 63, 68, 123, 149–50, 158–60, 161–64;

in *The Prelude*, 158–60, 161–64; psychological events as prototypes for, 40; repetition in as a critical problem, 38–40; in "Resolution and Independence," 95–96, 101–2; in Romantic poems, 37–38; scenes, 39; as self-recognition, 40–41; and self-transformation, 62, 64, 69, 96–97, 125–26, 149–50; and the sublime, 69, 123–25, 149–50; in "Tintern Abbey," 62–63, 64, 70–72; and traumatic experience, 40, 43–45; and the uncanny, 94–95

Reed, Mark, 137n

Reenactment, 51, 58, 114, 155, 158, 161. *See also* Acting out

Repetition, 25, 54–55; critical problems posed by, 38–40; and deferred action, 43; and moments of recognition, 39–40; and tautology, 122; of traumatic loss in Wordsworth's brother's death, 139; Wordsworth on, 54

Richardson, Alan, 6n

Ricks, Christopher, 140n

Romanticism, 35

Ross, Marlon, 6, 73n

Rudnytsky, Peter, 30n

Ruoff, Gene, 6, 10n, 88n, 93n, 113n

Rzepka, Charles J., 7n

Sacks, Peter, 147, 148

Salvesen, Christopher, 61n

Schafer, Roy, 32n

Schapiro, Barbara, 59n, 71n

Schiller, Friedrich, 35

Schwartz, Murray, 31

Scott, Sir Walter, 132

Self: defined in terms of art and psychology, 8; definitions of in recent criticism, 2–7; Wordsworth on possibility of knowing, 21–23

Self-dramatization, 8, 46, 57, 160; defined, 9–10, 28; and self-transformation, 8, 34, 46, 127; and stationing, 52–54; and traumatic experience, 42

Self-realization: as ideal in Romantic lyric 8; as unattainable ideal, 35–36

Self-recognition, 40–42, 158–60; Coleridge on, 40–41; Winnicott on, 40

Self-representation, 88; defined, 8; differences in, 105, 139–40; and family romance, 116; and poetic forms, 152–55; psychoanalytic model for understanding of, 28–36, 152; and self-transformation, 96–97, 102, 108, 153; Wordsworth's ideas about, 27–28. *See also* Strategies of self-representation

Self-transformation, 10, 102, 108, 127, 153, 157, 160; as aim of self-dramatization, 8, 34–35; in analysis, 34; dramatized, 142, 149–50, 157; and recognition, 64, 146; and the sublime, 69, 125–26

Shakespeare, 16, 20; *Hamlet*, 39, 84–86, 89n, 93, 125

Sharp, Richard, 132

Sheats, Paul, 12, 51, 62n

Shelley, Percy Bysshe, 2; *Adonais*, 134; "Hymn to Intellectual Beauty," 108; "Mont Blanc," 44; *Prometheus Unbound*, 37

Simpson, David, 5

Smith, Charlotte, 2

Southey, Robert, 50, 132

Spargo, R. Clifton, 102n

Sperry, Stuart M., 126n

Stationing, 52–54, 68

Stillinger, Jack, 22n

Strategies of self-representation, 67, 80, 102; apostrophe, 120, 143; dialogue, 97, 98, 102; identification, 101, 102, 163, 164; internalization, 59, 98–99, 102, 109; self-quotation, 97, 100–101, 102; splitting, 64–65,

79–81, 86, 95, 102, 109, 117, 142–43; staging, 82, 94, 95, 102
Sublime, the: dramatized, 69–71, 125–26; in the "Intimations Ode," 123–26; and new understanding, 69–70; in *The Prelude*, 162; psychological content of, 70–72; and recognition in "Elegiac Stanzas," 149–50; in "Tintern Abbey," 69–70, 72–73

Tennyson, Alfred, Lord: *In Memoriam*, 134; "The Lady of Shalott," 140; "Ulysses," 20
Thomson, A. W., 84
Thomson, James, 52
Transference, 29–34
Transitional self, 29–36, 46, 155
Trauma (and traumatic experience): as biographical background in Wordsworth's poems, 71, 142; and deferred action, 43–45; memories of, 130; and moments of recognition, 40, 42–43
Trilling, Lionel, 107n, 110n
Trott, Nicola, 123n
Tucker, Herbert, 27n

Vallon, Annette, 33, 78
Vendler, Helen, 27n, 59n, 110n, 125n
Virgil, 108–9

Waldoff, Leon, 21n
Ward, Aileen, 42n
Weiskel, Thomas, 69–70, 124n
Wilkie, Brian, 153n
Williams, Anne, 106n, 125
Wilson, Douglas B., 93n, 125
Wilson, Edmund, 42n
Winnicott, D. W., 9, 12, 40; on potential space and cultural experience, 30–31, 46, 102; on transitional object and self, 30–31
Wolfson, Susan J., 6n, 22n, 23, 107, 152
Woodring, Carl, 52
Woolf, Virginia, 73, 74

Wordsworth, Ann, 28–29, 33, 42n, 71, 130, 139, 148n; in *The Prelude*, 59
Wordsworth, Christopher, 132
Wordsworth, Dorothy, 7, 34, 78, 93, 95, 134, 148; as addressee in "Tintern Abbey," 55–58; *Grasmere Journals*, 77, 87, 110; as mirroring object, 72–74; as object of transference, 33
Wordsworth, John (brother), 93, 102, 128, 130–51, *passim*; controversy regarding, 131–32; death of 130–31, 142, 148n; death of as traumatic for Wordsworth, 139
Wordsworth, John (father), 89, 91–92, 130, 148n
Wordsworth, Jonathan, 125n 149n 159, 161
Wordsworth, Mary, 77, 79
Wordsworth, Richard, 132, 138, 139, 148n
Wordsworth, William: autobiographical experience in his poetry, 47–48, 77, 103–5, 131; as autobiographical poet, 15; biographical-historical (or empirical) Wordsworth, 1, 48, 63–64, 102, 155; and controversy regarding his brother John's behavior, 131–32, 137; and death of mother as traumatic, 42n, 71, 130, 139; and development, 7–8, 128; epistolary voice, 132; in France, 44, 78, 107; memory of death of father, 89, 130; and Nature, representations of, 58–59, 142, 148; on poet speaking "in his own person," 15–17; on the possibility of knowing oneself, 21–23; relationship with Dorothy Wordsworth, 73–74; representations of traumatic experience, 43–45, 71, 130; republican sympathies, 78; versions of in recent criticism, 2–7; and Annette Vallon, 78
—Poetry:
"Character of the Happy Warrior, The," 137

Descriptive Sketches, 161–62
"Elegiac Stanzas," 7, 29, 32, 79, 108, 128, 130–51; as autobiographical, 7; structure of, 142–43
"Elegiac Verses," 137, 138
Excursion, The, 16, 21, 50
"Fountain, The," 90, 98, 100
"Guilt and Sorrow," 21
"Home at Grasmere," 16
Intimations Ode, 32, 45, 67, 79, 111–29; 152, 156–57, 163; as autobiographical, 7, 104; family romance in, 116–17; structure of, 110–11, 111–29, *passim,* 152; versions of self in, 108
"Leech Gatherer, The," 24
Lucy poems, 3, 9
Lyrical Ballads, 49, 90
"Mad Monk, The," 112
Matthew poems, 17, 92
"Matron's Tale," 91, 92
"Michael," 10, 73, 90–91, 92
"Narrow Girdle of Rough Stones, A," 17, 98, 100
"Nutting," 10, 37, 38
"Ode to Duty," 10
"Old Man Traveling," 90
"Pedlar, The," 53
Poems, in Two Volumes, 104, 110
Prelude, The, 7, 12, 23, 64, 73, 91, 152–64; book 1, 21, 44, 78n, 81, 84, 106, 123, 155, 156, 157; book 2, 22, 124, 155; book 3, 106, 154; book 4, 99; book 5, 59, 130, 155–56, 157; book 6, 37–38, 100, 106, 157, 158–60; book 7, 21, 99, 123, 154, 157; book 8, 21, 91, 116, 157, 159, 160–61; book 9, 62n, 154; book 10, 44; book 11, 21; book 12, 44, 91, 157; book 14, 22, 37–38, 45, 84, 123, 157, 161–64
Recluse, The, 16

"Resolution and Independence," 10, 17, 22, 34, 45, 72, 76, 77–102, 104, 105, 107, 108, 109, 113n, 121, 128, 130, 153, 154, 156; as autobiographical, 7, 77–79
"Ruined Cottage, The," 4, 10, 53
"Thanksgiving Ode," 50
"Thorn, The," 12, 16
"Tintern Abbey," 16, 22, 25, 29, 32, 33, 34, 36, 38, 47–76, 78, 79, 104, 105, 107, 108, 109, 128, 130, 131, 152, 153, 154, 156, 160, 163; addressee in, 55–58; as autobiographical, 7, 47; structure of, 59–60, 64–65, 70; stationing in, 52–54
"To the Daisy," 137
"To a Highland Girl," 74
"Two April Mornings, The," 90
"When, to the Attractions of the Busy World," 102
—Prose:
Advertisement to *Lyrical Ballads,* 16
"Essay, Supplementary to the Preface" (1815), 16, 39
"Essays upon Epitaphs," 21, 26, 46
"Letter to a Friend of Robert Burns," 20
Note to 1800–1805 editions of *Lyrical Ballads,* 25, 49
Note to "The Thorn," 25–26, 27, 46, 54, 122
Preface to the edition of 1815, 24, 79, 83
Preface to *The Excursion,* 16
Preface to *Lyrical Ballads* (1800), 15, 24, 155
"Sublime and the Beautiful, The," 69, 72, 124n, 150
Wu, Duncan, 59n, 123n, 124n

Yeats, William Butler, 19